To David —
hope you enjoy the read

Pamela Masters
11/14/01

19⁹⁵

1st Edition & signed

THE MUSHROOM YEARS
A Story of Survival

PAMELA MASTERS

P.R. Simmons 25/4/44

HH **Henderson House** PUBLISHING

Published by:  **Henderson House**
P U B L I S H I N G
1390 Broadway, Suite B-295 / Placerville / CA 95667

Lyric excerpts of "Oh, What a Beautiful Mornin'"
by Richard Rodgers and Oscar Hammerstein II (p. 266)
Copyright © 1943 by Williamson Music
Copyright Renewed International Copyright Secured
Reprinted by Permission All Rights Reserved

Publisher's Cataloging-in-Publication
(Provided by Quality Books, Inc.)

Masters, Pamela
      The mushroom years : a story of survival / Pamela Masters.
--1st ed.
      p. cm.
      Includes bibliographic references.
      Preassigned LCCN: 98-93017
      ISBN: 0-9664489-2-8

      1. Masters, Pamela. 2. World War, 1939-1945--Prisoners and
prisons, Japanese--Biography. 3. Prisoners of war--China--
Biography. I. Title.

D805.C4M37 1998   940.54'7252
                                    QBI98-730

Printed and Bound in the United States of America by
Dome Printing, Sacramento, California

Cover Design—Pamela Masters/Brian Shepard

To Margo and Ursula,
and the memory of Mother and Dad
—and to all the friends of my mushroom years,
wherever you may be.
If you catch a glimpse of yourselves within these pages
it is intentional;
your contribution to my life is something
I have never taken lightly.

ACKNOWLEDGMENTS

To Angela Houston-Stewart of Richmond-on-Thames, in my beloved England. Ex-Foreign Office, and an encyclopedia of knowledge, she researched material for me that spanned the centuries. And Admiral Kemp Tolley of Maryland, whom I shook out of happy retirement. His background as the captain of a river gunboat on the Yangtse, his knowledge of the China Coast, especially the Gulf of Chihli, and his final station in post-war Japan, coupled with his delightful sense of humor and outlook on this crazy world, made me realize that nothing was too wild or impossible to contemplate. Then there's Jerome Steigmann of Phoenix, and his fabulous archives. All I had to do was mention a name or place and he'd send me invaluable background, maps, and information. Desmond Power of Vancouver, BC, slips in and out of a couple of the last chapters (if he recognizes himself); he helped me, inadvertently, to change the book from a family history project for my grandson, nephews, and nieces, into a book with a possible larger audience. Then there's Brad Carpenter, with his masterful editing skills, and zany marginals, who had me chuckling throughout the final edit. And as usual, in my happy way of always putting the first last, I have to thank Bob Greenwood of Las Vegas; if he hadn't waded through my original rambling manuscript and told me that there was a story there, I'd have probably dropped the whole thing.

AUTHOR'S NOTE

I guess I can't sidestep this any longer as too many people have asked me to comment on the story that Amelia Earhart, the aviatrix who vanished over the Pacific in July of '37, was interned with us in Weihsien Prison Camp.

It was in January 1992 that I received my first inquiry from friend and colleague, Jerome Steigmann, of Phoenix. The story was so intriguing I decided to research it. I found it started when one of the OSS paratroopers, a lieutenant, who liberated us on August 17, 1945, read a Los Angeles Times article written by a Patricia Morton back in June of '73. Morton, at that time, was an employee in the Special War Problems Division of the State Department. In that capacity, when many departmental files were declassified, she was able to obtain copies of them. One such document was a 17-page listing of the "Speedletters" sent via Chungking to the State Department in August 1945; they were from American internees in Weihsien Prison Camp to next-of-kin and business associates in the States. One letter in particular fascinated her: it was addressed to Amelia Earhart's husband, the well-known publisher, G. P. Putnam, and read, "Camp liberated; all well. Volumes to tell. Love to mother." It was unsigned—possibly as all messages were limited to ten words.

According to the lieutenant who read Morton's article, it triggered his recollection of interviewing a bedridden wraith of a woman, called "The Yank", who was being tended by a Catholic Sister named Mary Ann. By his account, she was kept in a stable, segregated from all the other internees, and was so weak she couldn't speak except in unintelligible whispers.

The lieutenant's sudden, belated conviction, that she must have been Amelia Earhart seemed really off-base, so I promptly got in touch with many old internee friends—one of whom had been in charge of assigning our living quarters. I was not surprised when each of them confirmed what I truly believed—that it would have been impossible for any person to be in the camp, let alone hidden, fed, and tended, without our knowledge.

Always tenacious, I found the address and phone number of the lieutenant and called him. He was as charming as I remembered him, and I couldn't help but realize how persuasive his story must have sounded to the fans and followers of Amelia Earhart. Before I hung up, I told him I would mail him a detailed map of the camp (see chapter 8) so that he could indicate the stable where "The Yank" was housed. I was hoping my letter and map would receive a response, but I never got one.

Still feeling that I had not done enough, I read up and researched everything I could find on Amelia Earhart. According to an article in the February '94 issue of the Amelia Earhart Society's newsletter, the OSS lieutenant described "the Jane Doe prisoner" as being almost skin and bones, and highly sedated on morphine brought to her twice daily by a Japanese "counselor", who was supposedly responsible for her. Although the officer learned that she arrived in camp under her own power, he never once saw her stand up, and according to the same article, "She left the compound in a litter a few days prior to the other prisoners in a Japanese BETTY bomber".

I found the story getting more macabre by the minute, raising more questions than it answered, and I couldn't help asking myself:

1. If she was a "Yank", and in such deplorable condition as the OSS lieutenant says, why didn't he call in one of the camp's many excellent doctors to examine her? Let's face it, the war was over: the Japanese had no control over us. We, especially the OSS, were completely in charge.

2. If she was a "Yank"–an American–why did he allow her to be taken out of the camp on a litter and flown off in a Japanese

bomber...to who knows where?

3. How could he think that the Speedletter to G. P. Putnam was confirmation of Amelia Earhart's being in the camp? As a wealthy publisher, with world-wide connections, he could have had other relatives and business associates in China who would wire him on their liberation from a prison camp. And there was no elation in his subsequent note of September 9, 1945, to the State Department, in which he stated flatly, "I have just received the message sent recently from your office and would like to file with you my new address, in the event any other messages are sent me from overseas." Then he listed his new address in Lone Pine, California. Not one word regarding the so-called liberation of his long lost ex-wife Amelia Earhart!

Further investigation in January of this year brought me in contact with yet another source: the author of an intriguing book on Amelia Earhart. To my surprise he too appears convinced that the lieutenant's story is plausible and that Amelia Earhart was in our camp. He gave me several graphic examples of crowded prison camp conditions, such as ours, where people and equipment were concealed and not brought to light until hostilities were over. I didn't point out that neither the people cited, nor the radio equipment involved, needed around-the-clock medical attention, but instead, I shot him the three points I have already listed: he either ignored them or told me I must be referring to the lieutenant's first, fictionalized account of the incident—to which I said, as far as I was concerned, *all* the accounts were fiction. He then asked me why it was that Weihsien was the only prison camp liberated by the OSS. "That's easy," I said, "it's because the map showed us 1,000 miles due west of our actual location, (See CONFIDENTIAL 2-page map of 2/1/45, chapter 15) and it took the persistence of the OSS to find us." He insisted that wasn't the reason; it was because Weihsien was a VIP camp—that's why Earhart had been interned there. I told him I was sure we would all have liked to have been considered VIP's, but we weren't, we came from every walk of life in the Orient. He wasn't impressed, persisting that the real reason the OSS liberated Weihsien was because they were on a special mission to spirit Amelia Earhart out.

I knew there was only one solution to this—I would have to find the OSS major in command of the sortie. Luck was with me. I located him the following week, and, after thanking him for his part in our liberation, I asked him point blank if he had been sent to Weihsien Prison Camp to free Amelia Earhart. He chuckled. He said, although he was the CO in charge, he never received any such orders: the first time he heard of Amelia Earhart supposedly being in Weihsien was in December of '97.

So, to all you researchers and writers involved in the Amelia Earhart saga, "Hang in there, the final chapter has yet to be written!"

To everyone else—so you can understand where I am coming from—you would have to have lived within the confines of a cramped city block with between 1,500 and 1,800 people to realize "there was no place to hide." Believe me, I tried many times.

And to all those souls who want to find closure regarding Amelia Earhart's disappearance, I empathize with you, but all I can say is, "Forget Weihsien—look somewhere else."

PAMELA MASTERS
(Bobby Simmons)

March 23, 1998
Camino, California

NOTE: I know that Weihsien was officially called a "Civilian Assembly Center", but, to all us survivors, it will always be remembered as "Weihsien Prison Camp".

CONTENTS

1

THE FATAL EIGHTH

Monday, December 8, 1941
Tientsin, North China

For one vivid moment I didn't feel the numbing cold, or realize the menace charging me with a fixed bayonet; all I saw was Ursula, safe in the British zone, and smoldering defiance exploded within me. Letting out an angry bellow, I slammed the side of the Jap's weapon with a heavily gloved hand, catching him completely off-guard. As the bayonet spun out of his frozen hands and he scrambled after it, I fled through the closing Concession gates, racing after Ursula, who was sprinting ahead with the prowess of a distance runner.

We covered several blocks before dodging out of sight into a *hutung*, where I bent over and clutched my thighs, panting into my thick scarf in an effort to pump warm air back into my freezing lungs. When I finally straightened up, Ursula was looking back up the street, her characteristic calm quietly taking over once more. "We made it—we're *safe!*" she said softly between gasps.

"Thank God he couldn't fire with a fixed bayonet," I said with a happy wheeze.

The strangest look passed over her face. "That's what *you* think!"

As realization hit, all my earlier bravado left me. *My God, we could've been killed!* Grabbing the grey brick wall of the narrow alleyway in numb horror, I couldn't help thinking, *Whatever happened to our happy morning trek?*

We'd left the French convent around seven-thirty with high hopes and a feeling of great relief. Today was the last day of our junior Cambridge matriculation exams. Last week had been the rough one, with five days of grueling, mind-numbing exams. To get this final day off on the right foot, my sister Ursula and I, boarders at St. Joseph's High School, attended early mass, ate a huge breakfast, and, after receiving a box lunch and a blessing from the Franciscan Sisters, laughingly stepped out onto Rue Sabouraud with the only other boarder in our little group: Thekla Andreadis, an attractive Greek from Shanhaikwan with Chinese papers.

The bursting dawn, flamboyant now in a sky of blazing colors, added to a glorious feeling of well-being. I looked at the several day-scholars who had joined us on the icy pavement beyond the convent's wrought-iron gates and wondered if they felt my excitement.

There was stocky Alice Kim, a Korean whiz-kid, whose homeland had been annexed by Japan after the Sino-Japanese War. Tall, slim Miriam Yueh, the daughter of a wealthy Mandarin merchant who had learned to hold on to his property and prosperity by collaborating with the Japanese. The last member, hard-faced, wiry Lena Solna, was a Czech with German papers and definite Nazi leanings.

On our way from the convent in the French Concession of Tientsin to the examination hall in the British Concession, we chatted back and forth, carefully avoiding any mention of politics, a taboo subject in the multi-national Franciscan convent. I always smiled when I thought of the dear Sisters *taboo,* as we still had been able to learn all the dubious affiliations and nationalities of the students who attended St. Joe.

When we got to Rue St. Louis, the boundary road between the

two foreign trading zones, we headed north, toward The Bund and the Hai Ho, or Hai River. After several blocks, we came to St. Louis College, the boys' school the French had named the street after, and stopped to peer through the high grilled wall to watch them drill on the ball field. We giggled when they noticed us and hurried on down the road. Further along, a delicate little Chinese man was doing his morning exercises, the climbing sun, now in a brittle blue sky, throwing his silhouette against a pink stucco wall. As I watched the subtle moves of his *t'ai chi ch'uan*, I was reminded of a ballet dancer in slow motion and stood fascinated while he turned and twirled oblivious to the world waking around him.

"Did you notice the time on the clock at St. Louis?" Ursula asked.

"Yes, it was just after eight. We should get to the Grammar School well before nine."

The examination hall was in the snobbish Tientsin Grammar School. A friendly rivalry existed between the students who attended it, and others like us, who were boarders at St. Joe.

"Let's cross over to the other side," Thekla said, eyeing Bristow Road, the name the British gave to their half of the street that bounded the west side of their zone. Although the Concession gates were at the intersection of the cross streets on the British side, the actual boundary line between the two trading zones ran down the center of the road, hence the confusing double name—Bristow Road on the east side, and Rue St. Louis on the west.

"No, it's got to be warmer here," I said, noticing the deep shade on the far side.

As I spoke, a stocky little figure trotted out of the dark shadows into momentary sunlight. Although his mouth was covered by a leather mask to keep out the biting cold, I recognized his build and the hated uniform he was wearing. "Hey! What's that Jap soldier doing over there?" I asked Ursula apprehensively.

"Looks like he's closing our Concession gates."

"He hasn't got a right to touch them," I said angrily. "We'd better keep an eye on him!"

The other girls didn't hear our comments as they bantered back

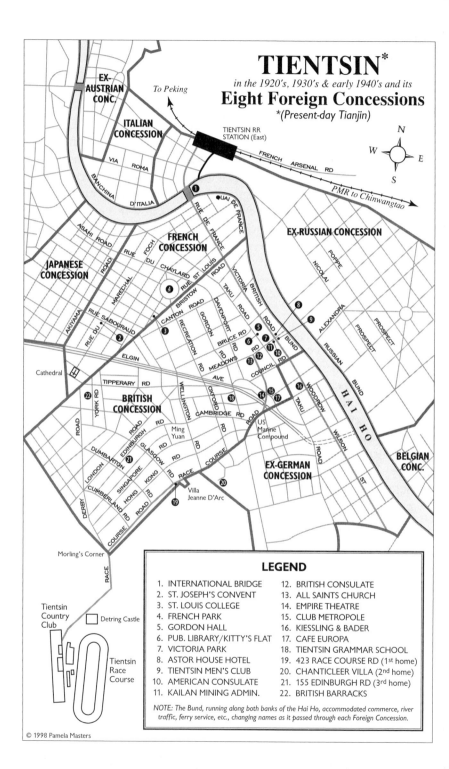

TIENTSIN*

in the 1920's, 1930's & early 1940's and its

Eight Foreign Concessions

*(Present-day Tianjin)

EX-AUSTRIAN CONC.

ITALIAN CONCESSION

To Peking

TIENTSIN RR STATION (East)

FRENCH ARSENAL RD

PMR to Chinwangtao

VIA ROMA

BANCHINA

D'ITALIA

RUE DE FRANCE

QUAI DE FRANCE

ASAHI ROAD

FRENCH CONCESSION

EX-RUSSIAN CONCESSION

RUE FOCH

RUE DU MARECHAL

CHAYLARD ROAD

RUE ST. LOUIS

VICTORIA ROAD

TAKU ROAD

BRITISH ROAD

POPPE

NICOLAI

JAPANESE CONCESSION

BRISTOW ROAD

CANTON ROAD

ALEXANDRA

PROSPECT

AKIYAMA

RUE DU SABOURAUD

RECREATION RD

GORDON RD

DAVENPORT RD

BRUCE RD

BUND

RUSSIAN

BUND

ELGIN

MEADOWS AVE

COUNCIL RD

HAI HO

Cathedral

TIPPERARY RD

WELLINGTON RD

OXFORD ROAD

WOODROW

TAKU

BRITISH CONCESSION

YORK RD

ROAD

CAMBRIDGE RD

US Marine Compound

WILSON ROAD

ROAD

EDINBURGH RD

GLASGOW RD

Ming Yuan

RD

RD

RACE COURSE

EX-GERMAN CONCESSION

BELGIAN CONC.

DUMBARTON RD

SINGAPORE RD

HONG KONG RD

RACE COURSE RD

ST

LONDON RD

Villa Jeanne D'Arc

CUMBERLAND RD

DERBY

COURSE RD

Morling's Corner

RACE

Tientsin Country Club

Detring Castle

Tientsin Race Course

N
W E
S

LEGEND

1. INTERNATIONAL BRIDGE
2. ST. JOSEPH'S CONVENT
3. ST. LOUIS COLLEGE
4. FRENCH PARK
5. GORDON HALL
6. PUB. LIBRARY/KITTY'S FLAT
7. VICTORIA PARK
8. ASTOR HOUSE HOTEL
9. TIENTSIN MEN'S CLUB
10. AMERICAN CONSULATE
11. KAILAN MINING ADMIN.
12. BRITISH CONSULATE
13. ALL SAINTS CHURCH
14. EMPIRE THEATRE
15. CLUB METROPOLE
16. KIESSLING & BADER
17. CAFE EUROPA
18. TIENTSIN GRAMMAR SCHOOL
19. 423 RACE COURSE RD (1st home)
20. CHANTICLEER VILLA (2nd home)
21. 155 EDINBURGH RD (3rd home)
22. BRITISH BARRACKS

NOTE: The Bund, running along both banks of the Hai Ho, accommodated commerce, river traffic, ferry service, etc., changing names as it passed through each Foreign Concession.

© 1998 Pamela Masters

and forth.

When our ragged little crocodile got to the next intersection, I noticed the soldier struggling with that set of gates; with a muffled grunt, he finally rolled them together and chained them shut.

"This isn't funny," I said. "If we don't hurry we'll be shut out of the Concession and we'll miss our last exam."

Alice Kim, finally noticing our concern, threw a strange look at Miriam, who silently shook her head. *What the heck's going on?* I thought, my scalp tingling. But the fleeting looks had already passed and their two faces slipped back into carefree grins and told me nothing.

"Don't worry," Ursula said quietly, "there's no way he can close off Victoria Road from Rue de France—they're both six lanes wide."

Victoria Road was the pride of the British Concession. A block up from The Bund, which followed the south bank of the Hai Ho on its west-east flow to the Gulf of Po Hai, it was lined with imposing banks, business enterprises, exclusive clubs, hotels—our favorite being the Astor House, our home-away-from-home—and merchandise marts like Hall & Holtz and Moyler Powell, where Mother liked to splurge when she came up to Tientsin to shop.

We walked another block at a brisk pace while the Japanese guard trotted up the far side of the road. I began to relax. Ursula was right, of course. We would be safe once we turned onto the boulevard's well protected length, with massive Sikh policemen handling the flow of cars and humanity at all intersections. Once we were in the Concession, we'd have to really move though, as we'd be many blocks from our final destination.

When we were approaching Taku Road, I noticed something ahead that quelled all sense of complacency: Victoria Road, still a long block away, was completely barricaded by a detachment of heavily armed Japanese soldiers. Our last chance to get into the British Concession had just vanished.

That's when Ursula and I dashed diagonally across the street to the intersection, racing the solitary guard as he headed for the last set of Concession gates.

*****

As the four breathless girls finally caught up with us in the narrow
hutung, I said sarcastically, "So you decided to join us after all."

"Hey, that was something you did back there!" Thekla said
admiringly, thumping me on the back.

I ignored her tribute. "How the heck did *you* get through? Why
didn't he challenge you?"

"He did, but Miriam explained we were students and he let us
through."

"So-o-o, why did he give *us* such a bad time?" It was all very
puzzling. Especially the emptiness of the street. Taku road wasn't
elegant like Victoria Road, but it was easily the busiest street in
Tientsin. Usually the narrow road was filled with hawkers crying
their wares, while mule and coolie-drawn carts, piled high with
produce and coal, would vie with bobbing rickshaws, weaving
cyclists and impatient cars. Today they were nowhere to be seen—
except for a few anxious faces peering out of *hutungs* as we had
been doing.

Ursula, cutting through my disturbing thoughts, asked the girls
if any of them knew what was going on. They all shook their heads.

I don't know if I sensed it, or whether it really happened, but I
could swear they all exchanged furtive glances. Then, remembering
how the guard had let them through with only a verbal challenge,
a red flag went up: *God, now we're going to have to watch them
too!* Could it be, that as day scholars, they really did know what
was going on, but wouldn't tell us?

Ursula took over once more. "We'd better hurry, as we're going
to have to do some backtracking. We shouldn't have come down
as far as Taku Road: it's going to take us a lot longer to get back
to the examination hall."

As we jogged east along the road, turning by a dark, abandoned
fish and produce market, an open truck loomed into view loaded
with men in uniform. For a moment, I felt relieved. But it didn't
last. Something about the scene seemed weird, and as we got closer,
I realized to my horror that most of the men in the back of the truck

were British, and they were being guarded by Japanese.

"Good God, those must be the Tientsin Volunteers! They look like they're prisoners. What's going on?!" The Volunteer Defense Corps, in existence under different names ever since the Boxer Uprising in 1900, had taken over the job of guarding British subjects in Tientsin after the last detachment of the East Surrey Regiment had been recalled in the summer of 1940.

As I spoke, the truck stopped and two guards jumped off the running-board to challenge a uniformed figure trying to hide among the empty stalls in the market. After a lot of shouting and stomping, the man came out with his hands on top of his head, and the Japs removed his side-arms and shoved him up roughly into the truck with the rest of the prisoners.

As it started to back up and turn around, I realized we'd be spotted. "They're coming this way! They'll see us, and we'll be caught!" I spun on my heel as I spoke and started to run.

"Hey, wait! Here's a *hutung*. Let's go down it; it's so narrow they won't be able to follow in the truck, and they can't leave their prisoners."

Miriam's advice sounded good, but I couldn't trust her or any of them. I kept hearing my parents' admonition, *"Never* be the cause of an international incident." *Lord,* I thought, *If we follow them, Ursula and I could either be kidnapped or, worse, be killed.*

Urs must've been on my wavelength; she gave me one look and we dashed back up Taku Road and around behind the market, zig-zagging in a southeasterly direction toward the Grammar School. We were only a few blocks from our destination when we ran around a corner and saw another truck, this time with a canvas cover, loading on more prisoners. We darted back out of sight and stopped to figure our next move. While we were planning our strategy, the girls caught up with us again, and in my paranoia, I started to feel trapped. For the first time in my life, I felt like a stranger in this country I loved and called home.

"Why don't you go in this store-front and out the back onto Gordon Road, then you'll be past the truck?" Alice Kim's suggestion made sense, but like Miriam's, it conjured up horrible consequences and I said defiantly, "Uh-uh! Not *me!*"

Back-tracking again, my heart doing a weird jig and my mind playing games, we circled the block, peering around each corner before daring to step out. Finally, spying the back of the truck with its load of prisoners heading away from us, Ursula and I darted out of the side street and sped down the road into the school yard—just as the clock struck nine.

I couldn't help smiling—*we'd made it!*

The little glow of pride I always felt when I saw the Union Jack—this time flying over the examination hall—completely erased the almost overwhelming fear I'd felt moments earlier.

As we snatched off our berets and hung them up with our coats and scarves in the outer hall, Mr. Foxlee, the headmaster, came out and greeted us quietly. "Good work. You got here. Your papers are on your desks. Good luck."

I walked down the aisle to my desk, as Ursula and the others slipped into their assigned seats. Foxlee, who had preceded us, moved up to the podium and, rapping loudly on the dark oak lectern, said, "You may begin now. You have three hours on this assignment. If you need anything, raise your hand, and the prefects will respond." As he finished speaking, he stepped down from the dais and quietly paced up the center aisle, leaving the prefects to watch us silently with arms folded.

As I looked over the papers that had been handed me, I forgot all about our strange escapade. Unscrewing my fountain pen, I started to write down the answers as I knew them. After what seemed like hours, I took a deep breath, flexed my shoulders, and looked up to rest my eyes for a minute. I got a jolt…*the prefects had disappeared.* I knew if I turned around I would be disqualified, so I kept on plugging along.

Then I heard it: a loud rumbling sound, heavy and metallic. Others heard it, and several heads bobbed up, only to bob down again and continue with the exam.

Outside there were shouts and the stomp of marching feet, followed by the clanking of metal, so heavy it shook the building. Then came the sound of grinding gears that needed oiling badly.

Through the din I heard abrupt, snapped commands in Japanese—then silence. Interminable silence. Finally, with a few false starts, gears started to grind again and the old building shook once more. Then all sound slowly died away.

Concentrate, Bobby, you're almost through.

As I finished the last question, I put down my pen and began reading over my paper. Outside it was deadly quiet.

"Time!" a prefect called in a loud voice, looking at his wristwatch.

Foxlee appeared. "Leave your papers on your desks please," he said. "The prefects will pick them up."

Ursula joined me as I took my coat off the rack and started out the building.

"Wonder what all the racket was about," I said, jamming my beret down on my head and stuffing my hands into my warm fur gloves.

"Sounded like tanks to me," she said.

Everything appeared normal as we stepped out into the frigid air. Then something made me look up at the flagpole. The Union Jack was gone. In its place the Rising Sun snapped furiously in the icy wind.

Ursula followed my glance and said, "Oh, no! Let's get out of here quick and try and get to Aunt Kitty's. We'll be safe near Gordon Hall, and maybe she'll know what's going on."

"Maybe we should go back into the examination hall and ask Mr. Foxlee what he knows," I said.

"Uh-uh! Let's get out of here! Hurry, before those girls latch on to us again! I don't trust any of them." I didn't stop to argue.

As we headed along "Canal No. 5", the irreverent name we gave the stinking canal that ran through the Concession along Elgin Avenue, named after Lord Elgin, one of Tientsin's illustrious earlier denizens, I heard my stomach rumbling.

"Is that you, or is it me?" Ursula asked.

"That's me, and I'm starved."

"Me too—and we left our box lunches in the hall."

"Do you have any money on you?"

"Nope."

"You think Monique might give us a bite to eat? I didn't see her at the hall today; she lives just over there," I said, pointing to an elegant grey brick house standing well back from the canal.

"No harm in trying."

Monique was a day scholar, and I really liked her. After France had fallen under the German heel in June of 1940, her parents had declared they were Free French and that they wanted no part of the new French government at Vichy that was collaborating with Germany. That made Monique a staunch Ally, as well as a friend. And she had told us we were welcome to visit any time we were in town.

Carefully looking up and down the street and seeing no Japanese, we darted over to her massive front door and rapped loudly. A servant came and peered at us through the peep-hole, then disappeared. As we stood waiting, a freezing gust surged down the canal, whipping at our legs in their heavy, black wool stockings. I shivered and shrugged deeper into my coat.

"Knock again," I said, my teeth chattering.

Ursula rapped louder this time. We could hear people talking inside, but no one came to the door. "I think we'd better go on," she said. "They're not going to open the door."

I started to get angry and banged on it with both hands.

I heard a scream, "Ma-*M-a-a-a!*", and Monique threw the door open. "Come in quickly," she whispered.

"Monique, we're so cold and hungry!" My voice broke as the warm air hit me.

"You cannot stay. The Japanese must not find you here." Her voice was pleading.

"Some bread and something hot to drink, and we'll be gone," I said, slapping my hands together to help the circulation. The icy wind had blown through my warm tabby-fur gloves as though I had none on.

"Monique, *please!*" Ursula begged.

"Stay here." She went to the back of the house, and I could hear rapid, low-key French being spoken—*that must be her parents—*

then I heard her say something in Chinese, followed by a sharp, "Vite! Vite!"

She came back still nervous and asked us, embarrassed, if we would mind eating in the kitchen. I looked at Ursula and shrugged, following her through the elaborate, over-furnished house out to the Spartan, pungent kitchen in the servants' quarters. The only time we had gone out to our kitchen at Chinwangtao was when we wanted Cook to make us cornstarch glue for some project we were on or to roast the peanuts we'd pulled up from the kitchen garden.

The Chinese cook, obviously ill at ease at our intrusion into his domain, pulled two chairs up to the old pine table and, turning to the stove, poured off two steaming cups of *cafe-au-late*. Then he put out a loaf of French bread, a bread knife, and a bowl of sweet butter.

"Thanks, Monique. We've never been so hungry...or cold."

"Cook is making you an omelette, then you must leave."

"I'm sorry we bothered you. I thought you were Free French and one of us," Ursula said contritely.

"No! No! We are Vichy French!"

"You weren't Vichy French last week!" I snapped rudely.

"Papa says we have no choice—the Japanese will kill us. We are Vichy French!"

Just then, there was a loud pounding on the front door. It could be heard all over the house. The cook grabbed our barely-tasted coffee and dumped it down the drain, threw the loaf of bread back in the bin and, opening the stove's firebox, pitched the tantalizing omelette onto the coals and slammed the door.

Monique's mother rushed in, while we stood up stunned, and started shoving us out the back door.

"Vive la France!" I shouted over my shoulder, as we plunged back out into the cold and ran for our lives, caught up in the hysteria of this wild, turncoat family.

The Japs didn't follow us, although we did nothing to conceal ourselves. In fact, there wasn't a soul in sight.

"This is unreal. Where *is* everybody?" Ursula asked.

"Everyone knows something we don't," I said, bewildered. "I

even forgot to ask Monique if we're at war. We must be, you know—all this doesn't make sense."

We crossed the canal over the bridge by Standard Oil's *Socony* station, and sped across the square in front of the Empire Theatre. The emptiness of the square, and the five streets leading into it, was ominous.

Trotting the several blocks to Meadows Road, we came to All Saints Church on the corner, where Margo, my oldest sister, had been married only four days earlier. I was still numb at the memory of that hurried wedding we'd been unable to attend. The lovely Gothic lines of All Saints did nothing to lessen the hurt within me. I tried to shake the feeling as we turned and trotted toward the imposing head office of the Kailan Mining Administration, the firm Dad worked for. The huge building, with its tiers of block-long granite steps and three-story Doric columns, always gave me a sense of Britain's enduring strength in the Far East. I knew that the security of Aunt Kitty's flat was now a matter of minutes away.

Just then, Ursula gave me a shove that sent me into the side entrance of the deserted British Consulate.

"What's up?"

"There's a whole battalion of Japs standing on the steps behind those pillars." she whispered.

"You're sure?" I asked. I couldn't see them for the wide columns and dense shrubbery blocking the view.

"Positive. I saw the sunlight on their bayonets. We can't go that way."

"But we're only a block from Gordon Hall!" Massive Gordon Hall had been a safe haven for foreigners in the British Concession since the nineteenth century, and was the bastion that saved them during the violent Boxer Uprising in the summer of 1900.

"It might as well be ten miles. Come on, we're going around the block again. Actually, it will get us closer to Aunt Kitty's little gate." I knew she was trying to sound encouraging, but it was falling on deaf ears.

We spun around and started back along the pavement, clinging close to the buildings. I still couldn't get over the fact that there was no one in sight in any direction.

Then, something caught my eye across the street, and I saw a curtain being quickly pulled closed. "We're being watched," I said.

"Friend or foe?" Ursula asked facetiously.

"How do I know? It was from behind a curtain." I could find nothing humorous in the situation, and the bleak emptiness of the streets made me feel we were the last persons alive on a dying planet.

The sun was lowering now, and although the wind had dropped, the air was piercing. The numbing cold and interminable empty streets made it feel like we were walking in an endless circle. Finally, a towering grey wall loomed up in front of us, blocking a three-way intersection.

"That's Gordon Hall," Ursula said. "We must be just west of Aunt Kitty's private gate."

Our haven, her flat over the city library, was enclosed within the formally laid out grounds known as Victoria Park that spread out before the imposing façade of Gordon Hall. Unlike the turreted hall that loomed behind it, the library was oriental in structure, with broad white marble steps, imposing red wooden pillars, and a graceful blue-tiled roof, tipped at the corners with grinning golden dragons.

We had come full circle. We were back on Taku Road, a few hundred paces west of Kitty's personal entrance to Victoria Park. As we eyed her gate that we knew so well, we got a jolt: a Japanese soldier was standing guard by it. He wasn't moving—just standing perfectly still.

"He must be freezing!" I said, and Ursula nodded.

"What now?" I asked.

Before I got a response, we saw him unsling his rifle, lean it up against the ornamental wrought-iron fencing that surrounded three sides of the park, and proceed to do some very energetic jumping-jacks. Ursula and I watched him furtively.

"We've got to get him away from that gate," I whispered.

Just then, as though some Higher Authority were looking out for us, he turned his back on the intersection and did some serious running-in-place.

"Now!" Ursula said, and we dashed across the street and slid into a shadowed recess of Gordon Hall.

He turned back our way, did more jumping-jacks, then spun back to jogging-in-place. The routine seemed to have a pattern, and I said a silent prayer.

"The only way we're going to make him leave his post is to make a disturbance across the street," I said, eyeing the huge plate glass windows of an import-export firm. "We need a rock to hurl at that glass."

The wind earlier in the day had blown the street clean of debris, and we could see nothing heavy to throw; then, Ursula's eye caught a broken piece of brick hanging slightly out from the buttress that was concealing us. She wiggled it loose and said quietly, "This should do it—we've got just *one* chance!"

The next time the guard turned to jog-in-place, Ursula flung the brick as hard and far as she could.

Bull's-eye! She shattered the plate glass into a thousand pieces. The guard let out a loud, "Buggayara!" and, grabbing his rifle, dashed across the street, while we made a bee-line for Kitty's gate. To our horror, he turned and noticed us, as we were slipping through the gate, and came running back, yelling in rage. Without losing a beat, I slammed the gate and shot the bolt, and we dashed for the library and the protection of Aunt Kitty's flat—pounding on the door and shouting to be let in.

Her delightful major-domo, who knew us well from our many earlier convent outings, let us in with a smile. As he locked the door behind us carefully, we peered up the dimly lit stairs to see Kitty, Mother…and Margo, all lit up by the soft light of the landing, like a trio of heavenly angels.

I pulled off my tam and tossed it up in the air, shouting in jubilation, "Ye gods, we *MADE* it!" Then I grabbed Ursula, and we danced around the amazed servant.

The next time I looked up at the landing, the three angels were sobbing uncontrollably.

2

DAYS OF INFAMY

The overwhelming relief of the previous night was still with me when I woke on the leather couch in Kitty's sun-drenched den. Before falling asleep after a heavenly hot meal, I'd been so busy trying to get out the story of our frantic day, I hadn't paid too much attention to the huge, overall picture of infamy that was unfolding around us. I caught remarks though. Like Margo saying that, as the port administrator's private secretary and Bentley Code expert, she had spent the last few days, before coming up to Tientsin for her wedding, sending and deciphering coded messages, trying to locate the many colliers of the British Moller Line. It was a last-ditch effort to divert the ships from Chinwangtao harbor, where they would have been sitting ducks for the Japanese. Luckily, she was successful.

In the seclusion of the convent, we'd known nothing of these cloak-and-dagger activities, or that the entire foreign community in North China had been on alert. To them, hostilities had gotten beyond probability—there was only one question left: "When?" To a person who was in love with history, the bits and pieces I heard that evening, and the fast breaking news that crackled over the shortwave radio the following morning, made me feel I had been robbed of some of the most exciting days of my life.

I could not believe the enormity of the Japanese attack on Pearl Harbor on December 8—which, because of the International Date-line, had occurred on December 7 in the Western world. How could it have happened? I could see the Japanese attacking our small enclaves and Treaty Ports in China; they'd been a thorn in their side ever since they overran the country in 1939, but to take on the United States? That gave me a completely new perspective on their military strength: it must be overwhelming.

To my chagrin, the ever-efficient Japanese soon found Kitty's shortwave set and confiscated it. An anxious week followed, while Mother tried to get us safe-conduct back to Chinwangtao, Margo tried to find out what had happened to her new husband, Jack, and Ursula and I spent our time trying to retrieve our clothes and books from the convent. I'm not sure who was more frustrated.

After several fruitless attempts to get to St. Joe on foot, only to be turned back at the forbidding Concession gates, we learned of a couple of boys who attended St. Louis College and had no trouble getting around Tientsin or the Japanese barricades. All they said when challenged was "Screwball!" Although it sounded too ridic-ulous to be true, we lost no time getting in touch with them. They suggested a less hazardous way to get to the convent, and one of them told us, "If any guards challenge you, all you have to say is the magic word and you'll get through."

"Why *screwball*?" I asked.

"That's Japanese for *schoolboy*," came the smart reply.

"But we're girls…" I said hesitantly.

"And they're Japs!" It was obvious from the way he said it that he didn't think they had too much between the ears, and the two strolled off laughing.

Following their instructions, we made a couple of very successful trips, walking to the convent and returning in loaded rickshaws, the magic password working like a charm. On the third and last attempt, we were finally challenged by a rather rough-looking guard.

Ursula, in the lead rickshaw, looked down at him and said with a smile, "Screwball", and waved her coolie on. It didn't work. The soldier glowered at her and barked threateningly.

Panicking, my rickshaw coolie dropped his shafts and the packages and paraphernalia that half-buried me shifted precariously. Frantically clutching them, and the sides of the tilted rickshaw, I wondered how long I could hold on before I slid unceremoniously to the pavement.

I looked across at Ursula. She was as cool as ice, staring at the guard with a questioning look of disdain. He became momentarily flustered, then stepping back, barked, *"Screw-GIRL!"* and grinning widely as though he'd said something very clever, he waved us on.

There was nothing humorous in Margo's quest though. She hadn't seen or heard from Jack since their wedding.

I remember the previous Friday evening, as I was talking to Mother Flanagan, our ninth grade teacher, Ursula came running up breathlessly, saying that Thekla had picked up a copy of the *Tientsin-Peking Times* on her way back from the examination hall and had read that Margo, and her latest beau, Jack, had been married the day before at All Saints Church.

I was stunned. I kept thinking, *Margo couldn't have done it— not without us! It must be a mistake.*

Thekla came over with the paper just then, and I snatched it from her. "Let me see that!" I snapped.

Mother Flanagan said, calmly, "You know we don't allow newspapers here. Roberta, hand it over to me."

"Mother, that's my *sister!* I have a *right* to know!"

"Yes…you…do," she said slowly, as she lifted out the society page and handed it to me.

Ursula and I read it together.

"Margaret Moore Simmons, daughter of Mr. & Mrs. George Simmons, and Sergeant Jack Roland Bishop, USMC, were married by the Reverend Simms-Lee on Thursday, December 4, 1941, at four o'clock in the afternoon, in All Saints Church. The bride and groom will be leaving for the States on December eleventh when the Fourth Marines pull out from their China station."

"What's the 'Moore' stand for?" Thekla asked inquisitively.

I looked at Ursula perplexed. Margo's second initial was the same as Mother's, a "G".

"I thought you told me once her second name was Grace," Thekla insisted.

"That's typical of the British," Ursula said, unruffled. "We often have several names. Margo usually only goes by 'M.G.', but her full initials are 'M.G.M. Simmons'. I guess the reporter just left out the 'G' by mistake."

"Well, I heard from a day scholar that she's not really your sister."

"That's absolute rot!" I said angrily.

"And that's absolutely enough!" Mother Flanagan interrupted. "Come on, we're going down to dinner. The other students must already be eating."

I was still numb as I followed them down to the basement refectory. I kept thinking of Thekla's remark. *How dare she say Margo isn't my sister! We three look so alike...we're all five-five, slim, with fair skin and dark brown hair.*

Ursula was closer to my age and a lot of fun to be with, but Margo was different. She was eight years my senior, and I held her in awe, my sensitive nature picking up her many moods but seldom understanding where they came from. One thing I knew, she wasn't able to cover her emotions as well as Ursula did.

I didn't talk much during the meal; I was too hurt and confused. I knew I should have been glad for Margo and Jack, but all I could think of was that she'd be gone before another week passed and that I'd miss her terribly. *Oh, Margo! Margo! Why must you leave?* I moaned silently. Then, without asking permission, I jumped up from the table and ran out of the room down the long, cold, tiled corridor to the dark stairway at the end of the hall. Racing up the stairs, flight after flight, I charged down between the long aisles of beds in the dormitory and threw myself onto my soft straw mattress, sobbing convulsively.

I don't know how long I cried; memories kept tumbling over each other. Some happy, some sad, but all touched by Margo, or

I-tse-la as the servants always named her. I remember Mother telling the story of how we all got our Chinese names. When Margo, the only one of us girls born in England, arrived in China, the servants called her *Ch'ao-chieh,* or "Little Sister", and everything was great till Mother came home from the hospital with a second daughter. The servants were genuinely happy with the new arrival, but didn't know what to call her, as there couldn't be *two* "Little Sisters". When the amah asked timidly if the new baby had a name, Mother said, smiling, "It's Ursula." As they all smiled at each other and nodded wisely, Mother turned to Dad and said, "They seem to approve of our choice." Chuckling, he told her, "They think you're very smart. You see, to them 'Ursula' sounds like *Erh-tse-la,* or 'Number Two'. From hereon out, I guess Margo will be *I-tse-la,* or 'Number One'." He was right. And when I came along eighteen months later, the servants didn't need any prompting; using the Chinese for one-two-three—*I-Erh-San*—they named me *San-tse-la.*

I was still crying into my soggy pillow when Ursula came up. "Mother Flanagan sent me up to see if you are okay."

"Is she mad at me?"

"No. She understands."

"I don't!"

"You mean about the 'Moore'?"

"Yes, that—but mostly for not telling us she was getting married."

"We couldn't have gone to the wedding. We had to take our exams. She knew that. Mother knew that. We would only have felt worse if we had known, trying to apply ourselves and not being able to concentrate on our work. It must have been a hard decision, but I know if you think about it calmly, you'll decide it was the only thing she could do."

"Well, where's she now?"

"Probably back in Chinwangtao, getting packed and ready to leave."

"Oh, no! She'll be gone before we get home for the holidays. I'll never see her again!" I wailed.

That's why I was so overjoyed at unexpectedly finding her at Aunt Kitty's flat. But now I was watching her go through all the emotions of loss that I had felt—only she was agonizing over whether she would ever see Jack again.

She had first told us about him when she took us to our favorite coffeehouse, *Keissling and Bader,* on her last trip to Tientsin in late October. While we were enjoying a frothy hot chocolate and wedge of cream torte, she regaled us with stories about Jack, a platoon sergeant in charge of a handful of marines at Camp Holcomb on the outskirts of Chinwangtao. From the tales she told, it was obvious that he was a terrible tease with a droll sense of humor. Somehow he had learned from Margo that Dad, who was the port accountant, had a minor job overseeing the company dairy. It was a token affair that required he drop in unannounced every once in a while to check on the Chinese workers, so they wouldn't try to tamper with the milk. One evening, when some marine brass came down from Peking, Jack took them to the club and introduced Dad to them as, "George Simmons, the local dairyman." Then, with a perfectly straight face, he turned to Margo and introduced her as "the dairyman's daughter." Margo was hysterical—Dad apoplectic!

Somehow I didn't think she was reminiscing about those fun times as she anxiously waited for word of him. When the International Red Cross finally located him—right there in Tientsin under Japanese guard at the old Marine Complex—the relief was quickly overshadowed by frustrating delays in trying to arrange to see him. When the day eventually arrived, Margo was so excited she just bubbled, and the Red Cross emissary who came to escort her said with admiration, "You look *beautiful!*"

I guess the Japs didn't think Jack should see her so happy, so they made her stand out in the freezing cold for several hours till her feet were blocks of ice, her hands numb, her nose blue, and her eyes running, then, satisfied she couldn't look more miserable, they ushered her in. They were only allowed ten minutes together, but in that short time Margo learned a lot, especially about the humiliating surrender of the marines at Camp Holcomb.

After their hurried wedding, Jack had returned to the camp and spent a hectic weekend with his platoon, packing base supplies and equipment and securing the facility prior to its scheduled closing the following week. He was working with a lieutenant, Richard Huizenga, who had come down from Peking with the last trainload of materiel.

Jack learned that that last shipment held several crates containing one of the world's great anthropological finds, Peking Man. Colonel William Ashurst, commander of the marines in North China, had ensured their safe passage to the States. In late November, Colonel Ashurst had received a visit from Dr. Henry Houghton, head of the Peking University Medical College, who told the colonel that he had the remains of Peking Man and asked if the marines could take them to the Philippines when they shipped out and then have them forwarded to a museum in New York. Intrigued, Ashurst agreed to handle the request, and when the several large unmarked crates arrived, he had them stenciled with his name. According to Jack, they, along with all the other materiel, were still sitting in railcars on the short spur line to Camp Holcomb.

The morning of December 8, while Jack and Huizenga were busy clearing out the base office, they heard the unmistakable rumble of tanks. Rushing outside, they were joined by the platoon, who started cussing in fury as they watched the Japanese tanks approaching down the long, straight beach road. Huizenga quickly dispersed the men to their battle-stations, then told the radioman to try and raise the legation guard in Peking, and failing that, to try Tientsin.

The only weapons the marines had to defend the camp were a few machine guns and whatever weapons they'd been issued. Although the situation was desperate, all the platoon wanted to hear was the command to "Fire!" It never came. The orders, when they finally arrived from Tientsin, were: "Don't shoot, except in self-defense. Comply with the Japanese demands!" The radioman had made them repeat the orders, and was told that Japan was at war with the United States.

As the tanks made their last turn towards the high, arched gateway to the camp, the lieutenant shouted, *"Hold your fire!"*

Margo said Jack looked positively murderous when he told how the Japs hauled down the Stars-and-Stripes and hoisted up the "Poached Egg". He ended with, "That's the first time I ever saw a marine cry."

There were tears in Margo's eyes as she wound up the story.

"It's okay, Margo," Kitty said, putting her arms around her. "You saw him, and he's all right. He'll be okay."

"I know…I know. I saw him. He's safe and unhurt. I guess I can't ask for much more…"

When Mother's persistence finally paid off and we boarded the train to Chinwangtao, I was ecstatic. We were going home! The city of Tientsin, which had grown from an imperial ferry crossing in the Ming Dynasty to a huge, sprawling metropolis, had always overwhelmed me, and although I'd felt secure within the British Concession, now even that safe haven was gone.

While I was making myself comfortable in our compartment, I suddenly realized that I had no reading material, and groaned inwardly at the thought of the long, boring trip ahead. Sitting looking vacantly out of the window at the frozen salt flats on the outskirts of Tientsin, I found my thoughts drifting back to the little Treaty Port of Chinwangtao and my family's half-century love affair with this strange land.

I thought of Dad, the only blue-eyed blond in our family, with strong features and a rather ruddy complexion—the latter marred by a livid birthmark that ran from his left eye to his lower cheek. It was strange how I never noticed that scar unless I deliberately thought of it; it was so much a part of him, he wouldn't have been Dad without it. I know he was proud of being the second generation of our family to live in China—first in Honan, where he had endeared himself to the Chinese by keeping a string of money-making race ponies, and later in Peking, Tientsin, and finally in the Treaty Port of Chinwangtao where he worked for the Kailan.

As port accountant in Chinwangtao, Dad worked the usual five days a week, with a lovely two-hour tiffin break every day. He made up for those casual hours by putting in an additional half day on Saturday and rounding out the week by looking in on the office on Sunday to be sure everything was running smoothly. He insisted a coaling port ran twenty-four hours a day, seven days a week, and that you had to be right on top of things at all times.

His father, George Simmons, Sr., had come to China in 1895, right after the Manchu court had signed the humiliating treaty that ended China's war with Japan. Although Grandpa was involved in railroads at the time, not coal mines, he found it hard not to be caught up in the intrigue that surrounded the origins of the Kailan Mining Administration, the huge mining enterprise that Dad would later work for.

After China's treaty with Japan, every little incident between China and a foreign power called for reparations. When two German missionaries were murdered in Shantung Province, Germany took it as an invitation to occupy Tsingtao, getting an exclusive ninety-nine year lease on mining and rail rights in that province. Tsarist Russia, not to be outdone, demanded Port Arthur at the tip of the Manchurian Peninsula across the bay from Chinwangtao, and France acquired Kuangchowan in South China, while Britain, as the dominating foreign power in the Orient, obtained a ninety-nine year lease on Hongkong and its environs, along with the port of Weihaiwei at the entrance to the Gulf of Chihli.

It was obvious the policies of the spineless Imperial Court would have bankrupted China if it hadn't been for two prominent Chinese, Li Hung-chang and Chang Yen-mao. Li was viceroy of Hopei Province and founder of the Chinese Engineering and Mining Company, a large coal mining operation in Kaiping, and Chang was director-general of mines in Hopei and Jehol provinces. Both men realized that if China was to recoup losses sustained through reparations, she would have to get technological help in mining her far-reaching mineral deposits. Li asked a British mining firm for assistance, and the company sent out an able young American mining engineer named Herbert Hoover.

Grandpa met and became friends with Hoover when they both lived in Tientsin. I remember snapshots of Grandpa, the railroad pioneer, and Herbert Hoover, the American mining engineer, in their homburg hats and three-piece suits with watch fobs and chains across their snug vests. Grandpa looking like a happy walrus with his flourishing white moustache, and young Hoover like a rather large cherub who'd been handed the wrong wardrobe.

Hoover—along with Gustav Detring, the German commissioner of customs in Tientsin, and Chevalier de Wouters, a Belgian financier—arranged for the British to purchase Li's Chinese Engineering and Mining Company in the violent summer of 1900 during the turmoil of the Boxer Rebellion. The purchase was made ostensibly to protect the mines from the Russians who were taking advantage of China's unrest to advance into Manchuria. Dad always insisted that whatever failings the Chinese might have, they knew how to use foreigners to protect their interests.

Detring and de Wouters, who headed up the loan drive for China's modernization, were considered nothing more than con men by many. And Hoover hardly faired better. His attempts to make the low-producing mining operation profitable left both Chinese and foreign investors unimpressed. Most westerners knew nothing of the corruption and "squeeze" that permeated Chinese enterprise, and still less about the superstition and sloth that riddled such undertakings. There were earth dragons to be pacified; ancestral tombs to be left undisturbed; and each morning, before the coolies would enter the mines, fire crackers had to be let off to scare away evil spirits.

When Hoover left China for good in September 1901, the huge Kaiping mines were completely under British control. Both London and local papers called it "the largest transfer of property to foreigners in the history of China"—part of the property being the tiny Treaty Port of Chinwangtao that would later become our home.

Later that year, Yuan Shih-k'ai replaced Li as viceroy of Hopei Province, and demanded that Director Chang get back the Kaiping mines; as both the Boxer Rebellion and a Russian invasion were now items of history, it was to be expected. When Chang's first attempts failed, he filed suit in England, and after several years of litigation, the case was decided in his favor. Although the British were successful in appealing that judgment, and the property remained in their hands, the court stipulated that the company had to be jointly managed by the Chinese and British.

Frustrated in his efforts to get back the Kaiping mines, Yuan Shih-k'ai started a rival coal mining company at Lanchow, and the animosity between the neighboring companies became bitter. It wasn't until after the Chinese Revolution of 1911, when Yuan Shih-k'ai was installed as the first president of the new Republic of China, that the battle between the Kaiping and Lanchow mines came to and end. The Chinese, realizing it was to their advantage to heal wounds and make money, merged the operations under the name of "Kai-Lan", a vast and profitable Chinese/British mining enterprise.

So it was, that years later, when Ursula and I went down with Dad to his office in Chinwangtao on Sundays, quite often George Wang, a Chinese accountant, would be there too. I wondered when I was young why such a small port needed two accountants; I discovered later that it was because of the Kailan's policy that, for every British managerial position, there had to be a Chinese counterpart.

Since the turn of the century, when the harbor facilities were built, Chinwangtao had grown into a picturesque port and summer resort. The pile of red rocks and ragged cliffs that had once formed a little tidal island, became a typical English coastal village with high roads and low roads, back roads, bluff roads, and beach roads—none with a name, not even the road that led up the steep hill from the port administrator's office by the railway tracks to the crest of the cliffs where the imposing, terraced club stood.

The exclusive island-aspect of the port was emphasized by the three points that attached it to the mainland: the railroad tracks to the south, that ran from the station in the native city out to the docks; the high earthen levee to the west, that held in a large pond where we skated in winter; and a picturesque little white bridge to the north where a highly decorated kiosk, which doubled as a guard-house, protected the road to the golf course and barred anyone coming down the Shanhaikwan beach road from entering the port.

As the old PMR headed northeast toward Chinwangtao, I thought of the little Treaty Port, not as I knew it would be, icebound and frigid, but with windswept bluffs, a shimmering sea, fishing junks bobbing on the bay, and the haunting chant of coal coolies as they loaded the patient colliers tied up to the dog-legged pier. My life hadn't started in Chinwangtao, but that's where memory began.

I remember Margo telling me when I was younger that Mother, or Gee as she was known to all her friends, had once dabbled in astrology, and when Margo was born in England in 1919, Mother was so involved with the ancient "science of prediction", she'd had Margo's horoscope drawn up through her twenty-first year by a noted London astrologer. As each one of the woman's predictions came to pass, Mother was convinced that the heavens held our future as surely as the sun warmed our days. And it was no surprise, when Ursula was born in Tientsin in 1925, that Mother forwarded the date and exact time of birth to the astrologer and asked her to plot a chart for her second child.

The Orient was in its usual chaotic state at the time, and it took almost six months before the papers finally arrived; when they did, Mother came down to earth with a thud.

The woman predicted the usual childhood traumas and illnesses, along with journeys and such, but the item that made Mother mad was the one that said Ursula would go to prison in China at the age of seventeen.

"The woman's off her trolley!" she exploded, "No foreigner goes to jail in the Orient. Not even for murder. Oh, we might stand trial, but we never serve a sentence. Dammit, we're *privileged*. Go to jail? Never! *This is rot!"*

Needless to say, Mother had gotten completely over that phase of her life when I was born a year later. According to Margo, it was just as well; Mother never did know what time I was born, a prerequisite to an accurate horoscope, as the year was 1927, and she and Dad, along with Margo, Ursula, and a few brave servants, were fleeing from Honan Province and the advance of Chiang Kaisheck's Northern Expedition, a supposed war of unification. The aim of the drive was to subdue the warlords who were ravaging the country and leaving it prey to communism, foreigners, and Japanese dreams of empire. I was almost born on a hand-car that Dad was pumping wildly along the railroad tracks, but his efforts got us to a mission hospital in Weihweifu just before the blessed event. Of course, I had no recollection of these life-and-death struggles or the turmoil that followed, and my earliest memories were always of the Treaty Port and its carefree lifestyle.

Our house, an oversized bungalow facing east across the Gulf of Chihli, was built over a honeycomb of steam pipes and root cellars. Typical of British homes in the Orient, the living area was separated from the servants' quarters by a central courtyard, with kitchens and pantries adjoining the dining room and main home. When we were little, our Chinese amah was the only servant who lived on our side of the compound in a tiny room next to our bedroom and nursery.

My favorite room was the immense indoor veranda that spread across most of the front of the house. During the long severe winters, it acted as a solarium, catching the morning sun and helping to heat the house. In the summer, the veranda windows were kept open, and impish sea breezes would whip through the screens, sighing and whistling as they ran down the long hallways and through the numerous rooms, twisting lacy curtains and playing with bed ruffles.

Summer evenings were spent on the outside veranda that sheltered the front door and was a continuation of its indoor counterpart—only there were no glass windows, just cool bamboo *lien-tzus,* that were raised or lowered to filter the sun. Two tiers of steps mounted up on either side of the veranda entrance, meeting at the top with a balustrade covered in tumbling red and pink geraniums.

Of all the seasons, summers were the most idyllic. When we were really small, Mother wouldn't let us swim on Long Beach, the name we gave the lovely, long strand where the summer visitors' bungalows were, because it sometimes had tricky undertow. It was then that we spent our mornings in the little cove in front of our home, running across the bluff and scrambling down the railroad-tie steps that clung to the cliff face, tossing our playsuits as we raced across the pebbles and warm, white sand. The beach was so private, we never wore clothes, playing as God made us, with only curved straw coolie hats to protect our sturdy little bodies from the sun's benevolent rays.

Spring was a rollicking time too, bursting on the scene like a happy jack-in-the-box. The first harbingers would be English violets, poking their heads out of charred ground cover and beckoning to their kin to follow. Then would come the stately acacia trees that climbed the hill behind our house up to Lady Walsham's Seat. By the time they gave their nod to spring, the ground beneath them would be carpeted with purple, mauve, and white violets as far as the eye could see.

Florence, Lady Walsham, who had been in Chinwangtao well before our time, must have loved the port as much as I did because she'd had a stone seat placed on its highest hill with a view of the bay, the misty reaches of the shoreline, and the rolling mainland with its soft, purple hills. When Ursula and I climbed up on the seat and played "conquerors of the world", we could see beyond the railroad tracks to the south to Camp Roberts (later named Camp Holcomb by the marines), a tiny American army outpost manned by a contingent of the Fifteenth Infantry, and further still to Peitaiho, a cosmopolitan summer resort that rivaled Chinwangtao in beauty.

In all the years I lived in the Treaty Port, I never saw a picture of Lady Walsham, who had scattered violet seed beneath the acacias. In my mind's eye, she would change from an ethereal, young Kate Greenaway beauty, dancing gaily through enchanted woods, to an austere, white-haired dowager, with a snorting pug dog, who handed out candy and kind words to good little girls. Many years later, I was to find that neither of these descriptions were accurate. She had been the adventurous wife of Sir John Walsham, who, in the mid 1880's, had been Envoy Extraordinary to the Emperor of China. When she visited Chinwangtao—probably coming over by donkey cart from Peitaiho or Shanhaikwan—she must have seen a beauty hidden in those "barren cliffs and ragged rocks" that no one else had seen. Maybe it reminded her of England. Whatever the reason, her thoughtful gesture of scattering violet seed turned spring into a time of breathtaking beauty.

Autumn was our only iffy season, sometimes mild, sometimes chilly, but always heralding the frigid, ice-bound winter that was sure to follow.

*****

The barely audible clickety-clack of the train wheels must have lulled me to sleep, because the next thing I knew Mother was saying something about us coming into the "home stretch" and how great it would be to see Dad again. It was already dark outside, and as I looked out at the frozen landscape, caught fleetingly in the light from the train window, I thought of the royal welcome awaiting us. Apart from Dad and the servants, there would be our chowdogs, Jane and Brewster, sniffing, bobbing, and jostling for attention. They knew when Ursula and I were home there would be walks everyday, regardless of the freezing weather—something Mother never had the inclination for, nor Margo the time.

They reminded me of bears. With winter, their coats became thick and lustrous; it didn't phase them a bit if they fell off an ice floe into the freezing sea—they would just climb out, shake the water off their coats, and keep on romping.

Winter was definitely the dogs happiest season. While the garden slept, and the bulbs and flower pots were stashed away in the root cellars, they would sit proudly out on the bare arms of the balustrade, like the lions of Trafalgar.

The previous year, during Easter break, we were enjoying the mid-morning sun as it warmed the indoor veranda, when, to our horror, a Japanese landing-party scaled the cliffs, yelling bloodcurdling *banzais* as the men charged across the bluff. For one terrifying moment, I thought they were going to scale the rock wall that surrounded our garden and charge right into our home, but they stopped at the wall and let out one more bloodcurdling yell, then waving their bayonets high over their heads, they ran and regrouped by the cliff's edge.

The whole realistic assault would've been completely terrifying if it hadn't been for our crazy, crouching dogs out on the balustrade, snarling and barking as ferociously as the Japs yelled, turning the whole exercise into a Mikado-like fiasco. The scene became even more grotesque when we noticed heavily be-ribboned officers watching the procedure astride huge Australian chargers. They were so short their legs barely reached the stirrups, giving them the appearance of little kids trying to play grown-up.

When I asked Dad how long the landings had been going on, I was told since the floes moved out to sea several weeks earlier.

"Why doesn't Mr. Chilton do something about it? This is a British Treaty Port; they have no right here!" I said indignantly. Chilton, the port administrator and Margo's boss, ran the little port with a strong hand that brooked no outside interference and earned him the sobriquet of "the benevolent dictator".

"He's advised both the British War Office and American Defense Department," Dad said, adding wryly, "They told him not to put undue significance on it 'as armies have to stay fit.'"

I was furious. My little Camelot was being desecrated, and no one was doing a thing about it.

"Don't get so mad. Chilton's told the Japs, if they persist, he'll have the whole Pacific Fleet sitting off-shore within the week." Dad rumpled my bobbed hair as he spoke.

"Will he?"

I liked that. *Nobody* pushed the British around. The more I thought of it, the more exciting it got—especially as we hadn't seen a naval vessel in ages. Dad was a little more cautious. "That's what he *says*," he countered.

"That'll teach 'em!" I said smugly.

But when Easter break was up, there was still no fleet on the horizon, and Mother and Dad were adamant that we return to school. "I'll write and tell you what happens," Mother said, trying to mollify me.

"But that's not the same as being here," I wailed.

"But it'll have to do, and that's final!"

I stewed for ten days back at the convent till Mother's letter arrived.

According to her, Bill Chilton played his most brilliant hand. Although, as an ex-naval commander, he had excellent ties with the Royal Navy, there was no way he could have had the British fleet in Chinwangtao in a week—or even ten weeks. He couldn't have had *one* ship sent up, and he knew it. But the Japs didn't. So he bluffed. Of course, it helped immensely that he stood head-and-shoulders above the belligerent little group of officers when they met in his office for the third and last time.

Before speaking to them, he turned to our civilian interpreter and said, "Mr. Araki, I want you to make it clear to these...gentlemen...that I mean every word I say."

Araki got the cold tone in his voice and nodded.

Then Chilton turned his droopy, bloodhound eyes on the officers, and looking scornfully down his long, prominent nose said ever so slowly and deliberately, "Gentlemen, would you allow a foreign power to scale the cliffs of Japan without using the full force of the Imperial Fleet to stop them?" He paused and looked each man in the eye, then resumed, "Well, I assure you, if you attempt one more landing operation in this Treaty Port, His Britannic Majesty's Royal Navy will blast your men off the cliff's face. Is that clear?"

It was.

They got the message. Not only did they call off the landings, they made profuse apologies for offending Bill Chilton, and especially for invoking the wrath of His Britannic Majesty's Royal Navy!

I was still smiling to myself at the outcome of the incident when the train started to slow down with a series of jolts. When it finally stopped with a hiss, I belted my coat, wrapped my scarf snugly around the lower part of my face, and stepped out onto the dimly lit platform.

When I saw Dad, a warm glow spread through me defying the icy cold, and while I gave him a whopping hug, a happy chant kept running through my head, *"We're home! We're home! We're home!"*

3

HOSTAGE

"Gee, you don't understand. Those bloody little Nips are forcing us to work for them. You and the girls are hostages. It's as simple as that!" Dad voice was sick with disgust.

I hesitated outside the dining room door, waiting for Mother's comment. She didn't speak.

I couldn't stand it. As I walked in, I blurted out, "What do you mean, we're hostages? What would they do to us if you *didn't* work for them?"

Dad looked startled; he hadn't realized I'd overheard. "Let's put it this way, Bobby, none of us in this port is willing to put it to the test."

Trying to change the subject, Mother said, "You'd better let Jung-ya know you're ready for breakfast."

As I walked over to the pantry to tell him, I glanced out the window.

"Where are the woods?" I cried in horror.

"The bloody Nips again! They cut 'em all down the day after war broke out. They had a crew of coolies in here, and they hacked and slashed till nothing was left standing."

"Why did they take the acacias? What could they possibly do with them?

"They needed them for pit props in the coal mines of Hokkaido."

"Pit props?!" I was stunned.

It had been dark the previous evening when we got home, and I hadn't noticed the devastation. Now all that was left were gnarled stumps and twisted suckers, reaching out of the snow like the flailing arms of dying souls. Looking up at the crest of the hill, I could see Lady Walsham's Seat still standing proudly, only now it overlooked a site of wanton destruction, and my long held disgust for the Japanese military turned into full-blown loathing.

I was barely six when I first saw their total disregard for human life and property. That was when they overran Manchuria, or Manchoukou as they renamed it, and hordes of refugees flooded over the Great Wall at Shanhaikwan to seek haven in Chinwangtao, away from strafing planes and errant bombs. Ursula and I had been the first to spot them, moaning and screaming in the acacia woods with legs and arms blown off, their bodies gutted with internal injuries. The less injured were trying to patch their wounds and staunch the flow of blood. We rushed home and told Mother, who alerted the hospital staff, then called all the women of the port, and the whole team worked tirelessly for days on end trying to save as many lives as they could.

That evening I had heard Mother talking to Dad, "Geordie, it's terrible. There's so much pain and suffering. Do you know, when they lose an arm or a leg, they pack the wound with mud and straw to keep it from bleeding? Doctor Grice says if they don't die from shock and loss of blood, we'll probably lose them to gangrene. He tried desperately to teach them hygiene as he worked on them, but I know it fell on deaf ears."

Dad said, "Gee, there's nothing kind about war. It's always tragic. Don't tire yourself too much. And don't grieve. The Chinese are hardy. They *will* survive."

Now, our lovely acacia woods that had once served as a well-camouflaged field hospital, had become victims along with us.

*****

We hadn't realized what a dense windbreak those trees had made; they had kept the chill of howling Gobi winds from sweeping over our rambling homes. Those same winds seemed now to come alive, like demons roaring down across the mainland and slamming against our homes, their fury kindled by their inability to fling us all into the icy bay. The charred stubble of the burned-off bluff turned into a black swirl, racing ahead of the onslaught, landing as soot on the heaving ice floes.

Our windows continually rattled, and fine sand seeped through the sealed double panes as though they had been left open. The house was always cold as the Japanese were not generous with coal like the Kailan had been. And, if in the past the port had seemed small, it was even tinier now, since we had an almost unobstructed view of every house and building.

Christmas was bleak and unfestive, reflecting the mood of everyone in the port, especially the bread-winners. Dad felt like a traitor. So did Margo. Their captors were past-masters in the art of group obedience. They knew they were in complete control and didn't hesitate to push that power to the limit.

In January, to bolster their sinking image and to gain acceptance in the world press, the Japs put us through the public indignity of forced attendance at a grotesque dinner of collaboration.

They took over our club, decked it out with British and Japanese flags, raided our excellent wine reserves, and threw a gala Japanese banquet with news cameras filming every move we made. As Ursula and I were both in our early teens, they considered us adults, and we had to attend.

I couldn't get over their strutting and posturing, watching as they grabbed onto different Britishers. With arms around their waists— most of them couldn't reach their shoulders—they'd beckon the cameraman to record the *entente* and feigned friendship for public consumption in Japan and throughout the world.

Mr. Araki, the Kailan's civilian interpreter and a close friend of our family, was run ragged translating toasts and other obnoxious sentiments as the evening progressed. The only light moment was when Araki came over to Margo, and taking her hand, said kindly, "I wish you happiness. I am so sorry. You…your husband…you did not even have a 'honey-week'." Bowing to him and his wife, Margo smiled her thanks, touched by his interpretation of a honeymoon being a two-week lunar event.

Mrs. Araki had been a famous Japanese dancer before she married, and although she was seven month's pregnant, the military insisted she entertain us that evening with a Japanese tone poem portrayed in motion. The number was long and dull, punctuated by fluttering fans and stamping feet, with a background theme played on an instrument that looked like a one-stringed lute. The monotony got to me, and to stop from falling asleep in the heavy atmosphere of smoke and sour body odors, I found myself studying this group of so-called conquerors.

I came to the conclusion that: 1) They couldn't hold their liquor. 2) They needed lessons in table manners: you don't *suck* soup. And they should be told that: 3) Napkins belong on the lap, not tied around the neck. 4) You excuse yourself before you pass out and fall face-first into your dinner plate. And 5) if a comrade *does* pass out in this inexcusable way, you help him out of the room; you don't leave him gurgling in the *sukiyaki* while you go on telling interminable stories of your feats of valor in the field.

It was while I was deep in my contemptuous musings that Cosmo Wentworth came into the room, holding a bottle of vintage champagne. He was the only bachelor in the port. Slim, youngish, with a dark handlebar moustache and a monocle, he looked, and was, the personification of an Indian army officer. He had come up from the sub-continent a few years earlier and had only worked for the Kailan a short time. He was bored with his job, and bored with the monotony and dullness of port life, and prior to the attack on Pearl Harbor, had been planning to return to his old post in India. I knew this infamous situation must be twisting his guts.

While I was wondering what he was up to, he turned and asked Mr. Araki to help him with a toast. Until then the Japs had been making all the obnoxious toasts while we quietly seethed, and I couldn't help noticing the port regulars' icy stares of disapproval when Cosmo started to speak, handing the open magnum of champagne to the Japanese aide seated by the general hosting the party.

Mr. Araki was startled too, but he gallantly smiled and hissed as he translated Cosmo's words: "This is the best champagne in the port. We, the British, on whose Empire the sun never sets, drink a toast to you brave soldiers of the Rising Sun."

The aide, who had finished filling the Japanese officers' glasses, handed the bottle over to one of our men to start filling ours, but Cosmo intercepted it and said, "No! We'll drink the common brand." He took the bottle out of the man's hand and handed him another magnum from which to pour, while the Japanese smiled fuzzily as they viewed our shocked expressions.

Cosmo gave us an imperceptible wink with his unmonocled eye, raised his glass, and shouted, *"To your health!"*

We didn't know what he had pulled, but we knew we had to show solidarity, so we all raised our glasses and quietly said, "Hear! Hear!"

While three more Japanese slid under the table, our new port administrator, Harry Faulkner—Bill Chilton had been promoted the previous year for his handling of the landing party fiasco—decided it was time to break up this embarrassing charade, so, at his signal, we all rose, bowed to our host, and left the room. When we were outside the club, waiting for our chauffeurs to bring the cars around, Cosmo cleared his throat loudly and said, "Thanks for backing me. Glad no one drank from that bottle. I took it out into the men's room when I had an urge and pissed in it!"

A few days after that uplifting incident, Cosmo disappeared. Dad was convinced he was on his way to India. He had a dark complexion and, without his moustache and monocle, could be quite nondescript. "He shouldn't have any trouble mingling with the natives," Dad said, adding, "He's an excellent linguist, and very resourceful; don't worry about him. Whatever he sets his mind to, he does."

It was a while before the Japanese learned of his disappearance, but, since he was single, there was no one to take reprisals out on. He was just another incident of war.

*****

After that, life turned into a monotonous grind. Ursula and I missed our studies. We tried to keep up but didn't have the necessary text books. We understood one required subject for our senior year was ancient Egyptian history, and the only source for that dry subject was the Encyclopedia Britannica in the club library. Studying from the Britannica has to be an exquisite form of self-torture, and we soon found ourselves ignoring ancient Egypt and wandering through the mystery and crime library donated to the club by the marines while they were getting ready to ship out.

It wasn't long before our days were divided between reading mysteries and taking interminable walks along the shore...or through the stubble that was once our lovely woods.

One afternoon in late February, Ursula and I, bundled up like Eskimos in huge fur coats with parkas and scarves protecting us from the freezing cold, took the dogs for a walk along the beach. The off-shore wind was frigid as we darted over the ice-floes following the dogs on their happy romp.

Before long they led us out beyond Castle Rock to the open sea, jumping from floe to floe with happy yelps. Finally, as I stopped to catch my breath, I looked up and saw a dark stick rising out of the ice-crusted sea about a quarter of a mile ahead.

"What's *that*?" I stuttered, pointing.

"A periscope!" Ursula said without hesitation.

Slowly it turned in our direction, and I felt my scalp creep in a weird way. Neither of us moved as it came around and lined up on us. As a part of the conning tower broke the surface, Ursula said excitedly, "That doesn't look Japanese, and it's not camouflaged."

One of the advantages of growing up in a Treaty Port was that you got to go aboard all naval vessels. I don't believe there was a ship in the British, American, French, and Italian navies we hadn't been on: light and heavy cruisers, destroyers, sloops, and submarines. The call letters on one of the last were the same as my initials, PRS; although they stood for *HMS Proteus*, I always considered it my personal sub! Looking closely at the dark color of the conning tower, we decided this sub was American and started to wave frantically.

It was useless. We couldn't get out any further, as the ice floes were getting too thin to take our weight, and the bay was too shallow for the sub to come in any closer, unless it surfaced completely.

"Damn! *Damn! DAMN!*" I exploded, as it slowly started to submerge.

"If only it could have come in closer," Ursula said, adding, "We'd better get home and tell Dad."

We raced back across the ice, the wind now slashing at our faces and whipping our scarves out behind us like pennants, the dogs all but forgotten in our excitement.

When we got home, I raced to the phone and asked the operator for Dad's office. Ursula grabbed the receiver from me and put it back on its cradle. "Hey, don't do that! The Japs in Dad's office might hear you. For God's sake, use your head!"

Mother, and later Margo, were intrigued with our story, but waiting for Dad to get back from the club was almost unbearable.

Finally, he came in, and Jung-ya, our houseboy, helped him off with his coat, asking if he wanted a drink before dinner.

"Whiskey-*chee*, please," he said, and then turning to Ursula and me, who were bubbling over with our pent-up news, he asked, "What the *hell's* got into you two?"

"There's an American sub in the bay," I almost shouted, speaking fast so that Ursula couldn't get a word in.

"A *what?*"

"An American sub. We saw it this afternoon."

"You're sure?"

"Absolutely," Ursula said.

After a long pause, Dad said cryptically, looking out of the living room window across the ice-crumpled bay, "That accounts for it."

"Accounts for what?" Mother asked.

"Accounts for none of the last ships reaching Wakamatsu," Dad said drily.

"You mean the sub's sinking the colliers?" Mother asked.

"It must be. All I know is that the manifests are signed off, and the ships leave port, but they never seem to get beyond the Gulf of Chihli. They just disappear. The Japanese aren't saying anything, but Araki told me on the q.t. that they are fuming."

"Oh, that's great! That's *g-r-e-a-t!*" I shouted.

"Where are they getting their fuel to stay afloat?" Margo asked as she joined the discussion.

"Damned if I know. The Chinese must be helping them."

"Do you think they were looking for the smugglers' beach and came up too soon?" I asked. The smugglers' beach was a strip of no-man's-land just north of Shanhaikwan, where the Great Wall ran into the sea, and through some foul-up, belonged neither to China nor Manchuria. Smugglers had been using it for years.

"Hardly," Dad said, "those smugglers are Koreans; they wouldn't be aiding an American sub. They're working for the Japs. They smuggle in drugs, and other contraband, and smuggle out silver to wreck the Chinese economy. One thing about the little Nips, they won't soil their own hands, but they're happy to use Korean thugs to do their dirty work for them. Hell, Customs says there are over a hundred heroin and morphine labs in Shanhaikwan alone, and another hundred between Chinwangtao and Peking!" The disgust in Dad's voice when he spoke of the Japanese invader was scathing, and somehow the sub-sighting got lost in a heated discussion of Japanese atrocities.

Although we spent almost every day down on the floes looking for the submarine, we never saw it again. We knew it had to be around though, as ships were still being sunk. I couldn't help asking Dad why the Japanese didn't send destroyers to flush it out and sink it, and he said that it was obviously just a minor irritation in their overwhelming war effort and insignificant as far as priorities were concerned. And it was also obvious he was silently thanking it for canceling out the stigma of his forced collaboration.

As spring approached, Dad said to Mother, clear out of nowhere, "Gee, do you realize the girls have never seen Peking, at least not so as they can remember it. The Lord knows what might happen to it, especially if the Pacific war spreads to the mainland. They've got to see it...*now!*"

"Oh, sure they do," she said placatingly. "Just get four gold-plated travel permits, and we'll be on our way!" Her sarcasm was like syrup.

But Dad didn't think he was being unreasonable at all when he asked Mr. Araki to see what he could do. I guess Dad's longtime friendship with Araki must have paid off, because his eloquent plea to the military on our behalf got us unheard of travel orders.

Margo was on a business trip to Tangshan. She, and her new boss, "Handsome Harry" Faulkner, were attending a policy session with the Japanese, who were doing what they were famous for, picking the brains of successful western businessmen. Their goal, realistically, was to learn all they could from us, so that they could take over the Kailan and we could be interned.

There was still a cold nip in the air the day Henry, our Chinese chauffeur, drove the four of us through the native city to the grimy station. He didn't trust porters, so he made several trips with our baggage, then stood beside the pieces as we waited for the old PMR to pull in from Shanhaikwan. The train had come down from Manchuria, and to our surprise, all the spotless panelled compartments of the first class car were empty.

As we took off, Dad thanked Henry for his help and told him to be sure to meet the evening train from Peking in six days time.

"Sure, boss," Henry said, touching his cap and moving off into the crowd.

"That's as good as telling him he has almost a full week to take each one of his nine wives for a spin in the car," Mother said, laughing.

"Come on, Gee, he's only got three wives," Dad said.

Mother's shrug was non-committal as we settled ourselves into the comfortable compartment.

There was no doubt Henry, like Dad, was a ladies man; I think that's why Dad and he hit it off so well. He had been a part of our lives for as far back as I could remember, and I guess he'd been with us several years before he plucked up the courage to ask Dad for a raise. Dad told him in no uncertain terms that his pay was entirely adequate, as he was single, and his living quarters and uniforms were supplied. Henry must've thought about that response pretty seriously, because three weeks later he told Dad he'd just got married! Of course, there was nothing for Dad to do but give him his raise.

A year or so passed before Henry tried again, this time hinting that his wife was very extravagant. Wary, Dad told him that that was tough; he'd got a raise when he was married and that was enough for two people. Henry mulled that over for a while and, a couple of months later, told Dad he'd just married wife number two. It was a charade that had a habit of repeating itself. After the third time, Dad dubbed him "Henry" and told him that was the name of a very famous English king. Henry was very proud of it, only he pronounced it "Henly", as he had the usual Chinese problem when it came to pronouncing "R's".

The train made only a whistle-stop at Peitaiho, as the summer resort was all boarded up, then headed west through the lovely rural countryside that had just started to sprout delicate shoots of green vegetation. At the busy farming town of Changli, a few peasants climbed into third class carriages, but still no one entered our car.

When we got to the Lanshen Bridge, the train came to a full stop, and several Japanese soldiers got off and searched the tracks and trestles ahead, looking for explosives. It was a ritual we'd been through every time we'd travelled to and from the convent. Once, while waiting for the "All clear," I'd watched horrified as coffins and bodies floated down the swollen river, churning among bloated cattle and uprooted trees, the result of one of China's never-ending floods. I remember thinking that particular explosive check totally ridiculous: who would put their lives in jeopardy placing dynamite under a swaying bridge that would collapse of its own accord under the onslaught of devastating nature?

Once more, after the "All clear!" as we crawled very slowly over the high, creaking bridge, we found ourselves holding our breath, and when our car finally left the span, we all sighed with relief and smiled at one another.

"You know, we go through this every time, but nothing ever happens," Ursula said.

"...to us," Dad corrected. "Last week they missed some explosives, and a car was derailed, but no one was hurt, thank God."

"Who's responsible?" I asked.

"Well, ever since the Nips took Manchuria in the early thirties, they've been trying to bankrupt China by smuggling out silver on the PMR. Chinese bandits and warlords learned about it, and the train became fair game. Now I guess it's the Communists, or Chinese resistance, if one can call them that—the coolies in the fields. They're trying to turn the tables on the Nips. Japan might think she's taken China, but except for the cities and a mile or so either side of the railroad track, she has no control. If the Chinese would only realize this, and the Nationalists and Communists really join forces, they could run the little Nips out so fast they wouldn't know what hit 'em!"

"Will that ever happen?" I asked.

"Never. They're too busy fighting among themselves—and snitching about each other to their conquerors. And don't think the Japs don't play one against the other."

As we rolled through the lovely farm country, we approached Kaiping, where Jung-ya had a family farm. We got to discussing it, and Mother said, "I can't believe Jung-ya was able to save up enough out of what we pay him to buy a farm."

"Oh, he came from Kaiping," Dad said, "so probably had a little land to start with. Now he has a regular farm—one of the biggest. Figure it this way: we pay him five dollars a month, and he has free lodging and, no doubt, helps himself to quite bit of our food..."

"Oh, no, Geordie, not Jung-ya..." Mother protested.

"Come on, Gee, they don't consider that stealing; it's a way of life. Anyway, it only takes a dollar a month to feed a family, two if you want to live high on the hog—so he puts three dollars a month away for a few years, and the next thing you know, voilà, he and his family are landed gentry!"

"I wonder why he stays with us if that's the case," Ursula said musingly.

"Because he likes us," I replied.

"I know how this sounds, but I think Jung-ya would give his life for us if the occasion arose," Mother said.

I got to thinking about it in my limited way, and I knew she was right, remembering how he always covered for us girls so we wouldn't get punished for some hair-brained prank; how he watched over us when Mother and Dad weren't home; and how he always remembered our birthdays with some little Chinese gift. We weren't his employers—we were his *wai kuo* family.

Ursula interrupted my thoughts. "You know, I've always thought it strange—his family hardly ever comes to see him."

"Well, they have to run the farm," Dad said. "I'll bet they are pulling in quite a bit from the crops now. Before long, they'll really be well off."

"I hope so," Mother said pensively. "Someone ought to be getting something out of all this mess."

When the train stopped at Tangshan, I got up, stretched my legs, and looked out at the gigantic coal hill hovering over the famous mines that had been a prime target in Japan's invasion of China. Tangshan was also the home of the Kailan's largest hospital. Dad told me Chinese coolies fought to work for the Kailan because the work was steady, the pay good, and medical care came automatically with the job. They felt secure, and their families, the core of Chinese culture, were able to stay intact, and as their sons grew up, they were able to work for the Kailan and build *their* families. It hadn't always been that way. Before the British took over the management of the mines, the Chinese would pay off bereaved families with a couple of bucks, because that was cheaper than shoring up the pits to save miners' lives.

I wondered how different it was now with the Japanese running everything. I hoped it was run by civilians and not the military, like Chinwangtao. I'd have to ask Dad.

My musings were broken by a soft sound. I glanced in the last compartment as I went back to my seat and saw a much be-medaled Japanese officer sitting by himself in silent contemplation.

When I got back to our compartment, I said softly, "There *is* someone else in this car. He looks like a Japanese general or something."

"Well, we won't bother him, if he doesn't bother us," Mother said with a smile, turning back to her book.

After leaving Tangshan I tried to read, but the telegraph poles chasing each other down the track were too distracting, and I couldn't concentrate. I found myself thinking of the general in the front compartment. My mind wandered back to the landing parties and the *banzai* charges, the horror of the Fatal Eighth, the ignominy of the collaboration dinner, and all the incidents that had led up to this moment. I felt a sort of noose tightening around us, and I didn't like it. The world had been our oyster for as far back as I could remember, and we were the privileged elite; now we were under house arrest, we had no control over our lives, and worst of all, Dad was working as a collaborator.

Dad had been in England, taking accounting, during his parents' earlier years in the Orient, and Mother, who insisted he was outstanding in his field, loved to tell about an incident in the mid-thirties when the Kailan's chief accountant in Tientsin wanted Dad to stop figuring in his head and use a calculator, the latest business machine on the market. Dad refused. He said there wasn't a machine made that could beat him, and he wasn't going to waste his time proving it.

The chief accountant was insistent. "If we train a Chinese clerk to use a calculator, I mean, really train him so that he's good, will you compete with him, and if you lose, will you use a calculator?" Dad grudgingly acquiesced.

Setting up the challenge took quite a while, as they had to thoroughly train one of Dad's most able Chinese clerks, who had always worked with an abacus, but he eventually became a whiz on the machine. Then the day of the test arrived, and they brought out two identical ledgers that had been painstakingly prepared just for the occasion. At the word "Go!", they both started. When it was all over, a few minutes later—with Dad finishing first—they had two different totals.

Dad was told his total was in error. He looked at them with scorn and said, "Run it through the damned calculator then, if you think you're so good!" They did and found Dad's total was the correct one. He was never asked to use a calculator again.

The train made a long stop over in Tientsin, so we all got up and took a walk on the platform. The crowds were still unbelievable, and the Japanese were throwing their weight around as usual, shouting unintelligible commands to confuse and terrify the Chinese.

When we got back on the train, Ursula took my seat by the window and I sat in the aisle seat. Looking forward, I noticed, if I peered out of the door, I could see slightly into the general's compartment on the other side of the aisle; I saw his sword flash a couple of times, then lost interest. Without the racing poles to distract me, I was ready to read and plunged into my book, forgetting about the outside world.

After a while, I excused myself and went to the lavatory. The tiny room was awkward to get in and out of, and as I stepped back into the cramped corridor, I staggered against the wall. Standing still for a moment to get my balance, I glanced into the general's compartment. A little steel dagger lay beside him on the seat, polished and sparkling in the lowering rays of the sun.

He didn't notice me; he was too busy working on his samurai sword. He was buffing it lovingly, and I knew before long it would have the same lustre as the beautiful little knife.

When I got back to the compartment, Dad asked if I'd seen our luggage. "Yes, the porter's already got it down, and it's by the doors ready to be unloaded," I said.

"Good. I hope the Wagon Lits has sent a car. You never know these days with the Japs running things."

I heard Mother make some comment, but realized I wasn't really listening—at least not to her. There were some strange noises coming from the general's compartment again: not loud, but weird.

I got up quietly and moved down the aisle, so I could look in, but he couldn't see me. I watched fascinated.

He stood up, took his samurai, put the hilt against the back of the seat facing him, bowed to some unknown god, and walked straight into the extended blade. He stood for a moment or two, the surprised look on his face reflected in the highly polished mahogany paneling above the leather seat, then he slithered to the floor, reaching for the smaller knife as he fell.

I rushed back to our compartment, as Mother was saying, "Get your coat on, Bobby; we've arrived."

Dad looked at me anxiously and said, "My God! What's the matter?"

"The...the...general...just killed himself!" I said, and felt myself beginning to heave.

"Easy does it," Dad said. "Try to take a deep breath."

I did.

"Feel any better?"

"Some. I'll be okay. What do we do?"

"Nothing," Dad said. "He just committed *hari-kiri*. That's very honorable. He must be someone very important, or he's just had a great victory. His act is an honorable end, most likely, to a distinguished career. I don't understand it...but then, we don't have to."

We looked out of the window as the train came to a stop. There was an honor guard out on the platform, and a crowd of Japanese dignitaries.

"Let's go out the other end, *quick!*" Dad said. "We'll leave the porter to get our luggage off. Come on, Gee; we don't want to be here when they find his body."

We sped out the far door, as the dignitaries entered the carriage.

I was still shaking and nauseous as I stepped onto the platform, and Dad started looking for the Wagon Lits limousine and a porter.

Soon the wave of nausea gave way to a feeling of misgiving. Although Peking had to be the most beautiful city I'd ever seen, even lovelier than Kyoto, Japan, which we had visited a couple of years earlier, austerity was everywhere, and the mood bleak and despairing. I could feel it in the masses of Chinese in the streets and see it in the faces of the foreigners. The only people cockily above it all were the Japanese. The military were everywhere, posing for pictures in front of shrines, temples, and palaces.

"Hail the conquering hero!" Dad said sarcastically, as we waited for a group of Japanese officers to have their picture taken before entering the Taoist temple.

As fuel was scarce, automobiles had been replaced by pedicabs and rickshaws, and the only car we drove in while we were there was the limo sent by the Wagon Lits Hotel to pick us up and return us to the station. Although pedicabs made sightseeing more leisurely, and we were quite comfortable with cushions and lap-robes, the harsh wind and biting grit made our faces feel like sandpaper at the end of the day.

I found Peking was like a gigantic Chinese puzzle, with cities within cities within cities. The walled city of Peking surrounded the Inner City that in turn encircled the Imperial City that enclosed the Forbidden City—each loaded with treasures and artifacts. Dad acknowledged that the Japanese couldn't subtract from that grandeur, but said he could see neglect of these national treasures at every turn.

We felt lost without a camera, though, and tried to make indelible mental pictures of everything we saw. It was a despairing feeling. We never did get to see the Ming Tombs, as they had been placed out of limits, and according to Mother and Dad, it was not a trip one could take in a pedicab anyway.

At the end of the third day, we were sitting in the lounge of the Wagon Lits—Mother and Dad having their usual evening cocktail—when we got a frantic phone call from Jung-ya.

The dogs were dying! They hadn't eaten since we had left.

Every evening, when Jung-ya had brought bowls of steaming *hsiao-mi*, or millet, and table scraps, one of us would inspect it, sometimes stirring it a little with a finger, then we'd say to the excited dogs, "Eat it! It's *good!*" and they'd scamper after Jung-ya to the pantry area, trying to snatch at the food before he could put the bowls down.

It was a ritual. And it was a ritual that had unintentionally been broken when we all were gone from the house at the same time. Not even Margo was home to put her seal of approval on the food bowls.

No approval—no dinner!

Jung-ya loved those dogs as much as we did, and it must have broken him up to realize they wouldn't take food from him without us blessing it.

Mother said, "Geordie, tell Jung-ya we'll be home late tomorrow, and tell him to be sure and let Henry know."

So ended our Peking vacation—memorable in a lot of strange ways, not the least of which was the reason for our early return.

4

MOSTLY MEMORIES

There was no escaping our disastrous change of circumstances. It hung like a funeral shroud over the little port. The horrible weight of collaboration was sucking the life out of the wage earners. I saw the look on Margo's face and Dad's at the end of each day, and could feel their self-loathing. We were at the mercy of the merciless and knew only too well what they were capable of doing.

Rather than dwell on the uncertainty of the moment, I found I was continually looking back on happier times and a life that had once been full of promise.

Like the summer when I was four and the huge ocean liner, the *Empress of Britain,* visited Chinwangtao. I'd seen the dredges working for days before its arrival, but their work was in vain. There was no way a ship of that size could berth in our shallow harbor, so it had to stand out to sea while the company tug, the *Fuping*, and a huge barge ferried the passengers ashore to a special train waiting at the pier to take them on a sightseeing tour to Peking.

Of course, Ursula and I had to watch the whole show, completely in awe at the size of the ship and the unending line of passengers boarding the waiting club cars, their strident cries of delight and continuous chatter drowning out the plaintiff, lilting chant of the coal coolies. While I was trying to adjust to the unseemly noise, I noticed Amah was nowhere around. I finally spotted her trying to follow us on her little bound feet. She couldn't reach the span of the railroad ties in one step, so kept tottering off them, her pointed shoes and tiny feet agonized by the sharp gravel of the rail bed. I giggled when she gave up and sat down on a capstan, watching us from a distance.

Turning back to the weird stream of humanity, I recalled Mother and Margo talking about tourists, and I got the impression they were strange, uncouth types that we should *never* mingle with.

I looked from them to Ursula, who was standing eyeing them, her face expressionless.

Suddenly I couldn't stand it any longer and burst out, "Oh, look! *Tourists!*", almost exploding with glee.

Ursula said quietly, "They don't look any different from us, but they sure dress funnily."

"Shall we tell Mummy and Margo that we saw them?" I asked.

"I don't think so."

"Do you want to go to Peking with them?" I asked, thinking how exciting it would be.

"Oh, no...not with *tourists.*" There was a hint of scorn in her voice as she turned and started walking back down the pier. I followed, jumping from tie to tie, wishing I was on that train.

Amah looked relieved when we came up to her, and carefully placing her little gnarled walking stick on the ground, she raised herself up from the capstan and slowly followed us along the tracks.

She was very sweet, but so slow. She reminded me of a turtle, or *womba,* as the Chinese called them. I had already learned that you never called anyone *womba* to their face—not unless you wanted a black eye or a busted jaw—as it was a horrible slur on their ancestry. But then I rationalized, Amah was so old it was doubtful she had any ancestors, so I couldn't offend her if I wanted to.

Dear Amah, she would sit quietly by the hour while we played with Moira Cobley, the chief engineer's daughter. She liked it when we played on the swings or in the sandbox with Moira, because then she could visit with Moira's amah, a much younger woman who was up on all the port gossip, Chinese and foreign.

Moira called her amah Li, and Li would give Amah "hair raising" facials while we girls looked on fascinated. The treatment must've been quite painful, but Amah told us that the further her hairline receded the more respect she would get in her old age. While we watched, Li would take about a foot of fine silk thread and stretch it taut against Amah's forehead, and somehow roll it between her fingers as she ran it up into the hairline. As it rolled, fine little hairs would wrap themselves around it tightly, and when she'd got a row of them twisted around the thread, she'd give it a sharp tug and pull them all out by the roots in a neat, clean line. Amah would give out a gentle moan, and Li would start on another row of hairs. The results were almost imperceptible at first, as Amah could only stand about ten pluckings at a sitting, but after several months her forehead appeared quite a bit higher, and after a year it curved back over her head, making her look very learned and wise. Of course, the ultimate goal was to be bald all across the top of the head, denoting wisdom of great proportions.

In exchange for Li's ministrations, Amah would make her lovely hand-sewn shoes; every-day ones had plain uppers, while dress shoes would be embroidered with flowers and butterflies in delicate satin-stitch. Without realizing it, I was getting my first lesson in the ancient Chinese custom of bartering.

How I loved those carefree days! Early in the morning I would run out to the play-yard to see the purple and white morning glories open up, and as the day progressed, I'd watch them twist up and hang like so many little umbrellas put away after the rain. Each escapade left me looking inquisitively around for the next, always totally without fear.

I found a whole different world out in the play-yard. A world of little creatures and insects, like lizards and wooly worms, praying mantises, and spiders. I loved them all, especially the last—there were so many of them in the bamboo mat roof over our sandbox. I'd pick up a brown wood spider and a long-legged green-and-

yellow one and race them up my arm. It never ceased to amaze me
that the little furry brown spider would always win, although its legs
were only half the length of the brightly colored one—it almost
seemed as though the green-and-yellow spider was scared of it.

Moira and Ursula were usually too busy on the swings to pay any
attention to my little game, pushing harder and higher to see if they
could make the swing sail over the top of its stand.

One day Mother came by, returning from a visit to a neighbor,
and looking over the vine-covered fence, screamed, "What are you
doing!?! Amah! Amah! *Stop her!"*

I looked around thinking Ursula must have flipped off the swing
or something, but Mother came charging through the gate and, with
one wide swipe, sent my little six-legged athletes flying into oblivion. I was completely bewildered and started to cry.

"Bobby, don't *ever* do that again! Spiders are deadly—especially
the brown ones!" She was shaking, she was so scared.

I started to wail. How could my little friends be deadly? I'd
played with them all summer, and they'd never hurt me.

But the joys of the sandbox died with Mother's scream.

I never played with spiders again. In fact, a few nights later I
had a horrible nightmare, where a spider grew into a giant and
chased me up a high mountain that turned into the coal hill at the
Tangshan mines, and when at last I reached the top, panting with
exertion, I found there was no other side—I was looking over a
precipice—and I woke up screaming in terror.

The following year Mother went home on leave. Mother and
Dad never took "home leave" together, as Dad always went to
England and Mother to the States. They also never took their leave
in the same year—or took us with them—that way each could get
a complete rest. When she got back, she told us we'd be starting
school in September.

"Who is going to teach us?" I asked, excited.

"I am," she said, rumpling my hair.

And sure enough, the first week in September, we found we were
in class with Moira and the port administrator's son, Alistair Chilton.

The sessions were held on the indoor veranda, with its flower-laden windows filtering the sun. Dad's *mu-jiang*, or carpenter, who was kept busy making filigreed end-tables, picture frames, and elaborate household furnishings, built four sturdy little desks with attached seats and built-in ink wells, and we all felt very important as we filed into class every weekday morning at nine on the dot.

Mother taught us simple math, careful italic printing that would later adapt easily to elegant Spencerian script, and reading. The last, she insisted, was by far the most important, because if one couldn't read, no other subject could be studied. And to emphasize this, we all had to read aloud daily.

She would pick someone to start, and after a paragraph or two, point her finger imperiously at another student, and he or she would have to carry on; this went on for a good hour, each student getting to read several times. Her teaching was phonetic; words were sounded out and broken down into syllables. She had no patience with anyone who glanced at a word and read it wrong because they didn't take time to sound it out.

Studying with Mother was fun. I found it exciting, and the hours we spent with her all too short. Mother insisted—possibly as she had other things she'd rather be doing—that, if we applied ourselves, we only needed to study in the mornings, so our afternoons were free to conjure up make-believe, to walk our precious dogs, and to enjoy the beauty that was all around us. We drew and painted primitive pictures, made dolls and doll houses, invented wild-and-wooly Rube Goldberg contraptions, and played games of derring-doo.

As we grew older, Amah had a habit of lying down with a headache whenever we did something really wild—like the time I roasted peanuts in Dad's monogrammed pewter shaving mug and it melted into an indescribable mess. And the spring we frosted mud pies with creamy white lime that had been left by a brick mason after a remodelling job, using Mother's favorite silver-plated flatware. Then there was the jam-making incident, when we used purple berries from the climbing ivy, and our arms were covered in a miserable rash all the way up to our armpits. Even that nas-

ty episode didn't dampen our spirits, and we darted from one exploit to another like bees in clover.

Margo spent the school months of those golden years attending
the Tientsin Grammar School, and as it wasn't a boarding school,
she stayed with our dentist and his wife, coming home for Christmas, Easter, and summer vacations.

I never saw much of her, except in the summer, and then because
of our age difference, I only saw her alone when she'd had a fight
with her best friend, Joyce Marsh. I really admired her and Joyce.
They were full of fun and mischief and could find more things to
giggle and joke about—only they always clammed up when I
arrived on the scene. It was frustrating and tantalizing at the same
time.

Late in the autumn of '33, Dad got transferred to Tientsin, and we
moved into a brick-and-stucco, three-storied house on Pao Mah Lu,
or Race Course Road. Mother said Dad picked it because it was
midway between the Tientsin Country Club and the Tientsin Men's
Club—that the imposing Kailan head office was half a block from
the latter was just an added bonus.

I had never left the little Treaty Port before, and nothing could
have prepared me for that trip to Tientsin. At every whistle-stop
along the way, I watched hordes of Chinese clamber aboard the
third class carriages, shoving, pushing, and cussing in a frenzy of
flight, with squawking chickens and bawling babies adding to the
din.

"What's happening?" I asked Dad at Tangshan, where the mob
seemed even more violent.

"Nothing. They've paid their fare, and they don't want to be left
behind."

I remember Dad pulling his head in from the window and saying
to Mother, "Dad would love to see this, Gee, *humanity* on the move,
and heaven help anyone who gets in its way!"

"It's as though they're making up for lost time," Mother said, as
the train squealed and started to pull slowly out of the station.

Through all the commotion and hubbub, Margo was the only one who was completely unmoved. She'd made the trip so many times, going back and forth to school, I don't believe she raised her eyes from her book the entire way.

At Tientsin's colossal station, the sights, sounds, and smells were overwhelming, and my earlier curiosity turned to outright fear. As we stepped off the train onto the milling platform, I grabbed Margo's hand like a vise, terrified I would be trampled to death at any moment. She glanced down at me with a look bordering on contempt, and I felt tears coming to my eyes.

"What's the matter?" she asked curtly. Then, noticing my eyes darting fearfully over the pressing crowds, she added, "Don't cry. There's nothing to be afraid of." I didn't believe her and held onto her hand even tighter as we started up the ramp to the pedestrian overpass that straddled the tracks. I'd never seen so many unfriendly faces in my life, and my fears didn't disappear until we got into the Kailan's waiting taxi and drove over the International Bridge and onto the wide Rue De France that ran the length of the French Concession.

Dad pointed out traffic policemen standing on little podiums in the center of busy intersections, deftly manipulating stop-and-go signals hanging over them like huge red and green Christmas lights. As Rue de France turned into Victoria Road, he said with pride, "We're entering the British Concession now."

Here, turbaned Sikhs with heavy beards took over the directing of traffic. They were so massive and threatening they didn't need traffic lights; they just scowled at the drivers and waved them through with a flourish of their huge, white-gloved hands.

That was the first time I stayed at the Astor House Hotel and looked with awe on Victoria Park and the crenelated mass of Gordon Hall. It's castle-like appearance was emphasized further the following morning, when a British regiment swooped out through the gates led by a marching band. The drummer at the head of the unit, beating a rolling tattoo, had a magnificent black moustache and wore a real leopard skin draped over his shoulders. I'd never seen anything like it and thought I'd burst with pride.

Later that day, we drove out to our new home on Race Course Road. When we got there, all our servants, dogs, furniture, and belongings had already arrived, and Dad was obviously impressed with the Kailan's thoroughness in handling the move.

There was only one dark room in the house; it was the rather large, long living room with a window at one end, almost covered in ivy. All the rest of the rooms had lots of windows looking out on every aspect of the city. I missed not having a garden though, unless a fifteen-by-twenty foot high-walled, mossy rock pile, with sundry shrubs and a resident snake, could be considered as such. Like most of the homes in Tientsin, it did have a roof garden— leading off Margo's little "penthouse". It was about the size of a badminton court, and it became a happy retreat for Ursula, me, and the dogs.

Dad soon realized that, as Tientsin was such a rambling city, we would have to have two cars, one for himself and one for the rest of the family. I remember them so well, "Fifi" and "The Duchess". Fifi was a little cream-colored Fiat with a dark grey landau top, lots of sparkling chrome, and a very decadent look. The Duchess was a huge Essex touring car, surprisingly the same cream-and-grey as Fifi. She was dignified and defiant, and rickshaw coolies ran like hell to get out of her way.

As it happened, Dad, who didn't drive, took the chauffeur and The Duchess, and Mother dashed around town in little Fifi, with us kids hanging out of the windows waving wildly at anyone who would wave back. I learned later that was taboo. Not our waving, but Mother's driving; foreigners had to be chauffeured or lose face. Mother, as usual, ignored protocol if it didn't suit her way of life.

Margo was a day scholar now, and walked to the Grammar School each day. Mother still taught us, as she had in Chinwangtao, because none of the primary schools in the city met with her approval. And, just as she'd done in the port, she rounded up several children to study with us, believing the competition good for us. Except for Moira Cobley, whose father had been transferred from Chinwangtao when we were, I didn't know or care much for the other kids, thinking them prissy and pompous. As always, class was from nine to twelve, with a snack break at ten-thirty. Mother did not provide snacks, but suggested the children could bring some fruit or cookies for break.

Christopher Lockhart, a freckled red-head with a horrible habit of sniffing after every other word, came to school one day with a banana for his snack, and while Mother was out of the room at break-time, he rang for Jung-ya and ordered him to slice the fruit into a bowl and top it with sugar and cream. When Mother came back into class, there was flaming Christopher sitting at his desk with a serviette tucked under his chin, diving into a bowl of sliced bananas and cream.

We were all out on the porch playing hopscotch, and happily chomping on apples and cookies and such, when Mother descended on him. "What is *this?*" she asked scornfully, pointing to the bowl of fruit.

"Bananas—*sniff*—and cream," he said happily, as he stuffed his face.

"I can see that. But where did you get the bananas sliced, *and* the serviette, bowl, sugar, and cream?" She spat out the last words.

"I ordered your houseboy to prepare it for me!"

"You did, did you? Well, don't do it again. *Ever!*"

"But I always have my bananas sliced with cream," he sniveled, his nervous sniff completely forgotten.

"Not in *this* house!"

"I'm going to tell my daddy—he's a colonel."

"I don't care if he's the Prince of Wales, you will eat a banana like any other child, or you won't *bring* a banana!"

As she turned away, she saw all our funny little faces contorted against the French windows, and she tried desperately to keep a stern face.

Now Moira was different. Her problem was an over-active imagination and a mother who played bridge seven days a week. She was such a forgotten cipher at home, she had to make up stories to justify her existence.

One day she came to class with eyebrows painted up into her auburn bangs and bright red rouge on her cheeks, chin, and nose.

It was all we could do not to laugh. As usual, the chauffeur brought her late, and as she came in, Mother gave her a withering look that slowly turned into one of incredulity.

"You're late, Moira."

"Yes, ma'am," she said softly.

"And would you mind telling me what you have on your face?" I saw Mother was trying not to smile as she spoke.

With a perfectly straight face, Moira said, "As I was leaving this morning, Mother said (imitating her mother's voice perfectly)— 'Come here child, you look pale…let me put a touch of color on your face.'"

"Moira, are you telling me your *mother* put that make-up on you?"

"Yes, ma'am."

I know Mother was just about to tell her not to lie, when she saw all of us giggling, and turned back to Moira and said, "No make-up is allowed in this school; you'll have to wash it off. *Now!*" Then she stood up and said, "Follow me!" and marched out of the room.

A few minutes later when they came back, Moira's face was still red, this time from the scrubbing Mother had given it.

Weekday afternoons, we still walked our dogs, taking each on a leash out to Morlings Corner at the south-east boundary of the British Concession, knowing that if they got loose and strayed they would be eaten by the hungry. One of our cats disappeared the first week we arrived, and I was horrified when Mother told me what might have happened. It took me a while to enjoy the warmth of my lovely tabby mittens again. Although the dogs were very good about being leashed, I couldn't help feeling sorry for them, as they never got to run and romp like they had in Chinwangtao.

There was something else that bothered me—the sight of countless beggars, maimed and disfigured, who cried for alms in the street and came around to our back door for handouts of food. There had been no beggars in the little Treaty Port, and I had a hard time understanding such poverty.

Tientsin was a city of contrasts. Of abject poverty and over-whelming opulence. Of homeless dregs of humanity scavenging for scraps, sleeping in vermin-ridden *hutungs,* and of fabulously wealthy Chinese businessmen, living in palatial, high-walled residences that took up entire city blocks. I remember the pre-funeral preparations of one such prominent merchant that went on for months. Hundreds of paid mourners, wailing and clashing cymbals, walked around the walls of his ostentatious residence for days on end, tying up traffic on all four streets. Finally, the whole thing was called off.

I asked Amah what had happened.

"Old man no want to die," she said simply.

Margo passed the residence every day on her way to school, and I heard her telling Mother about seeing the mourners being paid off as she came home that afternoon.

"It's funny," she said, "but they never had a real funeral procession…"

I interrupted her, proud of knowing something she didn't. "The old man wouldn't die!" I said.

"After all that expense, it's a wonder no one thought of finishing him off," she said bluntly.

We'd been at the Race Course Road house for over a year, when suddenly we moved. Looking back now, I think it was because Ursula and I loved to sit on the parapet of the roof-garden, high above the wide boulevard, waving at all the cars and busses that headed out to the race track come racing season. Although we had no fear of heights, it was obvious our antics were aging Mother and Dad fast.

One day in late autumn, they took us out house-hunting, and the first two we looked at were across the Hai Ho in the ex-Russian Concession. They were lovely places, but Mother pointed out wisely to Dad that they were too far from his clubs.

"Just think, Geordie, every time you want to go to the club, you'll have to take the ferry, and if it isn't running, you'll have to go the long way round via the International Bridge. You won't be happy, I know it."

As we clambered aboard the ferry—which was nothing more than a huge open sampan—for the return trip to the British Bund, the river got choppy, and we pitched and wallowed, and Mother, turning pea-green, leant over the side and wretched, then turned with a horrible look of embarrassment and said, "Geordie, it isn't going to work."

"I know, old girl, I'm sorry…we'll look elsewhere."

"Elsewhere" turned out to be closer to town, just past the Fifteenth Infantry's "Can-Do Field". The house, in a cluster known as the Chanticleer Villas, was approached down a long, dog-legged, brick-walled drive called Chanticleer Lane—the brick wall to the left enclosing homes and compounds on the perimeter of the ex-German Concession, the one on the right following the north boundary of the Chinese Jesuit Men's College.

I liked our new home, but it was much darker inside, as it was only two stories high and surrounded by trees, with several tall college buildings blocking its southern exposure. It also butted up against another big villa whose garden gates blocked the end of the lane, turning it into a cul-de-sac.

There definitely wasn't as much going on in the new neighborhood, but it did have a couple of big pluses: the dogs could play safely in the lane and tiny garden, and there were three German kids in the villa next door, two boys and a girl, ranging from five to ten years of age, or from just below my age to a year older than Ursula. Their names were Johann, Klaus, and Inge.

Every afternoon after lunch, we'd either run over and play in their garden, or they'd be over in ours. We built tree houses and forts, played hopscotch and jump-rope, and really enjoyed their exuberance and joy of life. They were a neat family, and Mr. and Mrs. Mueller were typical, loving, overweight Germans, who enjoyed nothing as much as their children, music, and good, hearty, German food.

Johann told us they had once loved their homeland more than anything else, but they didn't any more. "It's not the country," he told us, "but Hitler, and what he is doing to the German people. We will never go back to Germany while he is Fuhrer."

I didn't know just what he meant, but I enjoyed the game we made of fighting Hitler and his elite band of storm troopers, little knowing our childish games would soon echo a human nightmare.

That winter, like the one before, we spent Sunday mornings out at the French Arsenal, while Margo rode to hounds. I was so proud of her. She looked terrific in her beautiful cream-colored jodhpurs, shiny black boots, smart tailored jacket, and velvet hunting cap. There weren't many women riders, and none her age, so she really was the toast of the hunts.

Dad also basked in her reflected glory, which she nonchalantly took in stride, her gelding, Darby, prancing proudly with the horses of British taipans, Italian counts, and German barons, as if he knew he had the best rider there on his back. It was all very impressive, with the arsenal road lined with chauffeured cars, most flying their country's colors.

It was obvious Margo truly loved Darby. She would spend every free minute she could take away from her studies at the race course, where he was stabled, taking him for canters around the track. The cold winter gave him a lovely thick, glossy coat, and the few times Ursula and I went out to watch her ride, we were awed at how graceful she looked; she and Darby seemed one as they flew around the empty course.

Then spring came, and a long hot summer was predicted. Margo knew Darby would suffer with his heavy coat, so she had him clipped. I was dumbfounded after his grooming and said, "He isn't *black* any more!" It was true—he was a dark, dappled grey, but still just as handsome. Margo put her arm around his neck, and he nuzzled her happily. "He's still the most beautiful horse in all the world," she said proudly, and he nickered as though he understood every word.

A week later, he was gone.

I was told he died of pneumonia, and I wept with Margo at her loss. I soon got over it, but Margo never did.

She cried for ages, and I couldn't understand why. She wouldn't eat, and the looks she threw Dad at the dinner table were pure venom. It wasn't possible to blame him. He hadn't done anything; it was Darby who had caught pneumonia. I could feel something was wrong, but as Mother was away on home leave in the States,

I had no one to turn to. After a while, I learned to ignore the whole situation.

When the blistering summer of '35 arrived, it curdled the air in Tientsin, and the stench rising up from the streets and canals was nauseating. To make matters worse, Margo and I came down with chicken pox, and the excruciating rash that covered every inch of our bodies refused to respond to calamine, baking soda, or any of the old home remedies.

We weren't used to this kind of heat, and salty sweat ran into our open sores, making us miserable and short-tempered. Although the doctor had insisted that Ursula stay in our room to catch the bug and get it over with, she never got ill, but rather spent the time helping feeble Amah sponge us off and make us comfortable. Without Mother to help with our care, Jung-ya took over, making iced lemon-barley water and chilled gelatin desserts to tempt us to eat and drink so we wouldn't get dehydrated.

Slowly we recovered, and the day after the company physician lifted our quarantine, Dad shipped us all down to Chinwangtao for the rest of the summer.

As all the summer bungalows on Long Beach had been spoken-for years in advance, we got a suite in the Rest House below the club. The lovely little hostel handled about a dozen guests. A cool, flower-decked veranda ran the length of the building and overlooked a park with a playground surrounded by lilac bushes, yellow roses, and flowering shrubs.

Our rooms were in the front overlooking the veranda. Next to us was a quaint old Chinese gentleman who wore a long silk robe with a brocade jacket, a little black cap with a satin button on top, and hand-sewn slippers. After each meal, he would slowly walk up and down the veranda, rolling oiled walnuts in his delicate hands, and every couple of minutes, as he paced, he would stop and let out a long, rumbling belch, and quietly say, *"Ch'ih-pao-la!"*

The sound was sickening, and we would peer down at him from our window and shudder.

"Is it true he's worth eighty-five million?" I asked.

"That's what I hear," Margo said.

"Then he can afford to learn good manners."

"You don't understand, Bobby, he *does* have good manners. If you don't belch after a Chinese meal, you're insulting your host and the cook. What's more, it's supposed to be very good for you. I understand Chinese never suffer from indigestion."

"I'd rather have indigestion," Ursula said firmly.

Somehow, Chinwangtao wasn't the same that summer. Probably in part because Mother wasn't with us, but mostly because I was a visitor and had lost my sense of belonging. Mr. Cartwright, who had taken over Dad's position as port accountant, automatically got to live in our lovely old house, and I didn't care for him or his family

First off, they didn't like flowers, so all the colorful flower-beds that Mother and Jung-ya had planted were uprooted, and replaced by little pocket-sized lawns. Horrible, scraggly lawns. They had even filled in the fountain pool and planted it to lawn. I could tell the house wasn't happy. The garden wasn't happy. And it was obvious the lawns weren't happy, as they refused to grow.

There were no flowers on the balustrade or lining the paths that led to the garden gates. There was no color anywhere—not even the Union Jack was flying. I looked at the barren flagpole and wanted to cry.

The Cartwrights had two children, a boy and a girl, both in their late teens and both very tall. Albert was about as colorful as the garden, with pink-rimmed eyes, pale skin, and freckles. Agnes was easily as tall as her brother, with a beaky nose and long, dark, straight hair. Every time I saw her, she reminded me of a giraffe, especially with her wide hips and strange, lurching gait. I always expected her to tip her long neck and nibble the lower branches of the acacias as she passed under them.

I wished they'd all get lost, or transferred, or go home to England. Anything—but let us come back to our lovely home.

*****

Mother finally joined us in August, and when we got back to Tientsin at the end of the month, our sweet German neighbors were gone. I couldn't believe it when I pushed open their heavy garden gates and rushed up to the front door to tell them we were back, and found it hanging open.

I shouted, "Johann! Klaus! Inge!" and my voice echoed back at me. I called again and again; there was no answer.

I tiptoed in, going from room to room, hoping to find a clue. There was nothing. The heavy, old, over-stuffed chairs in the living room that had groaned as the sprightly boys and their little sister had bounced joyously on them looked forlorn and dusty. The grand piano sat mute where once Mrs. Mueller had pounded away with the deft touch of a pile driver.

I went up the great staircase to the bedrooms and found stripped beds, empty wardrobes, and limp curtains. All the children's clothes, toys, and books were gone.

As I stepped back onto the landing and looked at the graceful, long, curved banisters that wound down to the huge central hall, I couldn't help climbing up on them and taking one last flying run to the bottom. Swooshing off the end, I remembered the servants' quarters and decided maybe someone was out there who could tell me what had happened.

There was no one.

I went back through the house to the front door, turned, and gave one final look at the old place. The only signs of humanity were my newly made footsteps on the dusty floor. I softly shut the door and heard it lock behind me. I shrugged and walked slowly back home.

Mother and Margo were unpacking, and Dad was home from the office when I came in. As I ran up and gave him a hug, I asked, "Where are the Muellers?"

"I'm sorry, Bobby. But Mrs. Mueller died in surgery a couple of months ago. A few weeks later, Mr. Mueller passed away with 'flu complicated by a broken heart, and the German authorities shipped the boys and Inge home to relatives in Hamburg."

"That's not fair! They hated Hitler and what he's doing to

Germany. They never wanted to go back, not while he was Fuhrer!"
I said, remembering what Johann had called Hitler.

"What could the consulate do? There was no one here to take
care of them. No relatives. No one."

"I know it's hard, Bobby," Mother said, "but it was the only thing
that could be done."

*"Orphans…*how horrible! How lonely they must be…"

And then, remembering Johann had had a crush on Ursula, I
added, "Poor Johann."

"But they're together, Bobby. And they were always close.
They'll be all right. I know they will."

"Never! Not in Germany! Not the way they feel about Hitler!"

Not long after that tragic event, my prayers were answered. Mr.
Cartwright's contract with the Kailan was up, and he and his family went home to England, and we moved back to our beloved Chinwangtao. But the house didn't seem the same somehow; it was as
though it was trying to shuck off a bad memory. I got a strange
feeling that the Cartwrights must have been scared of the Chinese,
especially their servants, because they had put bars on our bedroom
window, and all the doors had double locks on them, even the ones
leading up from the servants' compound.

I couldn't get over it. When we went to bed at night, we had
always felt perfectly safe leaving Jung-ya to lock the outside doors
and shoot the bolt to the courtyard gate. We never thought of our
servants coming in during the night to rob us or do us in; they were
our friends, our Chinese family.

I loved to play in the compound, especially Sunday evenings in
the summer, when Cook would let me crank the ice-cream bucket.
Sometimes Jung-ya would be playing on his flute; he liked to do
that at the end of a long day when Mother and Dad were at the club.
The tunes sounded lonely and heart-wrenching, and I would squat
beside him and listen to them till he heard the car drive up on the
crunchy gravel. Then he would get up, put his flute away, slip into
his long white house-coat, and go and greet them.

Jung-ya was definitely "family".

And the bars on the bedroom window were something else. The

window looked out onto the flat roof of the boiler-room and across to the tennis court and pretty little copse that lay between our house and the club. Ursula and I often climbed out on it to escape from Amah; it was the only secret hiding place we had where even the dogs couldn't get to us.

When we asked Dad if the bars could be removed, as they made our room into a prison, he said he'd look into it. That's as far as it got, as the Cartwrights had had the iron frame and bars sunk into the wall so deeply it would've been a major project to have them removed. It was disappointing, but it couldn't mar our happiness at being home—or the joy of our dogs.

While Mother quietly cussed at all the weird renovations and decorating the Cartwrights had done to the house, Ursula and I, with Jane and Brewster, romped happily across the bluff and, scrambling down the cliffs, played on the incoming ice-floes. Later, we roamed through the forest and played tag around the barren acacias as they stood on a carpet of charred grass, flecked here and there with melting snow from an earlier storm.

As it was still late autumn, the forest caretaker, in his long padded coat and fur-lined hat with earflaps, was still burning the brush under the trees. We loved helping him, especially stamping out fires if they seemed to be getting out of hand. This simple ritual every fall was what made the ground so lush and lawn-like under the trees every summer and kept bugs and mosquitoes at bay.

We didn't have Amah any more; she had elected to stay in Tientsin near relatives. It was just as well, as we had run away from her so many times, Mother was on the verge of throwing in the towel. When we got back to Chinwangtao, she made us promise we'd always look out for each other and then told us we were on our own. Oh, the independence was wonderful!

The following winter was marked by the death of King George V and the ascension to the throne of his eldest son, the Prince of Wales, who became "uncrowned" Edward VIII. It was also marked by a change in Dad's attitude toward me.

I don't know if it was the thought of "royal succession", or lingering anguish at the memory of Tony, my little brother who died at the age of eighteen months; maybe it was my nickname, Bobby, that brought it on; but that year Dad decided to turn me into a tomboy. Strangely, I rather liked it at first, especially all the boys' things he bought me, like the workshop of carpentry tools that transformed Amah's old quarters into a veritable gold mine of intriguing projects. Actually, I started so many, it looked as though there was an army working in my shop rather than one individual. I was building a doll's house, a boat, and some furniture, not to mention a jigsaw puzzle, made of an old magazine illustration that I had laminated onto plywood.

One day I got stuck on the jigsaw, and as Dad was home, I asked him to help me. When he came into my cluttered shop, he gave one look and threw up his hands in disgust.

"Don't you ever finish *anything?*" he roared, as he stumbled over a three-legged stool that still had only two legs and, clutching the worktable, caught himself before he fell.

"Well, the reason there are so many projects is that I go as far as I can, and when I get stuck, I start another."

"You mean you stop just because you get stuck?" He sounded incredulous.

"What would *you* do?" I asked, almost in a whine.

"Dammit! I'd figure it out—that's what I'd do!"

"Supposing I can't?"

"But you *can!* You've got brains, *use them!*"

Then he proceeded to give me a lesson on contract bidding, bonuses for meeting due dates, and additional bonuses for beating them. "Write yourself a contract before you start a project. Give yourself a realistic date to complete it, and a bonus if you do it on time."

"What if I don't make it on time?"

"Then you have to pay a penalty. That's what the contractors do when they are hired to remodel our homes in the spring. If they don't meet the due date, the Kailan deducts a penalty from their estimate. Funny, they've never *not* made it on time, and almost always, they beat the due date by a week or so, so that they can get an extra bonus!"

With that, he sat down with me, and we worked out a contract for each project in the shop. Actually, when we went over them I found that I hadn't really got stuck on any of them, I had just lost interest and started something new. His approach put interest back in the projects, and by setting hard-and-fast due dates, I found the challenge came back too.

He looked at me when we were through and said, "Remember, everything has a beginning and an end—what you do in between is the challenge, and how it turns out is the kick in the pants you need to start you off again."

The following year it was Dad's turn to go on home leave, and he left for England in mid June. Actually, he only spent a few weeks in London with his folks and the rest of the time in Europe, mostly in the Montmartre section of Paris, where he and a talented artist, Lea Chapon, painted and sketched up a storm.

As good as Dad was at accounting, his first love had always been art, and he was one of the best. Being raised in a Victorian family of professionals, he had never been allowed to study art, let alone practice it, so he took out his frustration when he was on home leave by leading the life of a Bohemian in Paris and rendering meticulous little pen-and-ink sketches. It was due to this talent that I learned so much about his life. His little sketch books, usually only three-by-five inches, were filled with pictures. And, when time didn't allow for sketching, he would use his camera to beautiful effect.

Later, he took time away from his beloved Paris to visit Berlin, the city that had just hosted the Eleventh Olympiads. He came away impressed with the country's resurgence of national pride—and also with a wonderful collection of Telefunken records and a six-disc record-changer, the latest status symbol of music buffs. When he got home, I remember asking, as I helped him put away his new classical record collection, "Daddy, why do you have two sets of everything?"

"So I can alternate the records and have a whole movement play without having to get up to turn the discs over."

That was Dad all over. Nothing was too good for him.

I also remember the opening lines of the Christmas carol he was singing when he stepped off the *SS Scharnhorst*—

> *"Hark the herald angels sing,*
> *Mrs. Simpson's pinched our King..."*

referring to Edward VIII's upcoming abdication to marry an American divorcée. Not long after the formal announcement on December the eleventh, we learned that Edward's younger brother, the Duke of York, was to be crowned King George VI.

When Coronation Day, May 6, 1937, came around, Chinwangtao had its moment of glory. The bay and harbor had been dredged so that naval ships could berth, and on the great day, we all went down to Pier One to board the vessels that were lined up side-by-side, starting with the sloop, *HMS Bridgewater*, followed by a couple of sleek destroyers, and finally the heavy cruiser, *HMS Dorsetshire*.

All the officers were in full dress, emblazoned with medals, orders, and extravagant epaulets, and wearing much-braided cocked hats, while the men of the port were in dress-whites, some, like Dad, wearing Panamas to protect them from the sun. Mother and Margo, and the other ladies, wore gay, frilly voiles, floppy hats, and short white gloves. Everyone looked beautiful to me, as if they had just stepped out of a storybook, and the magic of the moment held me in its spell.

It wasn't to last. As we started to move up the gangplank onto the *Bridgewater*, a shrill whistle brought me back to reality. Margo smiled down at me when I gave a startled jump and said, "Hey, we're being piped aboard—I've always wondered what it would be like."

All the decks were lined with sailors so rigid they looked like cardboard cutouts, and I found it hard not to giggle when I glanced at their stern faces. Looking down to hide my smile, I noticed their polished boots and couldn't help wondering if I stepped on their toes whether they'd feel anything. Margo must've gathered I was up to no good, as she took my hand and gave it a gentle jerk and kept me moving along with the crowd.

That was the last light moment for what seemed like ages, as the service on the *Dorsetshire* went on for ever, and I was totally bored with the proceedings. I squirmed and wiggled, and found myself watching the junks and sampans bobbing about in the bay. Then I leaned forward and looked at Ursula, standing on the far side of Dad. She looked like a statue. I don't believe she moved through the whole service. *Why couldn't I be like her?*

Finally the service was over, and the Royal Naval Band broke into *Pomp and Circumstance*, and to my horror, I got goose-bumps. I was so embarrassed. I looked at my bare arms and legs and hoped no one would notice their pickled appearance. When the last note died on the noon air, a twenty-one gun salvo rang out across the bay, leaving me with knees shaking and Chinese junks scuttling for cover.

Then the rows of people on deck started to break up and mingle, and Ursula and I were told to go back to the car and tell Henry to take us to the Arnolds' house. It seems that while the adults were celebrating aboard ship, we were to take care of the Arnolds' four-year-old son, Eric, till the fireworks started, then we could join the grown-ups at the club to watch the display.

That was a real let-down as I loathed Eric Arnold. He was an only child who had come late in life and was sickly, spoiled, and totally devoid of manners. The day that started out like a fairy-tale soon turned into a nightmare that came to a climax at the dinner table. When a delightful homemade ice-cream dessert was served, Eric began throwing things at the servant, because the ice cream—which he had insisted was too cold—turned into a runny mess after he demanded the cook fry it. Ursula and I decided the situation was impossible and took off running for home.

"If anyone says anything about us leaving," Ursula said, "tell them the fireworks started early."

The real show that night was stupendous. There was a scaffold with a colossal "GR" and crown made up of thousands of brilliant lights high atop the hill at Lady Walsham's Seat. It could be seen far out to sea and on the mainland for miles in all directions.

"What's the 'GR' for?" I asked Margo as we stood on the club terrace waiting for the fireworks to begin.

"George Rex. Rex means 'King' in Latin."

"Do you know Latin?" I asked, impressed.

"Enough," she said with a smile.

She had changed since the morning, and her slim, off-the-shoulder evening dress, with its circular flounce that flared out below the knee, was stunning. She had curled her dark hair, which was usually worn in a smooth bob, and borrowed long, sparkling earrings from Mother. I wondered if Margo ever knew how badly I wanted to be eighteen like her.

Joyce Marsh came over and joined us as I was dreaming.

"Hello, sprout," she said and tousled my hair.

I shook my head angrily at her intrusion.

"I really like your dress, Bobby," she said.

I looked down at it and noticed it for the first time. It *was* pretty, even if it was just like Ursula's.

When we'd been in Tientsin, Dad had decided he wanted Ursula and me to dress alike, even though we weren't twins. He insisted it was very European and very chic. Mother had protested and pointed out that Ursula and I were different in a lot more ways than just age and size.

"As long as I'm paying the tailor bills, they'll be dressed the way I want," he had said with authority.

"Yes, George," Mother said sweetly.

So we dressed alike. Sometimes the dress suited me and not Ursula; sometimes it was the other way around. But Dad never seemed to notice. That evening we were both in simple silk dresses with princess lines. Ursula was wearing stockings with black patent shoes. I was wearing white ankle socks with pink roses on the cuff that set off my bruised shins and scuffed knees. Mother had tried stockings on me before, but I usually ran them before I got them on, so she dropped that item of my apparel and substituted anklets, or knee-socks, depending on the weather.

The evening had a nip in it as we all stepped out of the club and trailed over to the cenotaph on the cliff's edge to watch the fireworks display.

China was the home of fireworks and fire-crackers, with every event from the Dragon Boat Festival to New Year's being an excuse for a brilliant, noisy extravaganza, but I think even the Chinese had to admit that the *Ing Kuo-jen*, or English, had them beat this time, with one burst after another climbing higher and higher into the evening sky, exploding into stars, that exploded again and again.

As I watched the exciting display, Captain Arnold came into view with Eric on his shoulders looking like a precious angel, while Mrs. Arnold cooed and fussed around the two of them. I looked at the trio, then held my nose and pretended to upchuck; Ursula gave me a nasty frown. My little charade was interrupted by o-o-oh's and a-a-ah's from the crowd, and when I looked up I saw the time-released finale start lighting the sky. As each section of fireworks high on the superstructure of the Dorsetshire lit up, a picture started to unfold, ending in a beautiful display of the King and Queen with a giant crown hovering over them. I'd never seen anything so spectacular and stood in complete awe.

The following day we had a gymkhana for the ships' crews and the port teamed with sailors, wending their way to the site of the festivities on the flats out by the golf course.

It was like a great three-ring circus, with games of toss, tug-o'-war, soccer, obstacle races, dunkings, backwards donkey racing, and a hundred other events going on simultaneously, while beer flowed and food was consumed at a rate I'd never seen before.

I think what I enjoyed the most was the complete contrast from the pomp of day before, the officers and port regulars all "dressing-down" for the occasion. They ran the concessions and events like a bunch of carnies with nothing else on their minds than to make the day memorable for the crews of His Majesty's ships.

ERRATA - *first sentence, p73,*
should read: "That year, 1937,
rolled peacefully by, etc."

5

TIMES WELL REMEMBERED

The following year, 1938, rolled peacefully by in the little Treaty
Port, and although we didn't actually ignore the outside world, it
seldom seemed to affect our lives. In December, when Nanking and
Shanghai fell to the Japanese invader, Mother and Dad took it in
stride. In fact, that's when Mother decided we'd outgrown her home
tutoring, and we were told we would be attending a French convent
in Tientsin.

It was an icy day when we got out of the taxi on Rue Sabouraud
in the French Concession and pulled the long bell-chain outside the
convent gates. A little lay-sister came and, never once looking up,
opened the gates and let us in. On the portico, at the top of a tall
flight of steps, a Franciscan Sister greeted us and led us into a
Spartan little parlor, where we waited for Mother Superior.

When she arrived, I felt intimidated. She was tall and stately,
with a white, bloodless face, etched with minute blue veins; everything about her was stark and austere. After introductions and a
brief résumé on the conditions of our enrollment, she took us on
a tour of the school.

Her first stop was at the candle-lit chapel, where she genuflected briefly as she opened the doors.

I was speechless. I'd never been in a church in my life, and I'd never seen anything so exquisite. The high vaulted ceiling, held up by massive pink marble columns, formed a canopy of soft colors, and as I stood in awe, I could've sworn I saw angels sweeping through the pinnacles of the glistening white altar. As it was late in the afternoon, the sun was low in the sky, and the stained-glass windows were alive with vibrant colors that splashed across the pale oak pews. For one wondrous moment, I felt I'd seen the hand of God.

Then Mother Superior spoke, and the spell was broken.

She genuflected again, softly closed the doors, and led us down endless corridors to classrooms, the dormitory, the study hall, the refectory, the indoor recreation hall, and finally out to the high-walled playground lined with wisteria-draped pergolas. It was beautiful, it was friendly, and it was strangely exciting, but it wasn't Chinwangtao, and my heart yearned for the familiar life I had known.

The first night I cried uncontrollably as I burrowed deep into my soft, straw-mattressed bed. I was not alone. I heard sobs from every corner of the dormitory, while the Sisters moved from bed to bed, speaking softly and trying to make us feel at home. They allowed some of the older boarders, who had been there for several years, to come over and talk to us, and they teased us and spoke lightly of the good times to come. I found it hard to believe them, but finally, exhausted, I fell asleep.

The next day I learned what a real school was all about. What a change of pace, and what a schedule!

Not being Catholics, Ursula and I didn't have to attend morning mass, but were allowed to study instead. So, from six to six-thirty we studied; from six-thirty to seven we had calisthenics and drill in the recreation yard; then we had breakfast, prayers, and finally class at eight o'clock.

There was the Angelus at noon, followed by a big meal, an hour of recreation, and class through till four o'clock; then Benediction in the mystical chapel, and more recreation. We had study-hall from five to seven, then dinner, followed by more study from eight to nine-thirty—six days a week, with Wednesday and Saturday afternoons for art and music.

Strangely, I found myself enjoying the structured days. Even our meals—all but the evening one, eaten in complete silence—were a time for learning. Tables manners were drummed into us with a whisper, or a raised eyebrow. The Sisters were bound and determined that, when we graduated from St. Joseph's, we would have impeccable manners and be models of modesty and decorum.

I liked the idea. Maybe now I would become a lady, and my tomboy image would be a thing of the past. To this end I asked one of the Sisters if I could be called Pamela, my first name, as my second, Roberta, had been reduced to Bobby, and I hated it.

"Well, you don't have to worry, we won't call you Bobby, you will be Roberta," she said with a smile.

"But I hate Roberta too; it's nothing but Robert with an "A" tacked on. Why won't you call me Pamela?"

"Because it's not a saint's name."

"Neither is Roberta," I said petulantly.

"But Robert is," she persisted.

"In other words, if I didn't have a saint's name, I'd be nameless?"

"We'd give you one," she said with a smile.

I couldn't see any logic in this argument and asked, "How did the saints become saints—were they born that way?"

"No, they *became* saints."

"Then their names weren't sainted until they made them that way?"

"I guess you could say that," she said.

I felt I'd bested her, and said, "How about giving *me* a chance?"

"Roberta…I think you'd better get used to that name; it's a lot easier than trying to become a saint!"

After a year at St. Joseph, Dad suggested that Mother take us to the States on her next leave. At least I think it was Dad's suggestion. It was an open-ended leave. We could stay as long as we liked, as long as Ursula and I went to school.

The year in the States turned out to be a complete culture shock—from the Caucasian taxi driver who picked us up at the pier in San Francisco, to the bell-hops, the waiters, the shop clerks…the list was endless. I caught myself saying "Thank you" to many of them in Chinese, then stuttering awkwardly and repeating it in English. No doubt about it, China was my home.

We stayed with Grandma in her tiny house on Satsuma Avenue in North Hollywood, and I couldn't get over the fact that she had no servants. When she heard we were coming with Mother, she had a third bedroom added to accommodate us. Even with that addition, the whole house could have fit into Mother and Dad's bedroom in Chinwangtao!

As soon as we arrived, Mother enrolled us in school. Going from one that went from six in the morning to nine-thirty at night to a school that started at eight-thirty and was over by three turned into one glorious picnic.

We started in elementary school, because we didn't know American history and astronomy. We learned all that was required in six weeks and were then sent to brand new North Hollywood Junior High. Even there I ended up spending my days correcting papers for my homeroom teacher, Mr. Olmstead, while Ursula spent them collecting boyfriends by the drove.

I remember being truly shocked when we attended graduation exercises in June, and the rather tinny, new high school band had the audacity to play *Pomp and Circumstance* as a processional march. At least their rendition didn't give me goose-bumps as the Royal Naval Band had done at King George VI's coronation. I got used to *My Country 'Tis of Thee,* but still caught myself accidentally singing *God Save the King.* Other than that, I didn't make too much of an ass of myself, and when summer came around, I was more than ready for an exciting vacation.

Mother bought a car while we were there, a lovely '38 Plymouth sedan, and we spent the summer seeing California. We roamed the beaches, the deserts, and the mountains, and in August we took in the San Francisco World's Fair on Treasure Island. It had been built in honor of the new Golden Gate and Oakland Bay Bridges. The latter bridge was so long it stopped at Yerba Buena Island in the middle of the bay before proceeding on to San Francisco. The northern end of the island had shoals and was a hazard to shipping, so while the engineers were building the bridge, they had the shoals surrounded with a wall of piers and filled in the land to form Treasure Island.

The Golden Gate International Exposition, as it was formally named, had been running since the middle of February. When we visited it late that summer, many of the international exhibitors were closing down, because their homelands were either at war or on the verge of it. It was still very spectacular, with the Tower of the Sun and the Elephant Gates dominating the island. When we passed through the imposing gateway, I found myself in a fantastic electronic world of the future where the debut of radio pictures, the early name for television, held me spellbound. I was also intrigued by an atom-smashing cyclotron in the Hall of Science, and probably would have given it more attention if I'd realized then the part it was to play within the next decade.

All hell had broken loose in Europe while we were gallivanting around that summer. In September, Hitler invaded Poland—and England and France, who had guaranteed Polish independence, declared war on Germany. Russia, after signing a non-aggression pact with the Germans a month earlier, grabbed East Poland and attacked Finland. And that fall, Germany flexed its muscles preparing for the upcoming bloody "blitzkrieg" that would subjugate most of Europe in the first half of the following year.

Dad's letter in early December, full of holy torment, left Mother numb.

"We're going home," she said, as she read it through for the third time. Then added, "Geordie says we'll be safer in China than anywhere, and we must stay together. He's right, Mother. My place is with him. *Our* place is with him."

"Yes, darling, I know," Grandma said simply; then turning her little humped back on us, she reached in her apron pocket for a hankie, her shoulders shaking with sobs. I'd never heard Grandma cry, and I felt awkward as Mother held her close and said, "Don't worry, Mumsy, we *will* be safe."

"I know. I'm just being a baby. I'll miss you dreadfully."

There was no way we could know then that the pitching Pacific would turn the winter crossing into a nightmare. The ship, the *President Taft*, one of the smaller vessels of the U.S. President Lines, started out by taking an unprecedented seven days from San Francisco to Hawaii, then an additional nineteen days from Hawaii to Kobe, Japan.

The stormy seas weren't the only thing that made the trip memorable. We befriended a contingent of Catholic priests heading to their mission in Peking. Most of them looked like they were in their late teens, were from "Noo Joisey", and had Irish accents you could cut with a knife. One, Patrick, had a terrible crush on Ursula from the moment he laid eyes on her, and as they all wore slacks and sweaters on board, it was several days before she learned he was a "man of the cloth". Actually, it happened after Sunday mass, when he stepped out of the Social Hall in his cassock and bumped into us.

Ursula's face turned a blazing red when she saw him, and she tried to speak, but nothing came out. It was Patrick who broke the embarrassing silence with a mumbled, "I thought ya 'noo'…"

I giggled nervously.

Mother was sitting on deck sipping hot bouillon. She looked up as we came by and did a double-take. While Ursula and "Father" Patrick kept walking past, I flopped down on the deck-chair beside her and said maliciously, "That's one boy, or rather man, she can't have."

"You little stinker. He must still be in his teens; whatever made him become a priest? It's got to be a sin—he's so good looking."

"Poor Ursula," I said, in mock commiseration, "she told me yesterday she thought he was just wonderful."

"That'll be enough. They're coming back. Try to act naturally."

Mother smiled at Ursula as she dropped into the deck-chair on her other side. After a moment, Father Patrick sat carefully on the end of it and looked out at the roiling grey sea.

"You're full of surprises, Patrick," Mother said kindly, and he looked as if he were ready to cry; then she turned to me and said, "Bobby, go see if there's more bouillon—it's so nice and warming."

"Not for me, thanks," Father Patrick said. "I must be going".

He got up, and his cassock rustled strangely as he walked away. As he turned to step into the lounge, the wind whipped it against his lithe body, and Mother smiled and touched Ursula's hand. "Such a horrible waste," she said gently.

Ursula's face was stony.

The ship became sluggish in the heavy seas and hardly seemed to be moving. That night, at dinner, Mother asked the captain if we were on schedule.

"I'm afraid not. We'll be lucky if we make it to Honolulu by Wednesday."

"That'll make it seven days," I piped up. I should've kept quiet—that was only the beginning of our troubles.

Six days out of Hawaii we woke to the awful stench of crude oil. Ursula and I tried to look out of the porthole, but all we could see was a thick film of greenish-black sludge all over the heavy glass. Hurriedly dressing, we rushed out on deck to see what had happened. That was a mistake. That same sludge was all over the pitching deck, and we slid across it, slamming into the railing with rib-cracking force.

"Hang on and don't move!" a crew member yelled.

Then I noticed half-a-dozen men spreading sand over a thin film of slick oil. They told us later that a fuel line had broken in the night, and the roaring gale had quickly spread the slippery, smelly mess to every level of the ship.

As if that weren't enough, on the eleventh day out, when we should've been approaching the Japanese mainland, a strange orange sun tried to shine through the overcast sky, and as I looked up at it apprehensively, it raced wildly from the stern of the ship to the bow.

"What's happening?!" I asked.

The deck steward looked up at the sky and, noticing the weird phenomena, said laughing, "Oh, we've turned around. We're heading back to Honolulu."

"Why?"

"Guess the captain thinks it's nicer there."

"You're kidding?!"

He winked mischievously, and a few moments later the purser stepped out on deck looking very concerned. He cleared his throat a couple of times to get our attention, then said, "The captain offers his apologies—the rudder's broken. It will take a little while to repair it, and then we'll proceed on to Kobe. He regrets the delay and asks for your understanding."

I noticed now that the sun seemed to be circling the ship in a very erratic way. Of course, it was an illusion: It wasn't the sun spinning around the ship, it was the ship spinning around like a whirling dervish in the middle of the Pacific Ocean!

Several days later, after many false starts, we finally got underway. The going was very slow though, as the heavy seas never let up, and the weather got a lot colder. Some mornings there were icicles hanging from the railings, and the decks were treacherous again, this time with ice. Finally, on the nineteenth day, we limped into Kobe harbor, and the port pilot came aboard. He brought customs officials with him, and while he was bringing the ship in, they checked our luggage.

There was only one person who they gave a bad time: a very tall, red-headed American newsman, not surprisingly named Red. They saw his credentials and his camera, and they proceeded to give him hell. A belligerent little official gave him a shove in the stomach and grabbed his camera from him.

Red snatched it back.

The officer exploded and barked something in Japanese. One of his aides rushed off and came running back with a wooden crate, which he put down in front of the newsman. The customs official stepped on it and, reaching up, slapped Red back and forth across the face.

Bellowing, "Son-of-a-bitch!", Red grabbed the man's wrist and held him up in the air, knocking the crate out from under his feet so that he dangled off the ground, kicking and yelling like a spoiled child. A Japanese passenger, a businessman, came running over just as Red put the customs man down. The official immediately broke into an abusive tirade, and the businessman, hurriedly interpreting, told Red he was not to leave the ship under any circumstances; if he did, he would be arrested. Red shrugged and walked away.

As it turned out, we were the only passengers leaving the *President Taft* at Kobe; the priests were going on to Shanghai, then taking the train north to Peking, and the rest were booked through to Hongkong.

As we were leaving the ship, Mother asked the ship's officers if they would join us for a goodbye drink at the Tor Hotel that evening. Although the night was cold and damp, most of them turned up, along with a group of our passenger friends who were staying at the hotel till the ship was scoured of its smell and the rudder repaired. The evening was really relaxed, and after several drinks, one of the ship's officers told us how they "repaired" the rudder. Unbeknownst to us, they tried everything in the book, but each time the engines were started up, the rudder broke again. Finally, there was only one solution: crewmen were hung over the stern of the vessel, and they manually held the rudder in place. The freezing weather, and the strength required to do the job, made it necessary to change shifts frequently. None of us could get over the guts it must have taken, given the pitching sea and the icy winds, and when he was through telling his story, Mother offered a toast to the crew, echoing the sentiments of all the passengers there, with, "Here's to the best darn crew that ever sailed the Pacific!"

We had two days to kill in Kobe while waiting for the *Kokura Maru,* the ship that was to take us home, so we decided to go shopping at a delightful department store we had visited the previous year. When we found it again, we thought we must have made a mistake. The store was in almost complete darkness, the elevators didn't run, and the once loaded display cases and racks were just about empty.

As the day wore on, we noticed that the store wasn't the only place without electricity. Although the city was under a dense fog, there were no street lights, and the usual bustle of autos and taxis was missing too.

When Red stopped at our table that evening, Mother asked him how his day had gone.

"I know why that little customs official was so obnoxious," he said confidentially, as the waiter moved away. "I've spent a very interesting day snooping around in this blessed fog, and have come to the conclusion that something is definitely up. I was in Germany a couple of years back, and I found austerity and the hum of human endeavor everywhere, just as I found it here today."

"You're saying they're getting ready for war?" Mother said.

"I'd bet on it; and soon."

"But where? They've already taken China."

The conversation got heavier as they discussed possible targets for further Japanese expansion—never once dreaming of Japan's ultimate goal.

The next morning, after a big breakfast and a lot of goodbyes, we and our luggage were loaded into an old taxi that the hotel had been able to get for us. Kobe was still shrouded in fog as the decrepit vehicle wheezed and bumped down the hill to where the *Kokura Maru* loomed dark and dirty in the crowded harbor.

The trip through the Inland Sea was smooth and surrealistic. Ghostly little islands kept rising out of the mist like Oriental dry-brush paintings, only to disappear into the haze again. Every once in a while a melancholy foghorn blew, warning of rocky hazards.

The following day we stopped at Moji for cargo, then passed through the straits that separated Kyushu Island from Honshu, stopping one more time at Wakamatsu to pick up passengers before steaming out into the Straits of Korea. That was the end of smooth sailing. Raging currents and forty-foot seas pitched the ship up and down like a yo-yo; her keel would rise so high out of the water her screws churned air, then she'd crash down again and shudder, waiting for the next onslaught. Surprisingly, I felt no fear, only surging excitement.

Our cabin had two sets of bunk beds. Mother and Ursula had

taken the lower berths, so I had my choice of the upper ones. I picked the one with a view across the foredeck and, that night, watched in awe as the waves washed over the tightly battened hatches and flung themselves at our porthole, swirling and crashing like angry dragons.

Next morning when I woke up, the ship was still pitching. Looking out the porthole once more, I gave a surprised shout.

"Mother, *look*—there are people tied together with rope, and they're dragging bodies across the deck! What's happening?"

"My God, it's a rescue effort! A ship must be in distress, and we're hauling in her crew."

We hurriedly got dressed and went to the saloon to find out what was happening. Luckily the purser was there, and he told us that a tanker, designed to carry fluids, had foolishly been laden with timber and had split in two atop a big sea. The fore section had sunk in minutes, but we had been close by and were able to save the crew. The men being pulled aboard now were from lifeboats from the aft section that had managed to stay afloat for over two hours.

It was quite some time before we rounded the tip of Korea and headed up into the Yellow Sea, the ship settling down into a smoother run. Early on the fourth day, we approached Taku Bar at the mouth of the Hai Ho, and I knew our trip was almost over.

The weather was still numbing though. While Mother packed and checked our luggage in our little cabin, Ursula and I bundled up in layers of clothes and stepped out on deck to watch the final approach. The gulf, as usual, was full of ice floes.

The purser joined us as we stared at the land, and Ursula asked him why we were going so slow. He told us that the captain was afraid of running aground, as the harbor needed dredging.

Darn the captain, I thought, *doesn't he know I want to get home?* Just as we were reaching Taku Bar, he must've chickened out completely, as he dropped anchor and we had to wait for a tender to come alongside to take us in.

The long, barge-like boat had little or no shelter on its decks, and as luck would have it, when we were about a quarter of a mile from port, it got ice-bound, and we had to wait for an ice-cutter to make its way out to bring us in.

The layers of clothing I'd put on kept my body warm, but my hands and feet were frozen solid. Just when I thought it couldn't get any colder, the Gobi wind came down across the salt flats making me wrap my scarf across my mouth to keep the frigid air from sapping my breath. Then I looked at the Japanese standing there with us; they all had leather masks over their mouths, and I recalled Dad telling me that, due to their fish diet, most of them had rotten teeth and that their gold caps and metal fillings reacted to cold in an excruciating way.

As the sun slipped down behind the dirty city at the mouth of the Hai Ho, the tender finally nudged the pier. That's when I saw Dad, stomping and clapping his hands to keep warm. I waved frantically and rushed into his arms as we came ashore. He gave me an icy kiss and said, "Happy thirteenth birthday—and welcome home."

I felt I'd been away for centuries, not just a year.

Within a week of our being home, we were shunted back to St. Joseph's, where the grueling school days started all over again. This time it was much harder though, as we had picked up some very lax study habits while we were Stateside enjoying a school system that let the students, more or less, set their own pace.

Our first month's grades were a disaster, and we had to have special tutoring on almost every subject just to keep up with the class. It was mortifying and took all the fun out of our memories of North Hollywood Junior High.

During the year we'd been away, Mother Superior had been elevated to Mother Provincial, and we had a new Mother Superior. She reminded me of a female Friar Tuck: jovial, easy going, with a smile that could melt icebergs. She was an American and didn't care for her new title, so we were asked to call her Mother Montana.

Because of her easy-going ways and happy smile, I thought she'd be a pushover. I soon learned she might be fun—but she was firm— and I had to toe the line, or take the consequences.

Somehow we got through our unending studies and merciless

tuition, and the semester finally came to an end.

When we got home to Chinwangtao I was ready for total rest and relaxation and wasn't prepared for Mother's first words: "How would you like to have a friend stay with you for the summer?"

"Who?" I asked with a frown, handing my bags to Henry.

"Anne Newmarch."

"We don't know her," Ursula said. "*You* know her parents, but we don't know *her*!"

"Well, you're right, but she's a very sweet girl. Her father is ill and has to go home to England for some special treatment, and her mother wants to go with him. It's pretty serious, but they don't want to take Anne with them because of the war. That's why Dad and I offered that she stay with us"

"So it's all decided?" Ursula said.

"Well, we thought you both would be thrilled, so we went ahead with the plans. Anne is arriving tomorrow."

I looked at Ursula, and she gave me a shrug.

"You could at least show some enthusiasm," Mother said, perturbed.

Margo, who had come to the station with Mother, said, "Mumsy, if it doesn't work, Anne can always go to Tangshan and stay with her uncle, 'Ching' Muir."

"You're right, I'd forgotten him," Mother said, turning to us. "Tell you what. Anne will stay with us for two weeks, and after that, if it doesn't work out, we'll send her to Tangshan. But don't say anything when she arrives, she's gone through enough already."

The following day, we were back at the station, waiting for her train to come in. As we stood on the dusty, crowded platform, we watched about a dozen Japanese soldiers engaged in bayonet practice. It was very realistic and pretty horrible, with lots of grunts and yells, and although they wore padded clothes and face masks, their jabs and lunges left my active imagination seeing spurting blood and missing eyes. Dad was with us this time, and seeing me shudder, he reminded me that the Japanese always used scare tactics to keep the Chinese in line. The "entertainment" ceased a few minutes later when the old PMR rolled into the station, and we walked briskly up to the first class carriage to wait for Anne to alight.

When the steam subsided, there she was, standing head and shoulders above the little Chinese porter. Although she was only twelve, she was very tall, like her father and mother, with a blunt nose, wide eyes, and the most beautiful mop of curly, blonde hair I'd ever seen. At our wave, she came bounding over, talking a mile a minute and hugging us all as though we were long lost friends. Our family had never been very demonstrative, so we felt rather awkward, but that didn't seem to phase Anne a bit, and after a while, her bombastic *joie de vivre* had us all laughing and kidding along with her.

When we got to the house, Mother suggested that Anne call her and Dad, "Auntie Gee" and "Uncle George".

She thought about it for a second, then fingering her chin, she tipped her head slightly and said with a grin, "I don't know...I think 'Uncle Gosh' goes much better with 'Auntie Gee'," and turning to Dad asked, "Would you mind Mr. Simmons?"

Of course, Dad didn't mind; in fact, he was quietly tickled.

Then, when she learned we'd named the dogs Jane and Brewster, she said, "Oh, my, how *dull*!" and promptly renamed them "Yarramouch" and "Diddums-doo", and dammit if they didn't like their new names as well!

Our big, red tomcat, Willard, she left alone. He was named after a crazy port regular with flaming red hair and a massive beard, who roared around on a huge, noisy, motorcycle, and after she'd seen the gentleman, she agreed that the name was very appropriate.

Later in the afternoon, we introduced her to our next-door neighbor, Carlotta Maccini, and sparks flew the moment they met. Carlotta knew how to use her lovely dark eyes and lashes to great effect, and loved to swish her long blonde hair with a shrug of her shoulders. When she saw Anne, she gave her a disdainful look, then rapidly blinked her long lashes and flicked her hair, like a preening peacock.

"Carlotta, this is Anne Newmarch," Ursula said, adding, "Doesn't Anne have lovely hair?" That was a mistake.

Carlotta nodded acknowledgment to the introduction, and looking straight at Anne, said, "Mario says *I have* the most beautiful long hair in the world." She always called her father Mario.

"Really?" said Anne, "Then he hasn't met my Aunt Becky. Her hair is so long and beautiful, that even when she has it coiled in a bun, it still trails on the floor!"

She didn't even blush as she told that whopper, and poor Carlotta, whom Ursula and I never contradicted no matter how she boasted, stood speechless at the put-down.

"We're going to take Anne down to the beach and the tide pools. Want to come?" Ursula said quickly.

"No. I think I'll go riding with Mario," Carlotta said, and stalked out.

"Anne, how could you?" I asked incredulously.

"She needed it!"

After a splashing, giggling, fun time out on the rocks, we raced the length of Long Beach, waving to all our friends as they sat out on their bungalow verandas. On the way back, we stopped and introduced Anne to several of the kids, then hiked up the cliffs back to the house.

Dinner was rather late that evening, and when it was over, Anne bounced around giving everyone a big, goodnight hug before retiring. Mother and Dad were a little flustered at first, then they returned her hugs, and I could tell she had them completely under her spell.

Later that night, I woke up to the sound of soft crying coming from Anne's room. Getting out of bed, I padded down the hall and knocked gently on her door.

"Come in," she said, sniffing.

"What's the matter, Anne? Homesick?"

"No, worried. I hope Daddy's going to be all right; I love him so much." And she started to cry softly again.

I put my arms around her and gave her a hug, suddenly feeling warm inside.

"He's going to be fine, Anne. I just know it!" I said, then added impulsively, "I sure like you!"

I gave her another hug and slipped back to bed.

*****

Every morning in the summer months, Ursula and I would get up early and pick mushrooms to sell to the summer visitors. We had secret caches all through the woods, and by the time we'd picked several baskets, our tennis shoes would be squelching with dew, and we'd be covered in cobwebs. The next morning, when Ursula suggested that Anne join us in our exclusive enterprise, I knew she had been completely accepted into our family.

Later the same day, when we came up from the beach for tiffin, we found Mother and Margo sticking snapshots into one of the family albums.

"Let me see them!" Anne said excitedly.

"You take this one, it's full," Margo said, handing her one of the earlier albums from when Ursula and I were around two to four years old. Most of the snapshots were on the swings in the playground, or on donkeys being led by *mahfus*, but there were several of us, bare-ass naked, on our beach. Looking at them, Anne let out a happy yelp and said, "This is my favorite. You look like a couple of mushrooms!"

The shot was of Ursula and me, from the rear, holding hands and wading through gentle surf. The only thing we had on were curved, straw, Chinese coolie hats.

Needless to say, after Anne's first two weeks were up, there was no mention of her going to Tangshan to her Uncle "Ching".

Meals with Anne became friendly duels of one-upmanship. To her, there was no one as great as her engineer father, whose forte was railway bridges, and her mother's brother, Dr. "Ching" Muir, chief-of-staff and head surgeon at the Kailan's huge Tangshan hospital. Dad would smile at her bubbling pride and, not to let her steal the whole show, would tell her about Grandpa's pioneering of railroads in Hopei, Honan, and Shansi provinces, and how he and his colleagues had worked to link the major cities and provinces while contending with corruption and intrigue in the Imperial Court. From the mid-nineteenth century, Britain had wanted to expand trade with China, but the Manchu court was unwilling to let any foreigner interfere with the status quo. It seemed not to matter to them that, while some peasants in China had abundant food, others starved to death, because produce rotted in the fields for lack of transportation. China needed desperately to be brought into the current century, but the Imperial Court fought it every inch of the way.

While the eight major powers jostled for position, individuals like Grandpa saw all the inequities and buckled down to work to improve the lot of the Chinese masses. It's not surprising that in doing so, he fell under the spell of these industrious, uncomplaining people, who loved the soil and their ancestors with equal intensity.

"Actually," Dad went on, "the first permanent track laid in China, excluding the ill-fated Woosung Line at Shanghai, was only seven miles long, and ran from the Tangshan coal mines to Hsukochuang. The coal had to be hauled down the track on mule-driven carts, though, as the Chinese were afraid that noisy locomotives might disturb the spirits of their ancestors!"

Anne giggled. "Daddy told me about that—but didn't the English engineer in charge build a locomotive in secret out of all sorts of odds and ends?"

"The *Rocket of China*!" Dad said with a smile. "It might have looked like hell, but it paved the way for all that followed. You do know," he added, "that those seven miles were the start of the Peking Mukden Railroad—the PMR—and that China has never looked back since?"

Thinking of all the coal, produce, and people that traveled by train, it was nice to know Grandpa had lived long enough to see the fruit of all his labors.

We found when Anne was quiet, she was doing one of two things—drawing comic strips or writing plays. Being an only child, she continually lived in a world of make-believe, and the plots and twists her stories took were always ingenious. In this vein, she suggested one day, as we were coming home with our arms full of everlasting flowers we had picked down by the golf-course, that we should put on a musical. Her idea was to perform a Hawaiian skit with a love-sick maiden and blood sacrifices, culminating in a thundering ritual dance done in skirts made from the everlasting flowers. Ursula and I thought the idea great, and happily let her take over as writer, producer, arranger, star, and props.

After she'd written the playlet and sketched the makeshift sets, we sat down to make the grass skirts. The tough flower stems cut our fingers, and bunching and lacing them together with some of Mother's leftover yarn became tedious and sometimes quite painful, but the resulting short skirts with their flounces of everlasting flowers were truly lovely. As I held mine up and admired it, I could hear the round of applause I knew we'd get when we danced onto the stage.

When the great day arrived, we put the program on in the covered bleachers beside our tennis court, playing to the audience from the different levels, while they sat in lounge chairs looking up from the court. We invited all the kids in the port, the regulars and the visitors, many of the younger ones turning up with their parents or nannies. It was obvious, gathering from the applause we got after each act, that the show was well liked, but the finale proved, unintentionally, to be the greatest hit.

Rushing behind the grandstand to change into the skirts of everlasting flowers and leis made from Mother's glads and snapdragons, we knew we had a hit on our hands. After giving each other a quick once-over and a thumbs-up, we pranced up the bleachers to the thumping strains of the *Hawaiian War Chant*. We stomped and twirled and waved our arms in what we believed to be an authentic Hawaiian dance, and were most encouraged by the clapping and yelling from the audience. When the scratchy record finally ended, we each took a deep bow—only to find our skirts had disappeared!

Everlasting flowers aren't!

Late that summer, Mother put on her famous Harvest Moon party. She had thrown it every year since the early thirties, and everyone really missed it the year before, when we had been in the States.

One always knew when it was coming, as the British, American, French, and Italian fleets would find they had to be on maneuvers in the Gulf of Chihli just about then, and the sea would sparkle with all the sleek ships flaunting their brave colors.

That year the French and Italian fleets didn't make an appearance. I always thought the Italian ships were absolutely magnificent: slim and white, with piped music on all decks, and armaments placed like works of art. Dad snorted when I made this observation and said, "Only an Italian would make a fighting ship worthless by treating its weapons as works of art!"

That summer Mother went all out. She and Jung-ya had worked for weeks on the flowers and shrubs, and the garden looked gorgeous. Chinese lanterns twinkled over intimate little tables placed around the fountain, under trellises, and by rock gardens. The buffet was arranged on the outdoor veranda, where the servants could keep replenishing the table, and drinks were served at the head of the stairs leading up from the garden.

That evening guests started arriving from all over the little Treaty Port, the port regulars in their cars and the summer visitors in their private rickshaws. A few arrived on foot. Bill Chilton strolled over from his home on the cliff to be joined at our garden gate by Carlotta's parents, Mario and Elena Maccini. They were laughing as they came up the steps to the veranda, recanting some wild story that was going the rounds.

Mother greeted them and introduced them to some naval officers who had just arrived from the club, coming through the gate at the opposite end of the garden. Most of the men knew each other, as they'd played tennis together earlier in the day, and Elena enjoyed all their attention, going off with one officer on each arm. Bill, who secretly missed his earlier days in the Royal Navy, moved off with the captain of the British cruiser, while Mario asked Mother where Dad was.

She hesitated for a minute, then said, "Having his usual pout. He'll come out after the last guest arrives and be the life of the party, but he has to do this to me every time we entertain. It used to ruin my evenings, but I don't let it any more."

I believe Mario was the only person Mother ever spoke to about Dad—not counting Margo, of course. She always defended Dad to everyone else, but she and Mario seemed to have a mutual bond that made them very close. It had started when the Maccini's arrived in port and were entertaining for the first time. That evening, dinner was late, and Elena got upset, and she and Mario started quietly fuming back and forth in Italian. Mother noticed their guests were beginning to look embarrassed, so she went over and softly said, in Italian, that everyone was very understanding, and possibly if Elena and Mario spoke in English, no one would feel left out. That broke the ice. The Maccini's laughed and apologized for their unintentional rudeness. When the dinner arrived, it was superb, and no one remembered the incident, except Mario, who was still homesick for his beloved Italy. After that, he would come over often to visit with Mother and talk, especially about Florence, where Mother had spent a lot of time in her late teens, and where she had picked up the language. He found in her a confidante, and he needed one badly.

He told her his family didn't approve of Elena. They had been very influential in Italy before the rise of fascism and expected their only son to marry well. Elena didn't meet with their expectations, and although they tried to hide their disapproval, they weren't successful. Elena was very sensitive about her past, which kept cropping up in embarrassing little ways, and finally, she gave Mario an ultimatum: he had to choose between her or his family. Convinced that time would give her the polish and breeding his parents expected, he decided to leave Italy for the Far East and the post of Commissioner with Chinese Maritime Customs. The move worked to a degree, but Elena never felt really secure, and although Mario continually complimented her on her accomplishments, she felt she was a disappointment to him. "How can you instill self-worth in a person who's determined only to look at her faults?" Mario said in anguish. Mother returned confidence with confidence, telling Mario about Dad and his jealousy and philandering. But Mario didn't believe her. "I think you're wrong, Gee; he's really awfully proud of you."

That evening, realizing Mother was really seething over Dad's rudeness, Mario said kindly, "Believe me, Gee, I know George would be offended if he heard what I'm about to say—but your party is already a success and no one's even missed him." He gave her a hug, and she smiled grateful thanks, as she turned to greet latecomers.

As predicted, when the last guests arrived, Dad appeared at the top of the stairs, and looking at all the naval brass in their resplendent summer whites, he broke into *When I Was A Lad* from Gilbert and Sullivan's *H.M.S. Pinafore.* For a little man, Dad had a powerful big voice, and when he got to the finale with, *"I polished up the brasswork so care-full-ee, That now I'm a ruler in the King's Nav-ee!"*, the audience broke into roaring applause, and no one questioned his late appearance.

Of course, Ursula, Anne, and I had a great time. We found a beautiful spot from which to watch the festivities, yet not be seen— the window seat in the baywindow of Mother and Dad's huge bedroom. The room would have accommodated Grandma's entire home, and had once been three rooms. I can still remember when Mother had the walls knocked out and the room enlarged to its present size. When the contractor was finished and she looked it over, she said, "Before we move in the carpets, beds, dressers, and wardrobes, I want to throw a party. Look at that floor; it was *made* for dancing!" The next week, number two coolie went around with the chit-book, and everyone in the port received an invitation to a "Bedroom Party", possibly the first and only one of its kind ever given in the port!

Later in the evening, quite forgetting we were supposed to be in bed, Anne shrieked out, "Oh, look at that moon!", as the great white orb, larger than any of the lanterns, rose silently out of the sea.

"Shush!" Ursula hissed, putting her hand over Anne's mouth.

Anne pushed her away. "I won't shush!" Then, louder, she called out, "Auntie Gee, your harvest moon has arrived!"

Everyone stood up and looked over the rose-covered garden wall, awestruck at the majesty of the sight. Then they all started to applaud.

Mother made a mocking bow, and for a few moments, the moon seemed to swell even larger, as if it also accepted the applause, then it broke loose from the rim of the sea and sailed swiftly up into the late summer sky.

The voices ebbed and flowed, the silver and crystal tinkled, and music softly plucked at the evening air, weaving its magic over the scene. After dinner and liqueurs, everyone moved up to the indoor veranda, decked in hanging ferns and fuchsias, and danced till the wee hours to a continuous flow of music from Dad's much-envied record-changer.

When the party finally broke up, I heard Bill Chilton come up to Mother, and taking her hand, say, "Chalk one more up to Perle Mesta of the Pacific!"

The next night, after a dinner of delightful leftovers, we three girls went over to the edge of the bluff and sat with our knees drawn up under our chins to watch another moonrise.

The sea was in a different mood, with heavy swells and hissing surf, and the moon seemed to burst onto the scene almost angrily.

While we had been waiting for it, we'd talked about witchcraft, demons, and prophesies.

"My Mother's a Scot," I said proudly, "And she's *fae*."

"So's mine. It runs in our family," Anne said, not to be outdone. "In fact, Uncle Ching says *I'm fae!*"

"You *are?*" There was awe in my voice. I'd always wished I had inherited Mother's Scot attribute of premonition.

"Always have been," she said matter-of-factly.

The blazing moon looked down on the churlish sea just then, and to our complete surprise, laid out a silver map of Europe at our feet.

"Oh, my God! Look at that!" Anne cried.

Ursula shuddered. "I don't believe it!"

The waves broke; the pattern seemed to come alive; Germany turned black in the center of the map, spreading east over Russia, west and north over France, the Netherlands, Denmark, and grabbing at Norway. It tried several times to cross the Channel, but the

British Isles remained silver, as the sea rose higher and higher. Then, it crashed down into a deep valley, and the map disappeared.

"What did that *mean?*" Ursula asked, as the mounting moon now lightly touched the crests of the waves, leaving little fragments of silver sparkling along its trail.

"You saw how Germany spread out over Russia? That means they're going to take it, just as they've taken France, Belgium, and all the others," Anne said.

"But the Russians are their allies!" I protested.

"I know, but you asked me what it meant, and I'm telling you." Then she added happily, "But did you see that England didn't get gobbled up? I've always known it would never fall."

After that, the night turned ominous and rather sad, as we knew the summer was almost over, and as the young have done through the centuries, we made a pact as we sat there, that we would meet in the British Isles after the war, whenever that should be...*come hell or high water!* Then, we uncramped our legs, stood up and hugged each other, and loped home across the bluff.

"Shall we tell anyone what we saw?" I asked.

"No. That's our secret—until after the war," Anne said.

A week later we took her to the station, and she left amid frenzied hugs and tearful goodbyes, slipping out of our lives as she had bounced in—from nowhere to nowhere.

The summer of '41 started out rather quietly. There weren't as many visitors that year; a lot had left for Australia and other parts of the globe where life was a little safer and saner. I believe Anne and her parents, her father having recovered from his illness, were among them. I was already missing her; she had made our last summer such fun. Ursula didn't say much, but I knew she missed her too.

We tried to get over her memory by slamming a lot of balls around on the tennis courts and swimming a lot. It helped. So did playing mah-jongg with a group of kids on Long Beach. It wasn't as much fun, or as exciting, but it was relaxing, and we really needed to unwind after another rough school year.

We also did a lot of knitting for the war effort against Germany.

One afternoon, after a rather hectic tennis game at the club, I found Mother in the lounge doubled up with laughter.

"What's so funny?" I asked.

"Look at this sweater. The body would fit a ten-year-old, but not even a self-respecting ape could wear the sleeves without rolling up the cuffs! Oh, Lord, what am I going to do with it?"

"Knowing you, you'll re-do it, and you won't tell Rosie she botched the job," I said with a grin.

"How do you know Rosie was the culprit?"

"Oh, come on, Mumsy, who else could it be?"

"Well, you're right; and you're right again—I'll rework the sleeves and lengthen the body. Oh, nuts, I'll just unravel the darn thing and start all over!"

We all loved Rosie. She was utterly genuine, with no pretentious airs. A petite ex-trouper from London, with a strong cockney accent, she could belt a song with the best of them, and although she had never had a piano lesson in her life, her talent at the keyboard was sought out at every port function.

Although Ursula and I had enjoyed knitting since pre-school days, we'd only knitted clothes for our dolls, or sweaters for ourselves in a happy, leisurely way. With the war effort, I found myself pumping out a knee sock a day, or three pairs a week, interspersed with balaclavas, mittens, and time-consuming gloves. The oiled yarn that was provided us—I believe from Australia—had a slightly rancid smell and was rough on the hands, but as it knitted up almost waterproof, it was just what the navy and merchant marine needed.

There was only one thing I didn't like about continually knitting, it was B-O-R-I-N-G. The only way I could stand doing it was by going back to Dad's old work contracts and trying to break the time element with each new item I made, if only by a couple of minutes. After a while even that challenge wasn't enough, so I added another: I was not only going to be the fastest knitter in the port, my work had to be perfect. That meant there was no room for dropped stitches, or goofs of any kind. From that seemingly trivial personal battle, I became a perfectionist, something that would haunt me the rest of my life.

Unwittingly, Mother had a lot to do with it too, because she coordinated all the work and would never let anything leave the port that was not well made, hence the upcoming rework of Rosie's monstrosity.

Most of the work was beautifully done though, and if anything had to be reworked, Mother never mentioned it to anyone. It was a matter of honor. She would say of their effort, even Rosie's, "It's the thought that counts." And, I guess, that summed up just about all of our limited war effort.

One afternoon in the lounge, Mother was sorting and packaging the items that the women had dropped off earlier, getting them ready for shipment. Ursula put down her racquet and joined her, while I sauntered off to read the latest overseas edition of the London *Daily Mirror*, which miraculously still got through, albeit a couple of months late.

A human interest picture on the front page caught my eye. It was of three graves in a pine-studded cemetery. The caption read, *"Shanhaikwan, North China,"* followed by Rupert Brooke's immortal lines *"...there's some corner of a foreign field that is for ever England."* I was able to read the inscriptions on two of the grave markers; they were of British Tommies who had fallen in some long-forgotten skirmish, but all I could read of the third were the dates, "1928-1930". It was a baby! I suddenly thought of my little brother and took the coarse-grained photo over to the window and scrutinized it. There it was: "GEORGE ANTHONY SIMMONS", little Tony! Unbidden, tears filled my eyes, and I silently handed the paper to Mother.

Late in July we were surprised to hear from Father Patrick. He wrote that they had just completed eighteen months of Chinese studies and were entitled to a short vacation. We invited him to bring his friends and spend it with us, and were tickled when he arrived with Father Michael McCoy and Father "Windy", who had an unpronounceable Polish last name. They weren't to know it, but their short visit was the highlight of a very dull summer.

And, of course, the summer of '42 was turning out to be even worse, as we were now hostages in our own homes. There weren't any summer visitors either as they, like us, were under semi house-arrest in Tientsin and Peking, sweltering in the breathless heat that shimmered up from the hot macadam of the streets. There was no way they could get travel visas. Thinking of their plight and missing their presence, I couldn't help wondering how Mr. Araki had got us permission to go on our trip to Peking in early spring. I knew he liked Dad, always had, and Dad admired his integrity and guts. Japanese civilians were not thought of highly by the military who issued all travel passes; even intellectuals like Mr. Araki, who spoke several languages fluently, were treated like second-class citizens, allowing that if they had been better they would have been in uniform.

Dad's friendship with the Araki's dated back to their arrival in '38, which coincided with the arrival of their second child. To honor the occasion, Dad, who liked to write poetry, wrote a poem to the little girl, likening her to the sunlight over the bay, and her future to the joy sunlight brings to all that feel its warmth.

The proud parents were touched, and it made her special, even though they had wanted a son. And every year, come spring, Mrs. Araki would keep hoping for a boy, and keep having adorable girls, and Dad would keep writing little poems to welcome them into this troubled world.

Although once-crowded Long Beach was ours to enjoy, happy echoes of the past kept haunting us. It almost felt like the little port was in mourning. Even the coal coolies had stopped chanting. The only sound was the raucous caw of dispossessed crows, jostling and flapping at sundown in the few remaining trees near our house. I'd heard that crows looked out for each other, flying and foraging throughout the day, but when sunset approached, gathering for roll-call. If any bird was missing, scouts were sent out to look for it, while the others stayed in the trees until their lost friend was found, dead or alive. It was rather touching, in a noisy, messy sort of way; sometimes they'd still be cawing back and forth well after moonrise.

Even the curio dealers, who used to come to our door with their exquisite wares, stayed away; either too scared, or forbidden by the Japanese—I never learned which. Every summer in the past they had come to our garden gate with laden rickshaws, and had spread out their wares on the veranda floor on satins, velvets, and brocades. I would sit in awe as they laid out each item, handmade with the patience only Orientals understand, each one more breathtaking than its predecessor. Ivory, jade, porcelain, cloisonné, crystal, quartz, and soapstone, fashioned and carved by artisans as great as any in the Western world, only, in China, they were nameless and unsung. After they'd laid out the larger pieces, they'd produce silver and gold jewelry of every shape and description, inlaid with semi-precious stones, my favorite being cornelians and amethysts.

When the display was complete, I'd see Mother's eyes light up and watch the fun begin, as she bartered for the pieces she wanted. She'd feign nonchalance, that she could take them or leave them, but I knew that look, that yearning in her for all things beautiful. I'd look at the savvy old merchant too, in his long robe and satin cap, and get the definite feeling that he wasn't fooled by her attitude for a minute. At last, when she'd stretched the money from the "non-essential budget" Dad gave her to the last penny, she'd sadly let them pack up and leave…sometimes with an item I knew she was ready to kill for. Once in a while, if Dad was in the drawing room, she'd go to him quietly with the piece and try to convince him that it was priceless and fit for a museum, and that it would return dividends in the future. He never saw the logic in her argument though, and she would have to smile ruefully as she returned it to the merchant, knowing that Bill Chilton or Mario Maccini would grab it up as soon as they saw it, as they'd understand its full worth.

The curio dealers weren't the only travelling tradesmen. There were silk and linen merchants with beautiful handmade wares: lacework, embroidered linen placemats, table clothes and napkins, and delicate silk lingerie trimmed with satin appliqué, almost too lovely to cover with everyday outerwear.

I couldn't blame them for staying away, as I knew the Japanese would love an excuse to confiscate all their treasures. They'd been raping China, according to Dad, ever since they'd marched down through Manchoukou in the early thirties. They had swindled, bribed, and plundered, till there was nothing left but stoic resignation.

As the summer dragged on, Dad began to rage out of control, with Mother taking the brunt of most of his outbursts. Dr. Hope-Gill tried to tell her not to take the tirades personally, as they were caused by having to work for the Japs, and the stress was taking a toll on his heart. He insisted Dad wasn't mad at Mother, only she was the nearest thing to strike out at when the pain struck him.

There was no Dragon Boat Festival in August; I had always enjoyed that spectacle. It was one of the two days out of the year—the other being Chinese New Year—that the Chinese from the Native City would come up in all their finery to parade along the bluff road and watch the colorful giant paper boats floating out on the bay.

Later that month, we lost our beloved Jane. She'd been running on the bluff with Brewster and their latest little offspring, Victory—Vicki for short—racing in circles with the wind whipping up her shiny red coat. Suddenly, she let out a strange yelp and started to stagger. We shushed the other dogs, holding them in check, as we slowly led her home. She dragged herself to her favorite spot in the rock-garden under Mother and Dad's bedroom window, and lay there, eyes glazed, panting till her black tongue cracked. I brought her water and tried to get her to drink; it was no good. Ursula held her head and talked to her. She didn't know us. She was going, and there was nothing we could do to help her. I ran into the house and called Mother and Dad at the club. By the time they arrived, a few minutes later, she was gone. All Mother could say was, "God bless her. She had a lovely life…and she gave us love like no other animal ever did."

We buried her under the roses by the rock-garden, and we buried a part of our lives with her.

*****

The Japanese finally released Dad from his duties at the end of August, and the relief was overwhelming. The news was bittersweet though, as we knew we would have to leave Chinwangtao.

In early September, we were told to get our home in order and pack our housewares and personal belongings, as we were being sent to a furnished home in Tientsin.

Margo was not as lucky. She, with a handful of others, was not released, and she had to move into a room at the Rest House, a virtual prisoner. The other rooms in the hostel housed Japanese military personnel, who daily, by their presence, reminded her of her prisoner status. She kept Vicki for protection and company, and thoughtful friends had her over for meals, so that she wouldn't have to eat with her captors in the tiny dining room. It was a rugged time for her, compounded by the absence of any news of Jack.

Jung-ya was the only servant who asked to go with us to Tientsin. Cook and the coolies were too scared of the big city. And Dad and Henry had already had an emotional farewell several months earlier, when the Japanese commandeered our car.

On September 17th, we finally left—with fifteen years of memories all jumbled up with luggage, housewares, masses of paraphernalia, and one unhappy chowdog.

My heart didn't break when our little caravan of rickshaws started to move down the hill to the native city on the mainland, because I was sure we would be back. With the ready optimism of youth, I couldn't believe in finality. I turned and looked back over the tracks as we moved onto the road to the railway station and said, "Goodbye Chinwangtao…for now."

Dad heard me, and reaching over from his rickshaw, grabbed my hand and said, "Good girl, we *will* be back!"

6

TIMES BEST FORGOTTEN

No one talked on the train to Tientsin, we were all too deeply engrossed in our own thoughts.

I found myself wondering what life would be like in the city now that it was run by the Japs. Would we be allowed to go to school? I really missed not being able to finish high school. *I won't be getting any bonuses for completing my senior year on time,* I thought ruefully. I decided to give up thinking of the future, as each thought had to be left in limbo; only time would elicit an answer. Getting nowhere in a hurry, I got out my pirated edition of Eric Knight's, *This Above All,* and got lost in his great character studies.

There was no getting off the train to stretch our legs this time. Although the guards weren't sitting in our compartment, they were very evident whenever I looked around. It made the trip seem twice as long, and we were all ready to get off as soon as the train pulled into the station.

This time the old city definitely wasn't the same, and the weird feeling I'd had in Peking the previous spring took hold. I felt numb as we went through the British Concession. It wasn't ours anymore. Even the historic old street names were gone, replaced by numbers.

The "Poached Egg" now flew from every flagpole that had once been graced by the Union Jack, and slowly I found anger taking the place of anguish.

"We're going to take it all back you little buggers," I swore under my breath.

The feeling of bravado stayed with me all the way to our new home on Edinburgh Road—now Number 37 Road—where the rickshaw coolies dropped their shafts in front of a pair of massive red wooden gates.

The house turned out to be quietly elegant. Not the rambling, homey, bungalow-type we were used to, but a huge, three-storied affair, with a wisteria-draped entry yard, and a pretty, high-walled rose garden with a pocket-sized lawn.

The downstairs had a compact, oak-paneled den, a spacious living room that looked out onto the rose garden, and a dining room that could easily seat twenty. But the room I really loved was the library that led off from the dining room through a moongate; it had two walls lined with fascinating books and two walls covered in a rich, reddish-brown leather. To add to the feeling of opulence, there was mood-lighting throughout the downstairs rooms.

There were three large bedrooms on the second floor, and two bathrooms. The master bath was big enough for serious calisthenics, but turned out to be too cold to use in the winter, as we had no fuel to fire the central heating system. There were two more bedrooms on the third floor, and although they were icy in their remoteness, I turned one into my studio hideaway.

Up there, I would find myself thinking of the family that had built the house, the Winchells, wondering if they had gone on leave only to find they could not return, or if they'd just panicked and abandoned it with all its lovely furnishings, to become another luckless statistic of a foreigner's lot in the Orient.

And from my chilly perch high above the city, I could look down on the street and watch the beggars plead for alms. I knew that begging was a profession in China, but it still didn't help me to understand the cruelty of parents who could willingly deform their babies by tying string around some member of their bodies till it atrophied and dropped off. Sometimes they only tied members back, like shins to thighs, so that they would grow stunted and malformed, and the poor soul would have to kneel for the rest of his life, scooting around on a little wheeled tray like some performing circus animal.

I recalled Amah insisting that the worse they looked the richer they were, some even coming to their begging posts in their own rickshaws, and going home at night to a hot meal and a warm bed. I had never believed her.

Mother's first complaint, when the cook asked her for more *hsiao-mi* for Brewster, was reminiscent of those earlier days. "There's no way you went through fifty pounds of millet in just over a month. Brewster couldn't eat that much in *three* months!" she exploded.

The cook, looking bewildered, started to wring his hands and say, "But Missy…please Missy…".

Then Mother, realizing what was going on, said, "Okay, it's been a long time since I lived in this city. The beggars…I forgot the beggars. It's all right Cook, you may feed them—but only the ones at our back door, not everyone on the street!"

The beggars at our back door materialized every evening at "dog chow" time; it was their assigned turf, and the servants would fill their grimy, old, wire-handled tin cans with millet and whatever food scraps we had. Often, I'd see them scoot down the street swinging their stunted bodies on scrawny arms, or wheeling along on trays, to some less fortunate soul at another station who had not been fed, and they would share their steaming scraps. The scene always touched me.

I found out about completing my senior year in a hurry: the Japs wouldn't allow us to congregate in groups of any size, so school was out of the question. To kill the monotony of the days, Mother arranged for private tuition. I never did learn where the money came from for the classes, or for putting food on our table, as Dad didn't go to work. Typical of our life, I couldn't ever remember worrying about anything as mundane as money. If we needed it, we had it.

Although we appeared to be living as we always had, the days were shrouded in apprehension—mostly due to the ugly red-and-black arm-bands we had been issued. I loathed seeing mine attached to my warm fur coat; I felt it branded me as some sub-human species. I knew Ursula felt as I did, but as Mother never stepped outside the house, it was of little consequence to her. As for Dad, if it bothered him, he didn't show it.

He would get up in the morning as the spirit moved him, and Jung-ya would lay out his clothes and draw him a bath, as he'd done as far back as I could remember. Then we'd all sit down to breakfast. Ours was usually hot cereal, and once in a while eggs, but Dad had to have an English breakfast of croquettes, or kedjerree, or bubble-and-squeak—sometimes sauteed brains—with lots of strong tea and piping hot toast and marmalade.

Afterwards, we'd go our different ways. Mother to her household duties, Ursula and I to our classes, and Dad to some favorite haunt. And while Ursula and I would wrap ourselves up warmly and leave for class, we'd hear Dad hail a rickshaw and say, "Europa" or "Club Metropole" to the nimble coolie. To his chagrin the Tientsin Mens' Club and the Country Club were out-of-bounds now, so he and a few cronies would sip coffee in some sleazy little restaurant on Cousins Road or Dickinson Road, where once they would not have allowed themselves to be caught dead, and try to reel in some illusive rumor, or just talk about the "good old days".

The proprietor of the *Europa*, Isaac Zeligmann, was a Jew who had escaped from Germany late in the thirties, and he and his wife ran the little dump of a restaurant with hearts overflowing for the plight of the Allies. It was obvious that the arm-bands we wore really got to them, reminding them of the horror they had escaped from in Europe. In their broken English they tried to make everyone welcome, and Dad insisted, if Isaac's wife hadn't had her hand on the till, he would have given away everything in the place. He was just that way. Time and again, Dad would come home in the evening saying that some tragic musician, who had miraculously escaped from the maws of Hitler, had poured his heart out in music fit for the Met; for that, Isaac would feed him, or her, and help them find a place to live.

And, while Dad thus whiled away the days, we would be studying French with a Mrs. Warwick, or painting with Pierre Travers-Smith, a famous English water-colorist. Or, on a more practical note, taking Gregg's shorthand and typing from a very talkative Mrs. Norman, as Ursula and I had always wanted to be secretaries like Margo in the worst way, especially now that she had such a good-looking boss.

Of course, we didn't know how much Margo and Faulkner loathed being collaborators or the toll it was taking on them. It didn't help matters much that they did nothing but sit at their desks like so much window-dressing, and by the time December rolled around, they were both ready to climb the walls.

Then one day, just before Christmas, when Margo was about as low as she could get, the Japanese, who never lost an opportunity to make themselves look benevolent, asked her if she would like to go to Tientsin and spend Christmas with her family.

She looked at Mr. Araki, who was doing the interpreting, and asked, "Is this on the up-and-up?"

He looked confused, so she smiled and asked, "Do they really mean it?"

"Oh, yes, they do," he said with a smile.

"You *bet!* When do I leave?"

"You will travel up on the twenty-second and return on the twenty-sixth."

"Please thank them for me," she said, turning away so they wouldn't see her tears.

The twenty-second was cold and clear, and Margo rather enjoyed the trip until she arrived at the Tientsin station late in the afternoon. It never occurred to her that the Japs would use this occasion for propaganda, and when she stepped off the train and was met with news cameras rolling, she felt trapped. She stood in embarrassed silence while military brass gathered around her, chattering uncomprehendingly into the cameras, obviously making points for home consumption regarding their humane treatment of the enemy.

Although we weren't allowed to meet her at the station, we had been told when to expect her, and sure enough, as the time arrived, we heard a taxi come to a jarring stop.

Mother, Ursula, and I rushed out to greet her, while Jung-ya took her bags from the taxi driver. His face was beaming when he said, "Missy, Missy...so good see you!"

"So good to be here, Jung-ya," she said, her voice almost breaking as we all went into the house.

"My God, what a place!" was all she could say, as we led her into the huge living room. There was a fire going in the hearth, and tea and cake waiting on the low table in front of it. We couldn't get a Christmas tree, so had decorated a pretty cedar in the rose garden, just outside the picture window, and the late afternoon sun caught the tinsel and made it sparkle through the dripping, steamy window.

Brewster rushed up to her and sniffed her happily.

"I'll bet he smells Vicki," Margo said, as she sat by the fire and he put his head on her lap, eyeing her lovingly. "I left Vicki with the Joneses—their place has been our home away from home. When I left, she was happily exploring the house."

"How's she doing?" Mother asked.

"Fine. She's no longer a puppy really, although she still has a puppy's appetite."

"How's everyone at the port?" Mother asked.

"Okay...I guess." She hesitated for a moment, then said, "Actually, time waffles between excruciating monotony and downright panic."

"Panic? What do you mean?" I asked.

"The Japs have installed air-raid sirens, and when they start to howl in the middle of the night, we feel like a bunch of sitting ducks. After the first warning, we made plans to slip out of the port under cover of dark and to meet down at the golf club on the mainland—at least then, if the harbor were bombed, we'd have a fighting chance.

"Usually Vicki and I meet up with the Joneses near the Marshes' old house, and we hike on down together. So far, the sirens have always stopped before we got out to the golf course."

"Have you ever heard any planes?" Mother asked anxiously.

"No. And the damn Japs at the Rest House always laugh like idiots when they see me coming back in the wee hours with Vicki."

"Could be it was just a drill," Ursula said musingly.

"Well, as long as the little bastards think it's clever not to tell us so, we don't dare take a chance."

There was a momentary lull in the conversation, then Mother asked wistfully, "Has the *Corona* been back to port?"

"Not unless they've changed her name," Margo said, adding, "Actually Klette is taking it very well, though I bet he'd love to run their bloody ships up on the rocks!"

Olaf Klette, a very close family friend, was an independent Norwegian skipper who'd lost his ship, the *SS Corona,* to the Japs. On the Fatal Eighth, the *Corona* was being loaded with coal in Chinwangtao harbor—she never got away. The Japs not only commandeered her, they commandeered Klette as well, making him assistant port pilot, with an eye to him being senior port pilot when the Kailan's Captain Arnold was interned.

"What do you do at work?" I asked.

"Nothing!" She replied disgustedly. "I'm a pawn in their little game of keeping people in line. It's horrible. And the Rest House has to be the worst place I've ever been. Remember how we enjoyed staying there the summer we lived in Tientsin? Well, now it's a prison, and I'm the only prisoner. The Japs have taken over all the other rooms, and they are noisy and drunk most of the time. At first, I couldn't sleep for Vicki's growling. She'd hear them shouting and staggering up the halls, and she'd lie at my door snarling. I always lock myself in, and pull a heavy chair in front of the door. It's scary." Then she noticed Mother looking worried again, and added quickly, "Don't worry, Mumsy, I've got an overactive imagination. They won't do anything to me; it would spoil their image as humanitarians."

As we enjoyed the tea and cake, we caught up on more of the port news. There wasn't much, but it still made me homesick.

Margo jabbed the coals in the fire and held out her hands to its warmth, while Mother rang for more hot water. There was a pleasant lull in the conversation for a few minutes, then as Jung-ya came in with the water, Margo asked, "Where's Dad?"

"At the *Europa*, I guess," Mother said.

"What's that?"

"A little greasy spoon on Cousins Road where the Allies meet to talk about the good old days." I said.

"Dad can't go to the club?" she asked, surprised.

"Uh-uh. The Japs have taken over both the Mens' Club and the Country Club."

"How's he getting along without wheels?"

"Oh, he takes a rickshaw everywhere, and does a surprising amount of walking," Mother said. "Actually, I think he's a lot better off physically than he was. I guess everything's a mixed blessing."

"I noticed a red arm-band on the sleeve of your fur coat in the hall," Margo said, turning to me. "What's that for?"

"Didn't we write you? We all wear arm-bands. It labels us by our nationality, and scares most of the Chinese off. Come to think of it, it scares everyone but another arm-band away."

"We haven't been issued them in Chinwangtao yet. Guess there's really no need; there are so few of us and we're under continuous surveillance."

Dad came in the front door just then, stamping his feet and clapping his gloved hands together. While Jung-ya helped him off with his coat I heard him muttering his old favorite saw about it being cold enough to freeze the balls off a brass monkey.

Margo looked up as he came into the living room. He gave her a quizzical smile, and said, "I see you made it okay."

"Yes, it was an uneventful trip till the little Nips met me at the station with news cameras rolling," Her voice bristled with disgust.

"Those damn buggers—they never give up!" Dad snorted as Mother handed him a cup of tea.

"I want something stronger than that, Gee," he said, waving the cup aside.

"You're going to be out of booze if you keep this up."

Dad ignored her, and called, "Whiskey-*chee!*" to Jung-ya, who was still hovering in the background.

"How do you get booze here?" Margo asked.

"Black market," Dad said. "And it costs an arm and a leg." Then, changing the subject, he asked how things were at the port and if the Japs were still losing tonnage.

"If they are, we'll never know, as Araki's not saying anything that would jeopardize his job."

"Mrs. Araki pregnant again?" Dad asked with a smile.

"No. I believe they've finally given up trying for a boy."

"Just as well. If this war lasts much longer, he'd only end up being a *kami-kaze* pilot!"

Christmas was a time of mixed emotions that year. The joy of having Margo with us was mingled with the torment of not knowing where, or how, Jack was. Time flew, and before we got used to her presence, she was gone again. The whole episode seemed unreal; it was as though she'd never been there, and yet the emptiness we all felt after she left belied the unreality.

Somehow the winter of '43 crept inexorably on. Dad would come home evenings from the *Metropole* or the *Europa* with stories of our imminent internment, and tales of a civilian committee that was helping organize the round-up of all Allied nationals. Dad said they were awesome in their dedication.

It was imperative that no one was overlooked, as their lives would be hell if they were left behind. We *had* to stay together, that was our only strength. And the chore of finding all the Allies, some who were addicts and felons who didn't want to be found, was a challenge that the civilian committee had to overcome without letting our Japanese captors know that the situation was sometimes anything but one of happy cooperation.

Finally, on the twelfth of March, we were told we would be leaving for Weihsien Civilian Assembly Center on the twenty-third. We planned and packed, and unpacked, then packed again, knowing we would not be able to take much and trying to figure what we really needed and what we could do without. We should have known— a week before we were to leave, the ever-efficient committee came up with rosters of names, lists of necessities, and complete instructions for our debarkation.

On the fifteenth, Margo arrived in Tientsin with Vicki and the last of the port regulars: Harry and Eva Faulkner, Sid and Ida Talbot, Percy and Meta Jones, and Preston Lee. The only people left behind were the Bjerrums, who were Swedish and neutral; Captain Arnold, who, as a Manxman from the Isle of Man, insisted he was neutral too; and Captain Klette. Arnold was to learn, along with quite a few Free Irish in Tientsin, that the Japanese despised people who turned their backs on their country. They considered anyone from the United Kingdom as British, and if they denied allegiance to Britain, they were treated as "dishonorable prisoners of war".

While we were getting ready for internment, we were told if we packed our valuables into crates, made a manifest of their contents, and took them down to the Swiss compound, they would be locked in the godowns and secure for the duration.

Mother felt it was too good to be true, but after losing two complete homes to warlords before I ever came on the scene, she was willing to believe anything, so we wrapped, packed, and cataloged all our valuables, and on the designated day, Dad accompanied a mule cart loaded with the crates down to the Swiss compound. When he came home, he had a big smile and an itemized receipt.

"Guard this with your life, Gee," he said, handing the paperwork to her. "You have to admit these little Nips are civilized. I don't think it will be long before we'll be claiming all our things again."

It didn't take much to make Dad optimistic, but it was short-lived. Moments later, his happy mood ended abruptly with a pounding commotion out in the entry yard, followed by heavy kicking on our front door. Brewster and Vicki went wild, barking and snarling viciously.

"Chain them up!" Dad shouted to us as he called Jung-ya to open the door.

We didn't have time to chain them, so we rushed the dogs out through the sliding doors into the rose garden.

Ed Lewin, a civilian interpreter, was with the Japanese brass who came striding into our home. They went through the house from bottom to top, making notes of all the furniture that was left, and obviously checking accommodations for future Japanese occupancy. They finally came stomping back down the stairs into the living room. The dogs by now were in a complete frenzy, snarling and throwing themselves at the plate glass doors trying to get in.

The senior Japanese officer snapped something at Ed, who turning to Mother and Dad said, "The major wants your dogs. You are to leave them here, and they will pick them up after you leave for the internment camp."

"What's he want them for?" Mother asked suspiciously.

"War dogs!"

"But they won't attack unless we're here. They have been trained to protect *us!*" she exclaimed.

Ed explained that to the Japanese officer, who smiled and said something softly under his breath.

Looking worried, Ed said, "You are to leave the dogs—that's an *order!*" Then, following the major out of the house, he hung back for a moment and said quietly, "I'm so sorry; all I am is an interpreter."

As they stepped out into the biting cold, Mother looked at Dad and said, "That *does* it! I knew we were going to have to destroy the dogs, but we're going to have to do it *now!* I just know the Japs aren't going to wait till we're gone, they're coming back right away."

"Now, Gee, don't go jumping off the deep end. Dr. Hoch is coming later this week to do it, gratis. The Japs won't be back before then."

"You don't *know* that!" Mother shouted.

Dr. Hoch was an American veterinarian who had watched over and worked on all our horses, ponies, and pets. He knew the anguish we were all going through, and as he was the only one with the expertise and necessary drugs to put our pets to sleep, we welcomed his generous offer.

"Sorry, Gee, I won't help you," Dad said, as he gently mussed Brewster's ruff and went out to the entry hall and picked up his coat.

"Damn you! Take off then, you son-of-a-bitch, and leave me to do the dirty work!"

Mother turned and looked at Ursula, Margo, and me, as we stood open-mouthed at her foul tirade.

"Get out all of you!" she yelled. "Go! And stay away! I don't give a damn for how long. If you're wise, you'll be gone at least three hours. *Get out! Get out! GET OUT!*" Her scream turned into a wail.

"I'm going to see Iris," Margo said quietly. Iris was another war bride, whose marine husband, like Jack, was a POW somewhere in a Japanese military camp.

Ursula and I grabbed our scarves and coats and rushed out of the front door. As we slammed it behind us, we heard Mother call, "Jung-ya, I *need* you!"

When we got back that evening, it was dark outside. We wiped our feet on the scraper and timidly tried the front door. It was unlocked, so we tiptoed in.

Mother was sitting in front of a small fire, staring at the flickering blue flames. In her hand was an empty highball glass.

Ursula came in and put an arm around her shoulders.

Mother looked up, expressionless. She tried to speak. Nothing came out.

I rushed up and tried to give her a hug. She just stared.

Ursula looked at me over Mother's head and said, "We'd better get ready for dinner," and we both slipped out of the room.

As we passed Margo's bedroom, we saw her sitting silently on her bed. She didn't look up.

"The dogs didn't greet us; they must be gone," I said. And as realization hit me, I took a deep breathe and held it; when I finally let it out, tears came too, and I sobbed till I choked.

"It really *is* all over, isn't it?" Ursula said softly, adding, "We'd better go downstairs and be with Mother. She's been through hell."

I splashed my face with icy water, combed my hair, and put on a dab of lipstick, then followed Ursula down to the living room. Margo was already sitting on the hearth, hugging her knees, and

I blessed the darkened room for being kind to our puffy, tear-stained faces. Mother didn't look as though she had moved, but she must have as the glass in her hand was now half-full.

Dad came home about then, and I heard Jung-ya quietly greeting him.

"Whiskey-*chee*," Dad said, as he stepped into the living room.

Jung-ya mumbled something, and Dad shouted, "What do you mean—we're *out* of whiskey?"

That finally got to Mother. She turned slowly from the fire, tossed back the last of the drink in her glass, and in a slow, slurring voice, said, "I buried the last bottle with the two dogs—want to make something of it?!"

Jung-ya turned and left the room, and as he did, he staggered and fell against the pantry door. Mother smiled for the first time and said, "And Jung-ya helped me!"

The next morning when I came down for breakfast, the day was brilliant. The sky was a glorious, cloudless blue, and there was just a touch of hoarfrost on the shrubs in the rose garden. Then I saw the big patch of newly-turned earth, and the horror of yesterday came flooding back.

I knew Margo and Ursula were still asleep and that Jung-ya was serving Mother and Dad their morning tea in bed, so I quietly stepped outside, unmindful of the cold, and carefully stamped on the mounded earth. I went over it and over it, till it was almost flat, then carefully covered it with fallen leaves, so that it blended with the rest of the rose-bed. Then, passing under the pergola to the front gate-yard, I wiped my feet and slipped back into the house.

It was just after noon when the Japanese came back for the dogs, and my skin crept as I realized Mother's Scots' heritage of precognition had not let her down. This time Ed was not with them. In fact, they had no interpreter, and they didn't need one. They marched in through the house and slid open the plate glass doors to the garden. The Japanese major was the only one from yesterday, and he was accompanied by two soldiers.

He looked out into the empty rose garden, then turned belligerently to Mother. She looked him straight in the eye and slowly shook her head. He exploded! I thought he was going to hit her—but she didn't flinch. She just turned her back on him and beckoned him to follow her.

He ranted and roared as she kept steadily walking to the front door and out to the red entry gates. She threw them open and flung her arms wide, pointing down the street as she completed the gesture. She didn't need to speak Japanese; it was obvious she was telling him the dogs had gone.

He shook his fist in her face, and shouting to his two men, jumped into the command car. As the driver pealed out from the curb, we noticed two empty dog pens in the back, their doors banging open and shut with every jolt of the command car.

"Why didn't he search the house?" I asked, bewildered.

"Japanese never keep animals in their homes," Mother said. "The fact that ours were in the rose garden when he first came made him believe we didn't allow them in either. I guess he never thought of searching for them..." she ended lamely.

"He wouldn't have found them even if he had," Margo said sadly.

"We could have hidden them all along, and then left them with friends while we were away," I said disgustedly.

"No, Bobby, it wouldn't have worked—you know that. They would have starved to death, even if we could've found someone to take them."

She was right. For a moment, I'd forgotten their fierce loyalty to our family.

7

JOURNEY WITHOUT JOY

I'd always thought I knew most of the foreign community in the British Concession of Tientsin, but when the evening of March the twenty-third finally rolled around it was obvious I had absolutely no knowledge of the scope of the Allied Nationals in that city. They converged on the drill hall in the old British barracks from every part of the teeming city, speaking in tongues I could barely distinguish: Dutch, Belgian, Greek, Spanish, Russian, Danish, and umpteen Oriental dialects that defied interpretation.

Among them were a handful of Free French; many White Russians with British papers; a couple of Cuban hai-alai players caught without a way home when war was declared; and members of a Puerto Rican baseball team in the same boat. There were businessmen with their families from every occupied country in Europe, who had stayed in the Far East thinking they would be safer there than in their devastated homelands. They had gambled and lost, and kept looking at their precious children and stoic wives with anguish in their eyes.

There were Eurasians, the half-castes and pariahs of society, most with more beauty and breeding than the snobs who black-balled them. There were a few dope addicts with a look of panic, as they knew their lives of make-believe had just come to a terrifying end, and they would have to face the future without opium or any other blessed type of oblivion. Their noses were running, their hands shaking, and their skin, normally a pasty white, seemed to have taken on a queer bluish-green tinge in the eerie light of the compound. Some had been holed up for so long, they knew none of their countrymen and were known by none. These were all people who, for varying reasons, had decided to stay after their governments had repatriated their embassies and consular staffs.

For the British though, there was an added incentive: they had been asked to remain at their posts to safeguard Britain's interests in the Far East. Dad, and the others in the Kailan complied willingly, as they had invested heavily in their adopted country, loved it, and knew no other life.

Among those being jostled about by the arrogant Japanese were agents for large American oil, auto, and tobacco companies, British shipping magnates, and representatives of banks of all nations, who had traded in the Far East for almost a century. I recognized one such Dutch banker with his rosy-cheeked brood of seven, as three of his girls had attended St. Joseph's as day-scholars.

There was only one distinguishing mark on all of them, from the lustiest babe-in-arms to the oldest, feeblest adult—the demeaning red arm-band. We had been told by the Japs if they were lost, or became illegible for any reason, that our futures as honorable prisoners of war could change drastically. As much as we hated to do it, we embroidered them with bold black thread to ensure that the poorly printed characters would not fade and become indistinct, then we embellished them with our national flags, defiantly turning these symbols of infamy into badges of honor.

As I looked at the milling crowd in the barracks compound waiting to be shipped off to the prison camp, I noticed quite a few blue-and-white flags of Greece, some black-red-and-yellow flags of Belgium, the tri-colors of France and the Netherlands, with the majority emblazoned with either the Union Jack or Stars and Stripes. Some, less artistic, but no less proud, embroidered the name of their homeland on their arm-bands—that's how I knew the baseball players were from Puerto Rico.

The time-consuming, oft-embarrassing operation of the frigid night was the meticulous checking of every single piece of luggage. We each were allowed one suitcase that we could carry; the rest of our luggage—beds, sheets, blankets, dishes, pots and pans, and other simple household miscellany,— had been shipped on ahead. I wondered if the Japanese had searched it as thoroughly as they were searching us now.

It's pretty hard to put the precious accumulation of sixteen years into one suitcase, but somehow, I did it. I even snuck in my favorite Winsor and Newton water colors and a couple of sable brushes. I didn't know where I was going, or if I would be allowed to paint, but I knew I couldn't leave without my colors and a few sheets of art paper. I was glad to see my favorite instructor, Pierre Travers-Smith, chewing on his unlit pipe. I thought of the gallery of water colors he'd left behind, and my heart went out to him.

I saw Mother turn and look heavenward in a silent prayer as a Japanese guard closed her suitcase with a snap and barked something. He shouted again, and I realized he was pointing at me. I came over and opened my case. He unstrapped the carefully packed layers and quickly, but thoroughly, felt through the contents. He found the box of water colors and brushes, pulled them out, and looking up, smiled, then put them back in the case. For a moment, I wondered if he was laughing at me. As he moved on to Margo's luggage, I turned to Mother and asked quietly why the heaven-sent prayer.

"He didn't find my Kuan-yin!"

Mother's exquisite porcelain Goddess of Mercy, a gift from a generous, infatuated warlord, had survived two lost homes—now a third. Was she to be a good omen? Then remembering Mother's sturdy Sheffield-steel kitchen knives that she hadn't trusted to be shipped with the crated household items, I remarked, "He found your nice, sharp, kitchen knives, though."

She shrugged, accepting the loss along with all the others that had stacked up in her life, and said, "No matter. I guess they were too sharp. He thought they could be used as weapons."

*****

Finally, we were shoved into lines, roughly four-bodies abreast, and a long, motley stream of people started moving out into the street. Only the very young with their mothers, the old, and those ill or incapacitated were allowed to ride in old army trucks; the rest of us had to walk. Now I knew why we were only allowed one suitcase: that was all we could carry on the long march to the station.

We had been at the barracks since early evening. It was now the wee hours of the morning, and the streets once more were deserted as we trudged down them, heading toward the International Bridge and the railway station I knew so well.

We'd no sooner started out than Jung-ya emerged from the shadow of a *hutung*. Coming up to Mother and Dad, he reached for their bags and said softly, "Master...Missy...I cally for you."

They smiled their thanks, and without thinking, handed their suitcases over to him. A soldier rushed up out of nowhere and hit Jung-ya across the head with his rifle butt. As he fell to the ground, the guard snatched the two cases from his unresisting hands and shoved them at Mother and Dad, shouting and waving his rifle and stamping his foot.

The message was clear to all who witnessed the incident.

I felt sick as we were forced to move on with Jung-ya lying unconscious on the freezing pavement. There was no way we could help without jeopardizing him and everyone else. Margo's face crumpled as she turned for a last look, and tears ran down her icy cheeks. Ursula showed no emotion. As I watched, Dad reached for Mother's hand, gave it a squeeze, and brushed her cheek with a silent kiss. Then, as I felt a lump rising in my throat and thought I was going to choke, a shrill, melodic whistle rang out in the night, to be joined by hundreds more piping lungs, and the theme from *Colonel Bogey,* from a battleground on the other side of the world, rent the silence of the sleeping city.

The Japanese guards shouted and barked at us, but finally, frustrated by the *to-hell-with-you* spirit they were witnessing, they gave up. All they'd been ordered to do was get us to the station, and the last thing they wanted was a confrontation. So, being good soldiers, that's just what they did.

Traveling by train for so many years, and seeing the seething crowds jammed into the third-class carriages like so much cattle, I never dreamed that one day I would be in their place. The only good thing about the stifling arrangement was that body heat helped us thaw out, and our numb hands and feet started to tingle with feeling once again. I knew I should have been tired, but I wasn't. I felt both energized and disoriented; all I could do was look at all the faces around me and wonder where they came from.

Three truculent guards came into the carriage, shoving us out of their way as they marched through. As most of us barely had standing room, I was pushed into a stall and fell over a pair of long, hard legs. I tried to get up only to be knocked down again. "Dammit, that's enough!" I hissed, clawing my way up through a tangle of limbs, leaking baby bottles, and smelly fur coats. After a couple of futile attempts, I grabbed a pair of folded arms and finally pulled myself erect, only to look into two of the palest blue eyes I'd ever seen.

I don't know how long we just stood there, inches apart, staring at each other. It seemed like centuries. I couldn't look away, and those pale eyes never blinked. I felt a blush creeping over my face and tried to turn around, but I couldn't move.

Then he spoke. "You all right?"

I nodded.

"I know a place where you can sit," he said, and started to shove slowly through the crowd in the aisle while I followed mesmerized. We were almost through the carriage when I found my voice and said, "I can't leave this car. It was assigned to us. I'm with my family."

"We're not leaving—we're joining Nico."

With that he pulled the heavy connecting door open and stepped out onto a tiny platform into the early morning cold. Nico, whoever he was, was sitting on a rough wooden bench attached by angle-iron brackets to the metal railings, seemingly oblivious to the weather.

"Hello," I said, seeing his smiling face and feeling instantly at ease.

He looked surprised for a moment, then asked my escort, not rudely, "Who's she?" his breath trailing steam in the frigid air.

"Ask her," the pale-eyed stranger said.

That's how I met Guy Woodruff and his side-kick, Nico Kamilos. Guy was tall, slim, and angular, with dark unruly hair and Slavic good looks. Nico, stocky and muscular, had the build of a pugilist. I found myself thinking, *If they lived in Tientsin how come I've never seen them before?*

It didn't take long to figure out that the two of them were life-long friends. There was a quietly-seething arrogance about Guy. He appeared to be mad at everyone—everyone, that is, except humorous, down-to-earth, unflappable Nico. As we talked I watched them bounce off each other, sometimes like a couple of comics, and at other times like ferocious combatants. They were fun, they were exciting, and they were different in every way from the few privileged boys I had grown up with. I soon caught myself getting entangled in a fiery philosophical discussion, and realized with a shock that Guy's almost insolent manner came from his being an avowed communist.

I remembered one of our livelier dinner discussions at the convent. Mother Asteria, a Franciscan Sister with patrician features, had been presiding, and several Russian seniors from Harbin were trying to provoke her by comparing the Communist party with Catholic convents and monasteries. She listened politely, then said slowly, "There is a big difference…a *very big* difference. We live our lives for the glory of God. The communists have no God; they live for the glory of the Party. We offer up our worldly goods to the church and try to live a life of Christ. The Russian people did not *give* their worldly goods to the Party; they were confiscated. They didn't choose the life they live; they were forced into it. They're not allowed to pray to God for strength; they're told He doesn't exist. They're told their only strength is the strength of the

Party. I'll agree the concepts are similar, but the actuality is as far apart as the poles."

Not to be put down, one of the girls said, "What about their idea of women-in-common?" There was a wicked smile on her face as she added, "No marrying. Just switching and swapping. Could be fun!"

Mother finally exploded. "That's enough—we'll have none of that!"

Ursula, swallowing her last mouthful, looked up and said, "Communists sound like a bunch of spoiled brats trying to do away with authority."

A quiet aristocrat, whose family had lost everything when they had to flee Russia, said, "Don't you believe it! The Party has replaced one type of authority with another, and if Stalin's purges can be believed, the new authority is worse than anything Russia has ever known."

Suddenly I realized Guy was talking about me and calling me an unmitigated snob who never gave a thought for the masses and their suffering. "I bet your old man exploits the coolie class, and you live off the sweat of their bodies!"

I found myself getting angry at his dumb clichés. When he used the expression 'coolie', I immediately thought of the coal coolies in Chinwangtao and how Dad had fought to prevent the Kailan from putting in mechanical handling. He knew it would've cut the company's costs considerably and allowed the coaling of twice as many ships in the same allotted time, but thousands of coolies would have been out of work and unable to provide for their families. It had been a long, and sometimes bitter, battle, joined by all the personnel in the Treaty Port, but to the Kailan's credit, management bowed to the argument, and the slow, manual loading of colliers was allowed to continue.

"You don't know what you're talking about!" I snapped. "Communists are nothing but frustrated capitalists. Given a couple of bucks, they'd join our ranks any day!"

"That's rot, and you know it!" he exploded.

I saw Nico looking uncomfortable, but I didn't give a damn.

"I tell you what—this is the 'Grand Experiment'. Here we are, all on our way to a prison camp with all our worldly belongings in one suitcase, and a few bucks in our pocket. And, when it's all over—whether you like it or not—the rich will be richer, and the poor will be poorer, not because anyone exploited anyone, but because that's human nature. Communism doesn't allow for human nature."

"You're nuts—but you're on. How much?"

"I don't want to exploit you," I said sarcastically, "all I want is for you to admit that I might be right." I knew I sounded smug, but damn it, who was he to criticize a way of life he obviously knew nothing about.

"Well, a good fight's a great way to beat the cold," Nico said, trying to defuse a situation that was getting steadily out of hand, but Guy and I weren't listening and just stood glowering at each other.

Luckily, a few minutes later, the three guards came by, going back through the cars, and our mutual loathing found a new target. When they saw us on the platform, they shouted and started shoving us around. I felt my spine stiffen and thrust out my jaw, but it was a vain gesture. It was obvious what they wanted, and it was obvious that we had to obey, so we stepped back into the car.

The warmer air of the carriage had a muggy, almost cozy quality, and the racket had subsided to a gentle murmur of voices. Most of the overwrought children had fallen asleep, too tired and exhausted to whimper, and the older people had been helped into more comfortable positions, so they too could get some rest.

Once again, as our little group broke up and I moved off by myself, I felt a strange feeling creeping over me: Here I was on a train, not knowing exactly where we were going or what was going to happen to us, but through it all, I felt no fear. Everything was an adventure; the excitement had even made me forget I hadn't eaten in sixteen hours. Cook's last act before being paid off had been to fix us sandwiches. Mother had had him pack them individually, so we could put them in our pockets in case we got separated on the trip. I forgot about mine until my stomach finally reminded me. Still, not knowing how long our journey would be, or if we'd get fed when we arrived at our destination, I only ate half of mine.

As I ate it, I carefully stepped over luggage and bodies and went back to where I'd left Mother, Dad, Margo, and Ursula. They had found seats, and although they were squashed, they looked comfortable. Margo and Ursula were talking softly to a couple of attractive brunettes in their late teens, and Mother was gazing out of the window. I couldn't tell if she was asleep, but Dad was: snoring gently, and grunting now and then as the train lurched over uneven track and the drafty windows rattled.

For some reason the scar on his face was more pronounced that night, and I wondered if all the hours out in the cold, and the trek to the station, had aggravated it. I found myself recalling how when we were in the States, Mother had spent many hours searching for a cosmetic that would help make the scar less noticeable. She brought several shades of cream and powder-base formula home with her, but after Dad had applied them with varying success, I never saw him use them. I remember watching him from the hallway as he tried the different products and overhearing his wistful words as he got up from her triple-mirrored dressing table: "Gee, I know now why I love the Chinese so much. When *they* call me 'Scarface' it's a term of respect. Lord, why isn't the rest of the world as gracious?"

As I looked at him, I realized I loved him dearly, even though he was no saint, and my mind raced back through all the visits Mother and Margo made to Tientsin when we were at St. Joe. When they came up, they always got special permission to take us out for dinner or shopping or the movies, but Dad never came to see us. We usually found out he'd been in Tientsin from one of the day scholars: their parents would see him at work or at the club or with some beautiful Russian at some swank restaurant. That was Dad. I knew it didn't mean he didn't love us, just that he always looked out for himself first. I was positive that in some earlier life he must have been a Russian Lothario, because he couldn't stay away from beautiful Russian women. They held a fascination for him that turned him into putty. I don't know if Mother knew about all of them, but he was quite fabled in Tientsin's foreign community.

It always seemed strange to me that, except for his roving eye and love of music and art, Dad had to be the epitome of the stuffy Victorian, with all the narrow-minded puritanism that came with the men of that era, and it struck me as amazing how he could have married a liberated soul like Mother. He told me he met her when he took thousands of Chinese coolies over to the Western Front in World War I to dig trenches and graves for the Allies. Mother was an ambulance driver. He said it was macabre—if she couldn't get to the field hospital in time, he took over. It was a gruesome, unending job, and somewhere in that nightmare a bond was welded that would last them a lifetime.

I remember, when he was at home, he was very much the lord of the manor, and in most instances, Mother played the dutiful wife; but when he was away on business or home leave, she would have a ball. That's not to say she let Dad repress her when he was home. Far from it. I can remember disagreements that turned into arguments that turned into ketchup throwing, dish slinging brawls. That the dining room had to be re-papered and re-painted at regular intervals was living testimony to our exciting meals. Mother never matched Dad throw for throw; she had much more fun baiting him, then feinting like a good boxer when the dishes came her way.

I always wondered who started this free-wheeling lifestyle—whether Mother did it to get back at Dad for his affairs, or Dad did it because he was jealous of Mother's popularity.

Because Mother was the only woman in the port who played billiards or snooker, the skippers of the British and Scandinavian colliers enjoyed playing with her. She became quite a pro, and the old-timers would love it when some new officer came up to the club. Setting him up, they'd say that Mother liked to shoot a game or two, then intimate they didn't care to play with her. After a discreet pause, they would suggest if the new officer wanted to score points and be invited back, maybe he should offer to take her on—then they'd sit back and watch the ensuing rout!

Come to think of it, that was the only time Dad wasn't jealous of her. His pride in her ability, and his enjoyment at the luckless newcomer's plight, kept the green-eyed monster at bay.

Looking at her now, I couldn't tell if her eyes were focussed or if she was looking back over a lifetime of memories—many, like now, where she had been uprooted from her home, her friends, and her servants, never to see them again. Was she thinking of little Tony—alone in his untended grave under the shadow of the Great Wall?

In her checkered early life, she had lived on every continent except South America, but China seemed to dish her out more heartaches than all the other places combined. One thing it had taught her was how to accept, and although she must have been going through all kinds of hell, she didn't show it. She had a deep, abiding philosophy—I couldn't call it a specific religion, as it embraced every concept conjured up by man...or God—but it gave her an inner strength that she was able to draw upon when the going got past the bearable mark. I could see she was wrapped in that special strength now, and I left her to her thoughts.

Just as I was drowsing off, a thought came to me that hit me like a brick. I found myself poking her and saying, "Where are we going?"

Jolted out of her reverie she snapped, "To prison!"

"And how old is Ursula?"

"Seventeen," she said impatiently.

I didn't respond, letting it sink in.

It was almost a full minute before she said, "Oh...my...*God*!"

I couldn't sleep after that. I was still taut as a bow string—so totally engrossed in the moment, I could think of nothing else. Although Guy had disappeared into the crowd, I kept seeing his pale blue eyes and hearing his mocking tirade. As my mind kept playing and replaying our meeting, Nico came up and asked if I would like to meet his father and sister.

When we got over to where they were seated he didn't really have to introduce them; the three of them were so identical, they could've been punched out with the same cookie cutter. And when he said his father was a baker, the irony really hit me. They all had chunky bodies, pugnacious faces, wide smiles, and little black raisin eyes that twinkled with hidden laughter. I could see Nico was the center of their little world, and the two of them looked on him with unabashed love.

"Where's Guy?" the old man asked.

"A safe distance from here," Nico said. And then, in answer to his father's questioning look, he added, "Bobby and Guy have been fighting over communism. I thought they were going to come to blows."

I laughed a little nervously, feeling strangely out of water with my new acquaintances. I didn't know how Mr. Kamilos felt on the subject of communism, or any other "ism" for that matter, and trying to change the conversation to something safer, asked, "What's that you're carrying in your coat?" The package, wrapped up in layers of cloth and sticking out of his fur-lined jacket like some precious booty, had me intrigued.

"That's his culture," Nico said.

"His *what?*"

"His culture. Yeast."

When he saw I still looked blank, he added, "It's a yeast culture for bread. It has to be kept warm and alive. He's hoping we'll have bread in the camp and that they'll let him be a baker again."

When I told him I didn't know anything about bread making, the old man's face lit up, and he started giving me a half-Greek, half-English explanation of how to care for yeast cultures and how to make bread, with Nico and his sister helping out when he got too bogged down with the language. Finally, when I broke away, I couldn't help thinking there was a lot more to the bread I ate every day than I had ever realized. *So that's a trade*, I thought, *and I've been talking to "trades people"*. Then I found myself blushing furiously, as I recalled Guy calling me an "unmitigated snob".

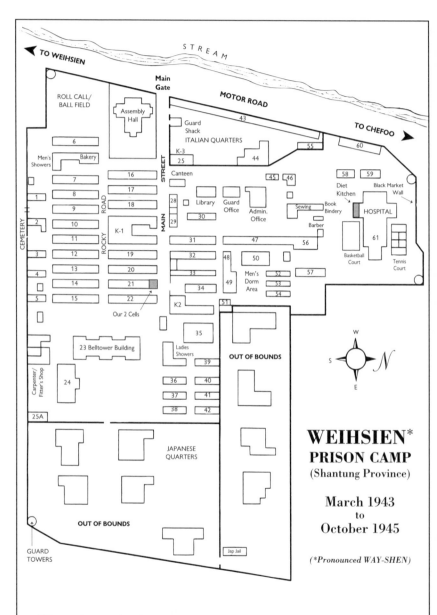

This map does not show the acacia trees along Main Street, through the cell compounds, and scattered throughout the grounds (including the guards' housing complex), nor the tall pines and firs that surrounded the assembly hall. The only areas void of trees were a wide sweep along the electrified outer wall and around the forbidding guard towers, and the roll-call field.

© 1994 Pamela Masters

8

WEIHSIEN PRISON CAMP

I hardly remember the walled city of Weihsien with its massive gates and cobbled streets. It's all a blur to me. A stop on the way to a prison camp for the crime of being in the wrong place at the wrong time. We did get one break though: there were trucks waiting for us at the station—not enough to take us all to the camp at the same time, but still trucks—a blessing, as it was late in the afternoon and a cold rain was falling.

The ride over bleak, rutted country roads was slow and tedious, and several trucks high-centered and had to back up to find surer passage. It took almost an hour to cover the three mile trip to the camp, and when we arrived, the tired old trucks groaned and skidded as they turned under a huge ceremonial gateway with bold characters inscribed beneath its dripping, ornate grey-tiled roof.

"The Courtyard of the Happy Way," Dad translated, reading its incongruous message of greeting. "Happy? That's not what I'm feeling now!" His comment was greeted with several "Amens" from fellow travelers.

Climbing out of the truck, I almost fell, stepping into slick, slimy mud that sucked at my sturdy walking shoes, trying to drag them off my feet. As I steadied myself, grabbing a tarp-hook on the side of the truck bed, someone handed down my suitcase and said, "Welcome to Weihsien!"

There wasn't much to see. Misty rain, dripping trees, rows of soggy grey brick buildings with tiled roofs, and the smell of rotting human excrement. *Oh, happy way! Oh, happy day!* I thought facetiously, as I found myself being herded along like so much cattle to one of the larger administration buildings.

It was just as well I hadn't eaten all my sandwich on the train, as we'd no sooner stepped in out of the drizzle than we were told that our first meal would be breakfast the following morning, if volunteers would step forward to help with the meal. I wonder if Cook ever realized how great the remaining half of that sandwich tasted...

Somehow we survived that first freezing night. Not surprisingly, accommodations had not been made, so we slept on hard wooden floors, literally collapsing where we stood, curling up in our disheveled clothes, too tired to care. Within minutes, grunts, snorts, snores, and whimpers faded into nothing as we passed out in complete exhaustion.

Breakfast the next day in the steamy community kitchen was skimpy and pretty foul: weak Chinese tea and bread porridge. The latter made with sour bread that had been soaked in boiling water and stirred to a mush, as it was too stale to serve any other way. With no sugar or cream to add to it, it was almost inedible. While we were eating, a committee member came in and told us that, when we were through, we were to go to the athletic field for indoctrination, housing, and work assignments.

The field wasn't hard to find as it was the only large, tree-less area in the camp, and through the years, it was to become the site of most of our outdoor group activities and daily head-counts. Located in the southwest corner of the prison camp, its two six foot-plus exterior walls were of grey brick, topped with several feet of electrified barbed wire. An ugly guard tower with gun slots buttressed the outer corner, and I noted with a chill that there were machine guns mounted in the slots trained directly on us. As I looked up at the forbidding sight, two young guards in black uniforms stepped out of the tower and placed their rifles against the waist-high railing. They looked as though they were in their teens, like me, and as they laughed and joked and punched each other on the shoulder, the incongruity of the situation hit me. Somehow it was hard to think of those kids as my enemy.

Margo came up just then, mad and out of breath. "Where the heck have you been?" she snapped, "You're supposed to be with us so we can be assigned living quarters. Come on, hurry up!"

I followed her to where Mother, Dad, and Ursula were gathered, and withered slightly under their reproving stares.

As the last stragglers trailed onto the field, there was a loud squawk from a public address system, and the droning buzz of conversation around us stopped. After a few more crackling sounds, a voice called out, "Attention, please! Attention, please! This is your Commandant! Welcome to Weihsien Civilian Assembly Center!"

"Call it anything you want," Dad said under his breath, "it's still a prison camp!"

I couldn't see the Commandant because of the crowds, but I could hear him, and his English was excellent.

"I am a repatriate from the United States," he went on, "and I was in Hot Springs Assembly Center in Virginia before I was sent back to Japan. I want to tell you something,"—he paused to get our complete attention—"while I was at Hot Springs, I was always treated with courtesy and respect, and I aim to see that you receive nothing less."

I felt, rather than heard, a murmur of approval run through the crowd.

"But remember…" here he paused once more for effect, "if you want to receive courtesy and respect, you must cooperate. Provocation and disrespect will be treated harshly.

"One more thing. This camp is not Hot Springs. If your rations are short, ours will be too. If you are cold, we will be too. In short, we are all in the same boat; whether we're all rowing in the same direction remains to be seen."

He sounded firm, but fair.

Then, he introduced the captain of the guards and interpreted as the stocky officer, with arms well down to his knees, stood stiffly to attention and barked his orders. He also wore a black uniform, and I learned later that it designated that he, like the young guards, was a member of the consular guard and not an officer in the Imperial Japanese Army. I wondered if they would prove to be as obnoxious as their khaki-clad cohorts.

He told us that the arm-bands we had been issued while under house-arrest were not valid in camp. We would be assigned new numbers and new tags, which we were to wear at all times, and each morning, there would be a roll-call. Through the years, we were to find ourselves responding with a "Here!" to the guards shout of, "*Yon hyaku kyuu juu nana, kyuu juu hachi, kyuu juu kyuu,*" Ursula, me, and Margo, reduced to 497, 498 and 499.

Before we left the roll-call field, all the single men and women were told to report to the respective dormitory areas, and heads of each household to the administrative office compound to be assigned cell numbers—only they called them room numbers. Meanwhile, most of the committee responsible for our orderly move to camp pitched in once more to organize work details.

All those not preparing food were to be assigned to cleaning up the camp. The rains of the day before, which had gone on through most of the night, had left the main roadway a quagmire. I found that the stench that had greeted us on our arrival was from overflowing latrines, augmented by piles of soggy garbage in various phases of decomposition.

Somehow I missed the cleanup detail and found myself peeling potatoes with twenty others in the community kitchen—dubbed "Number 2 Kitchen" or "K-2"—where we'd had breakfast a couple of hours earlier. With so many people, and so few potatoes, the job was soon done, and I left the kitchen compound and stepped out onto Main Street, the name some enterprising individual had already posted on the road leading up from the main gates.

The sun had finally come out, and to my surprise, Dad was standing across the street from me in the entrance to a cell compound.

"What's up?" I asked, as I waved to him.

"Come see our new living quarters," he said.

I darted around the deeper puddles in the road and stepped through a pretty, little gateway into a long, narrow compound studded with nostalgic acacias.

"We have the first two cells," Dad said, as he led me to them.

Mother had just completed sweeping out the first one, and she handed the broom to me, saying, "Oh, there you are! Give this to Margo and tell her when she's through with it to hand it down the line." Then she turned to Dad and said, "The light doesn't work. We'll need a lamp-bulb before tonight. See what you can find...or swipe."

I smiled at her remark as I moved on to the second cell, handing Margo the broom as I stepped inside. As she took it and started sweeping, she said, "For God's sake, wipe the mud off your shoes before you come in! This is all we've got to call home for Lord knows how long—let's keep it as neat as possible."

"Where's Urs?" I asked.

"Rounding up our cots and bedding."

"And all the good-looking guys in camp!" I said with a laugh, as I turned and saw Ursula coming through the gateway, followed by two good-looking strangers pulling a wobbly handcart loaded with all our worldly possessions.

"Good girl!" Dad said, eyeing the unwieldy stack, then turning to the boys, he offered, "Hey, let me help you."

"That's all right, sir—just tell us where you want them."

I wasn't to know it then, but I'd just met two of Ursula's most ardent admirers—soon to become rivals: tall, unassuming Alex Koslov, and his complete opposite—stocky, conceited, Grant Brigham.

As the day progressed, I learned that Weihsien had originally been a university campus, and that the long cellblocks had been student housing. Each block consisted of a row of twelve small rooms, measuring nine-by-twelve feet, that looked out onto a narrow, tree-studded compound and the back of the next row of rooms. The compounds were connected at each end by latticed brick walls and decorative gateways.

Each room had a door and standard window in front, and a little, high, clerestory window at the back for air circulation. They hadn't been used by students in years, and before we arrived, had housed soldiers of the Chinese Puppet Army. The rooms had all been badly neglected; the white plastered walls were peeling and in need of repair, and the only electrical fixture was a ceiling lamp, hanging from a frayed cord.

When we moved in, Margo put her canvas cot under the front window, and I fitted mine, foot-to-foot with it, along the right wall. Ursula's cot was across from mine on the left wall. There was a high, three-foot long shelf with a rod under it at the end of Ursula's bed to hang our clothes on, leaving just enough room for a crate to sit on and the door to open. It was very primitive, and along with the communal biffy a hundred feet down Main Street, it was to be our home for nine-hundred and thirty-five days.

As soon as I had made up my cot and stashed my suitcase under it, I stepped out into welcome sunshine to explore. I found the camp divided up into a myriad of compounds and courtyards with airy latticed walls, many graced by moongates and pretty tile-roofed gateways, enclosing administrative offices, kitchens, two-story classroom buildings (now made into dormitories), and living quarters. There was an all-pervading flavor of the Orient throughout, and I couldn't help thinking that it must have been a lovely place once.

Going through one more little compound, I stepped out onto a basketball court with a large, L-shaped building on two sides of it. Surprisingly, it did not have an Oriental flair, but was a tall, three-storied affair of solid Western design. I was wondering what it housed when I felt a gentle tap on my shoulder. As I turned, I saw Dan Friedland, an old friend from convent outings.

"I knew I'd find you, if I kept on looking," he said with a lop-sided grin. That's what I'd always remembered about Dan—his tall, gangling, good looks, and that infectious smile. I'd met him one weekend when Aunt Kitty wasn't feeling well and had asked if we'd mind staying with the Blessings. Claire, their daughter, was a day-scholar at St. Joe, and she and I were always at logger-heads. I felt she tolerated our company that day, because her parents made her, but after the first outing, the scene changed: Ursula had hit it off with one of the boys in Claire's group, so from thereon, we were always invited to join them on our monthly outings. I still felt like a tagalong though as Ursula was the one with the boyfriend; it wasn't until Dan, with his zany American sense of humor, made me feel like one of the crowd that I got to enjoy those Sunday excursions.

"Where were you on the train?" he asked. "I looked for you, but I never saw you."

How could I tell him I was fighting with a rabid communist and hadn't given him a thought! I was really glad to see him now though, and I told him so.

He grinned and asked, "Know where you are?"

"Haven't the foggiest."

"Well, that there building there," he said, affecting a drawl, "is the hospital."

"Really? I was trying to figure out what it was when you came up."

"Well, now you know."

"Bet the rooms in it aren't as tiny as the one that was assigned to us."

"For your information, all the cells are the same size, so don't go around feeling you're being dumped on. Next thing you'll be saying is you don't feel well and need a stay in the hospital!"

I laughed. "You read me like a book!"

"Just one of my talents," he said in mock modesty, adding, "Actually, what *are* you doing here?"

"Just nosing around. Think I'd better start looking for my cellblock though, before Margo and Urs think I've gone over the wall."

"Where is your cellblock?"

"Just off Main Street, directly across from Number Two Kitchen."

"I'll walk you home."

Dan led me through a courtyard, then we ducked through a

gateway into the mens' dormitory compound. I felt he had done it on purpose just to watch me blush at all the catcalls coming from the tall dorm windows. "Why is it, when men get together and a girl comes by, they always have to make such a darn racket?" I said angrily.

"Ignore 'em," Dan said laughing, as he waved to a group in recognition.

"Are you in a dorm?" I asked, as we crossed a secondary road and stepped into the K-2 compound.

"No. Mom and I have a cell down near the assembly hall. Actually, it's a couple of rows back from Number One Kitchen, where the Peking and Tsingtao people eat."

"Is Number Two only for Tientsin-ites then?"

"Seems so."

When we got to our cell, Margo and Ursula weren't there, so I just showed Dan where it was, and he suggested I come to his cell and meet his mother.

Stepping back out onto Main Street, I stopped in disbelief. The Franciscan Sisters, who owed allegiance "to no one but God", were cleaning the women's latrines! I hadn't even realized they were in camp. Mother Flanagan, her beautiful habit pinned up at her waist and her flowing coif tied securely back, was swamping out the "honey pits". And, as I stood there with my mouth open, Mother Superior, or rather, Mother Montana as she liked to be called, came out of the stinking shed, wiping her sleeve across her sweating brow.

I rushed up to them and said breathlessly, "What are you *doing* here? I thought you were Franciscans!"

"So did we," Mother Montana replied, "but it didn't mean any-thing to the Japanese."

"Why are you on this filthy detail?" I asked indignantly.

"Because we asked for it," she said simply. "Somebody had to do it—who better than us?"

Mother Thomas à Becket, a Scottish spitfire and my ex-eighth grade teacher, and Mother Joanna, who taught the seniors at St. Joe, came down the muddy street just then, carrying a large bucket of disinfectant between them. They had put a short pole through the handle of the bucket, and each had an end, gliding along in perfect unison.

"Some people are *pigs!*" Mother Thomas said, spitting out the words in obvious fury. Although she had pinned up her skirts too, there was dirt on them, her coif was awry, and her bright hair was sticking out in wisps like little red flames.

"Here, let me help you," Dan said, reaching for the bucket.

"Thank you, young man," Mother Thomas said, her voice suddenly prim, "we're just going to set the bucket down, scoop out the disinfectant, and drop it into the pits. We're almost through. No need for everyone to get dirty."

"You're sure you're okay?" I asked.

"Uh-huh," Mother Flanagan said, then added, "We've got to hurry as several women have been back at least three times to find out when we'll be through." Then she laughed, "When you gotta go, ya gotta go!" She winked at me and turned back to work, as Mother Thomas gave her a withering look.

"The Blessings and the Adams are in this compound," Dan said, as we proceeded up Main Street past K-1. I glanced in the compound and saw the two girls Margo and Ursula had been talking to on the train.

"Are those the Adams'?" I asked.

"Yes, Bea and Lettie. Claire is next to them, and their folks are on either side."

I didn't see Claire and figured she was either at work or in the cell fixing it up.

"And here's my compound. The Collins' and the Hazletts have six cells between them. Then me and my mom; a couple of missionary families; and a Mrs. Woodruff and her son. Man, she's a wild-looking gypsy!"

When I heard "Woodruff", my knees turned to jelly.

"Come on in, and meet my mom," Dan was saying.

"Oh, I don't think so...I look a mess," I said lamely, suddenly feeling horribly shy, and desperately trying to put miles between myself and the chance of meeting Guy.

But I was too late! I felt another tap on my shoulder and turned.

It was Guy. He had followed us into the compound and was standing there, a beat-up old felt hat planted on the back of his head, his pale blue eyes mocking me.

"You don't look any worse for last night," he said.

I just stared at him, strangely seething inside.

"I'm Dan Friedland," Dan said quickly, sensing something was wrong.

"Guy. Guy Woodruff."

"You've met?" Dan asked, turning to me.

"Yes, we've met. Actually, we collided!"

"You could say that," Guy said sarcastically.

Dammit, why was he so biting? I was too dumb to realize that probably my attitude had something to do with it.

"Hey, Guy, I need you!" a voice sang out.

"Nuts, that's my mother—better be going." He sounded almost human for a moment, then he was gone.

I turned to see what his mother looked like. *Oh, Lordy, Dad better not see her.* She was *very* Russian. Wild and sensuous, with masses of unruly hair. I was wondering if she had pale blue eyes like Guy, when Dan, following my gaze, said smiling, "All that and fascinating green eyes as well."

"You must've been reading my mind."

"My mother likes her. Says she's salt of the earth, whatever that means. I get the feeling she wouldn't like her as much if Dad were still around."

"She doesn't have a husband…?"

"She does. Seems he left on a business trip the summer of '41, and she hasn't heard from him since."

I was glad I stayed to meet Dan's Mother—I liked her immediately. She was a striking lady and a stereotypical Jewish mother—fussing and gushing, and apologizing for not having coffee or tea to offer me.

"I didn't come for tea or coffee, I came to meet you," I said, and she glowed happily. I knew now where Dan got his great disposition.

When I returned to my own cell, about an hour later, Margo was there looking really down in the dumps.

"Do you know, all I've got to remember Jack by is this pair of collar pins of his globe and anchor..." her voice trailed off, and I could feel her anguish.

I gave her a reassuring smile and looked at the pins. She had polished them till they shone.

"You know, they're kinda neat. I'd like to blow one up and make it into a poster or something."

"Would you?"

"Sure, if I can find some heavy paper that's large enough."

The more I thought about it, the more I liked the idea. There was no doubt I needed a project or I'd go squirrely, so I went nosing around the camp again to see what I could find. I lucked out at an office in the administration building and swiped a large sheet of white chipboard. Figuring it would have been used for some "blah" bulletin if I hadn't taken it, I convinced myself I was doing everyone a favor.

A couple of hours later I had rendered a huge globe and anchor with an eagle on top. I had fun highlighting it with my precious paints, and was really proud of the job. It needed something more though, and then it struck me: I carefully lettered "SEMPER FI" under it, in chiselled Roman caps. Margo's smile, as she happily hung it over her bed, made my day.

We had been in camp almost a week when I finally met the last of the inmates in our block. They were interesting people, some more so than others. In the cell next to us were two Australians, Major and Mrs. Collishaw, of the Salvation Army. They were followed by the Tucks, an American missionary and his wife, both well over six-foot tall, from the interior of China. Then, the Allans, Jock and a very pregnant Emma and their little son Douglas; we had made Jock block warden by popular acclaim earlier in the week. Then came the Beruldsens; there were four of them. Followed by Mark and Gladys Tabor; he was an American in his late twenties, she British, in her early forties. The next two cells were taken by the

Hattons with their four kids—more missionaries. And in the last cell was Mrs. Carver, a British widow from Peking, and her lovely Eurasian daughter, Deirdre. Mrs. Carver never spoke of her late husband, but friends of ours from Peking said he had been a very wealthy Chinese businessman.

For the next several weeks, when I wasn't peeling vegetables in the kitchen, I was down by the main gates watching the new arrivals come in. One group, from a remote mission in the interior of China, really stood out. As they trudged up through the gates, they gave us, and the camp, one look and stopped right in their tracks. A gangling youth peeled out from the group, looking positively consumptive, and climbed up on the low retaining wall that surrounded the assembly hall grounds, and before we realized what had hit us, he was shouting, "Hallelujah! The Lord has sent us to this pit of iniquity to save these souls from the filth of their lives!"

I was so naïve I thought he was telling us they were going to help clean up the physical dirt of the camp. But as he raved on, coupling the fires of hell with the filth of our lives, I quickly changed my mind. I could see now they were going to be the type that were long on words and short on action; I was told we had quite a few of those in camp already.

"That's what they call hell-fire-and-brimstone," a voice said at my side, and I turned to see Peter Fox, a friend of Margo's, who visited our cell quite often.

He was an intriguing soul, with a rather lurid background, if the stories he told could be believed. He was Eurasian, much to Dad's disgust, and had been raised in India and French Indo China. He was several years older than Margo, and had served a stint in the French Foreign Legion in Annam. He told us their biggest enemy in those days was boredom, and their escapades to dispel it could have filled a book. His racy storytelling, punctuated with little giggles, had us girls in stitches, and Ursula and I knew he was just the tonic Margo needed to get through those dark early days.

I remember the first time he came to our cell and, peeking in, saw the "SEMPER FI" poster over Margo's bed and said, "You believe in letting a guy know where he stands from day-one, don't you?" Then he giggled.

He had a brother, Mike, who was a wire-service correspondent, and a very good one according to his earlier by-lines, but his ego and temperament were so opposite to Pete's, not to mention his looks, that every time I saw them together I had trouble reconciling their relationship. Luckily, barb-tongued Mike didn't spend much time around us, and that's just the way I liked it.

Two of the civilian camp committees, housing and work assignment, interrupted the zealots before a second speaker could climb up on the wall, and told them to report to the office for living quarters and work detail.

I learned later that they told the assignment committee they felt they could help the camp more if they were allowed to do the Lord's work, and then asked if they could call a prayer meeting in the church.

They were advised they would have to get in line if they wanted to use the assembly hall, as there were denominations ahead of them that had prior rights.

I believe that's why I had such a soft spot for the Salvation Army. When all the denominations in the camp had made their demands for Sunday in the church, starting with six-thirty mass for the Catholics, and going through the day, every hour on the half-hour, with Episcopalians, Lutherans, Methodists, Baptists, Presbyterians, Fundamentalists, and umpteen minor sects, there were no hours left in the day for the Army. With quiet understanding, they simply said, "The Lord will bless Thursday for us. Thursday will be our Sabbath," and from that day forward, the whole camp was able to enjoy their loud, jubilant music and attend their service on Thursday if they chose to.

It was right after the hell-fire-and-brimstone evangelists came to camp that a group of priests arrived, their long robes dusty and disheveled, inappropriate white pith *topis*, or sun-helmets, tucked under their arms. They looked vaguely familiar. Then, as a tall slim priest dusted himself off and looked over the heads of the little group, I recognized Father Patrick and time spun backwards—landing with a happy thud in the summer of '41.

I remembered when we heard from Father Patrick that summer and he asked if he could visit us, I'd looked at Ursula and said, giggling, "He sure is a glutton for punishment."

I hadn't been able to read her face, but she completely ignored my remark and said, "I think that would be nice."

"Why don't you write and invite him yourself?" Mother said.

"Come on, Mumsy, you know Urs hates to write letters; think you'd better do it, or we'll never see him!"

"Okay. He says they've got the first week in August off." Then to Ursula, "Guess they'll be here for your sixteenth birthday—that might be fun."

"Do we get to introduce them to the summer visitors without telling them they are Fathers?" I asked with a giggle.

"What makes you think they won't be wearing their cassocks or Roman collars?" Mother said.

"Well, they didn't on board ship, except on Sunday, so I bet they won't now."

"Bet you're wrong!" Ursula said, flouncing out of the room.

But, for once, I wasn't.

Ursula and I went down to the station to meet them—Father Patrick, Father Michael, and Father Windy. They wore tee-shirts, slacks, and sneakers, and carried duffle bags, looking like proverbial college kids coming home on vacation.

The minute Father Pat laid eyes on Ursula, he blushed crimson and stammered. Father Mike must've been aware of the situation, because he stepped in and started to tell us what a pleasant trip they'd had, and how nice we were to invite them.

Mother and Margo greeted us when we got home. Although we had told Margo how the priests dressed aboard ship, I could tell she was taken aback at their casual appearance, but she smiled broadly at the introductions, and offered to show them to their rooms.

"We're having iced-tea on the outside veranda. Come and join us when you've freshened up," she said over her shoulder as she headed back.

"What do you think?" I asked her quietly.

"I don't know. They seem very nice. Father Patrick is a knock-out."

"And Father Mike's kinda neat," I said, "but I like Father Windy. He might be short and homely, but he's lots of fun."

After the milling crowds of Peking, the priests had a hard time getting used to the sparse foreign population of the Treaty Port. It was a reverse culture shock.

We spent the following morning down on Long Beach, riding the breakers and lying around in the sun. When our summer friends came down to join us for volleyball, we introduced the three Fathers to them as Pat, Mike and Windy, and at noon, when we broke up for lunch, they left us and headed back down the beach to their bungalows.

That afternoon, after a brief nap, Ursula suggested that we go up to the club and play some tennis. "I know it's warm," she said, "but we have to play now, as all the courts fill up after five when the port regulars get off work."

"Oh, it's not too hot to play," Mike said, "But we don't have any racquets."

We told them that was no problem, as there were a lot of spares for guests up at the club.

As the others played tennis, I had a hectic afternoon acting as "ball girl". It was obvious they hadn't played the game in ages, and the ball went all over the place, so when five o'clock rolled around, I told them to call it quits, and we climbed up to the terrace and ordered cold drinks. Ursula and I had sodas, and the Fathers each had an ice-cold beer. We hadn't been sipping them long before a group of summer visitors arrived—the mothers of our volleyball friends.

I tried not to laugh when they spied our three guests, but they were so obvious. Their husbands came down to the port every fortnight or so, and between times, they were starved for male companionship. Even the navy had been scarce that summer, so three new unattached men must have looked really enticing.

Once again, we introduced them as Patrick Noonan, Mike Mc-Coy, and "Windy"; then I sat back and watched the women flirt outrageously.

After a while, it was obvious the Fathers were becoming really uncomfortable. Thinking this time we'd probably gone too far, I looked questioningly over at Ursula. Picking up her racquet, she nodded and said it was time to be going. As we got up to leave, one of the women gushed, "You *are* coming to the movies tonight, aren't you?"

"Oh, I forgot it was Thursday," Ursula said, then asked, "What's playing?"

It was one of the better offerings of the season, so I knew we'd all go—there was so little entertainment in port except for the weekly movies.

Thursday dinners were always prompt and early, as the show started at eight sharp. That evening after dinner, the men excused themselves while we got ready. When they joined us in the living room a few minutes later, they were all in their black suits and Roman collars, and I shook my head and said, "You do realize you're going to ruin the evening for a bunch of swooning summer visitors!?"

"What have you girls been up to?" Dad asked smiling.

"Nothing," I said guilelessly.

"I'll bet!"

The evening was so lovely we decided to walk up to the club, and except for the happy chirp of crickets and the occasional hoot of an owl, the night was velvety in its stillness. As I trailed behind the little group, staring up at the stars, I found myself anticipating the upcoming encounter.

I was not to be disappointed.

When we walked into the auditorium, and the women saw the three priests, their looks of disbelief sent out a mild shock wave. I wanted to burst out laughing; instead I looked over at Ursula. I could feel her gloating as she eyed their embarrassed stares. Grinning, I went over to her and she whispered smugly in my ear, "I know *exactly* how they feel!"

Ursula's birthday fell on Sunday that year, and she decided to celebrate it with an elegant Chinese meal topped off with Jung-ya's fabulous watermelon sherbet.

Sunday morning, Henry took the three priests to mass at St. John's, the little Catholic church in the native city, and while they were away, she opened her presents. We'd decided not to let on that it was her birthday so that the Fathers wouldn't feel embarrassed at not bringing her a gift.

Later in the morning, when they got back, we went for a ride by the dunes near Camp Holcomb. We were all on little China ponies, except Margo, who was riding her beloved Sammy. Ursula and I fitted our ponies quite well, and Windy didn't look too bad, but Pat and Mike were a joke—theirs toes touched the ground!

"This is kinda like riding a bike," Pat said. "I guess when I want to stop I just drag my feet."

After some hysterical attempts to adjust Pat and Mike's stirrups, we gave up, and took off laughing.

In the distance the view of Chinwangtao and the harbor was breathtaking. Junks were bobbing on the waves, the sun catching their huge, slack sails. Little two- and three-man sampans were weaving in and out around them, their oars throwing up silver spray. And, along the beach, fishermen with bloodless, water-logged legs were casting great nets expertly out into the surf and slowly hauling them back in, silver fish flipping and flashing under the restraining nets.

We drank in the scene for a while, then rode on, winding our way around clumps of coarse reeds and wind-scoured shrubs. About twenty minutes later, Margo asked if we knew the way back to the *mahfus* and the car.

"Sure!" we chorused.

"Great! You head on home then—I'm going for my ride now," and with a gentle command to Sammy, she took off down the wet sand, pounding through the creeping wavelets that lapped at the beach. One minute she was there, the next minute she was gone— past the last of the dunes and on to the tall reeds that hid the mouth of a small creek. I saw Sammy cross the creek with a leap, and then race on toward Peitaiho.

"That's some riding!" Windy said with admiration, and I felt a happy glow of pride.

That evening Cook surpassed himself with the Chinese banquet he laid out. There was dish after dish of Mandarin delicacies, topped off with steaming platters of *chiao tzes*—big Chinese dumplings, filled to bursting with a lovely, spicy pork filling.

"You've got to leave room for Jung-ya's watermelon sherbet; it's like nothing you've ever had," Mother said.

With dessert, Dad called for champagne to toast Ursula's special day, not realizing our guests knew nothing of her birthday. After the priests got over their surprise, Mike offered a lovely old Irish toast—

> *"May the road rise to meet you,*
> *and the wind always be at your back.*
> *May the sun shine warm upon your face,*
> *and may God ever hold you*
> *in the hollow of His hand."*

To which we all said, "Hear! Hear!"

And dear Pat, getting really tongue-tied, blushed fiercely and stammered a simple, "Happy birthday."

When dinner was over, the men excused themselves to say their office, and went to their rooms.

I was uncomfortably full and curled up on a chaise on the outdoor veranda and watched the clouds brush the face of the moon. I could hear the murmur of Mother and Margo in the living room, and once in a while a comment from Dad. It was so peaceful, it was hard to believe there was a war going on the other side of the world. Ursula came out of the front door just then, followed by Jane and Brewster.

"I'm going to take the dogs for a walk and try and jog dinner down," she said.

"I'd go with you, but I can't move," I said, as I stretched out on the chaise and groaned.

I heard her go down the steps, and the click of the garden gate, and then I must have dozed off.

When I opened my eyes again, the clouds had disappeared, and the moon was casting a ghostly light on the swaying grass of the bluff. Ursula suddenly loomed up on the cliff's edge: she had come up the steps from the beach, and the moon touched her, making her appear ethereal.

The dogs came into view then, darting back and forth happily, and chasing each other around in circles. Ursula started to laugh at them and clapped her hands, skipping after them across the grass. It was all very fairylike and unreal.

I don't know what made me, but I looked at the windows of the indoor veranda that led off from the guest rooms, and I saw Patrick. He was standing watching Ursula with a look of untold anguish on his face. He didn't move for a long time, and as she approached the garden gate, he slowly crossed himself and stepped back into his room.

I pretended to be asleep when she came up the stairs.

She came over and shook me lightly. "Bobby, you'd better get to bed—you'll catch a chill out here," then shushed the dogs inside.

I was up having breakfast with Dad next morning when Pat came into the dining room.

"I hear beautiful singing. What is it?"

"The coal coolies loading the ships. Some days, like today, the wind blows from the south and you can hear them. It is lovely, isn't it?"

"I'd love to see them," he said wistfully, and I told him we'd watch the loading as soon as the others were through eating.

Breakfast seemed to last forever. Dad and Margo had gone to work long before the last stragglers came in to be served.

"If you don't hurry, we're going without you," I said.

"Going where?" Ursula asked sleepily.

"To watch the ships being loaded. Pat's never seen coal coolies load a ship, and he likes their singing."

"Ah, that's what it is," Windy said. "It's beautiful."

"Some people think it's monotonous, but I don't."

As soon as the meal was over, I called the dogs and started for the front door.

"Race you to the cenotaph—catch me if you can!"

I ran down the veranda stairs with the barking dogs at my heels, then tore out through the gate and under the tall acacias—running past the administrator's house and out onto the headland where a huge granite turtle stood silent and alone.

Legend had it that a Ch'ing princess had thrown herself off the cliff over unrequited love, and that the turtle cenotaph marked the spot where she had drawn her last earthly breath. I loved the story almost as much as sitting on the old turtle's back to watch the loading. The sound of the chanting was always much clearer from my high perch.

"Why, they're like ants swarming all over that ship," Pat gasped, catching up with me. "And those gangplanks are so narrow, do any of them ever fall off?"

"Very seldom," Ursula said, joining us. "I can only remember one time. Dad said by the time the work crew had climbed down to retrieve the body it had been half-devoured by rats."

"Oh, God, I never heard about that!" I said, shuddering.

Ursula looked embarrassed. "I shouldn't have said anything. I'm sorry." Then, turning to the men, she added, "I guess you've learned in China human life is cheap. A man is worth less than a mule. When a man dies, or is accidentally killed, the family gets five dollars. But if a man loses his mule, he's paid fifteen."

"I've learned that's the Chinese law of supply and demand," Windy said drily.

We watched the coolies working in pairs, a shoulder pole between them, with a huge basket of coal agily balanced in the middle of it. The ones with loaded baskets swarmed up one plank, while the ones with empty ones ran down the other: a continuous stream of humanity, moving to-and-fro to the beat of a haunting chant.

As I eyed the priests coming up from the main gate, Father Windy broke out of the little group and ran over and gave me a big bear hug. "You're looking good. How long have you been here?" he asked, seemingly not surprised to see me.

"Since March twenty-third—whenever that was."

"What's it like here," Father Patrick asked shyly.

"You'll find out soon enough," I said, then added, "At least we're all here together."

"Yeah, that's a blessing."

I looked up Main Street and saw the inevitable committeemen approaching.

"It doesn't take our assignment committee long to find able-bodied workers," I said with a laugh. "You don't know it yet, but you're just about to volunteer for some nice, stinky detail!"

As the committeemen introduced themselves, and the group headed for the bachelors' dormitories, I turned to Lisa, a tall, slim English girl I'd just met, and told her how neat the Fathers were.

She looked dubious and said, "Priests are no fun."

"You'll find these are. They're not like those evangelists—they're just like us, and not much older." And, as we sauntered along, I told her how we'd met them, deciding not to mention Patrick's crush on Ursula: time enough to see if it still existed when they met again in camp.

9

THE ANT HILL COMES ALIVE

For a person who'd always found enjoyment in being alone, a pleasure that had been mine in abundance in the solitude of the Treaty Port, I found no such balm in the camp. Even the convent, with its structured lifestyle, had left me many moments of welcoming solitude. It was to be a while before I learned the art of escaping—not physically from the confines of the stark grey walls, but mentally tuning out the world around me. That would come later. But I did find myself—in the place of self-absorption—studying all the people around me, especially those who affected my life.

For instance, it didn't take me long to figure out who was running the camp, and it certainly was not King Kong, the name we derisively gave the captain of the guards. After his initial rather unfriendly "welcome", for want of a better word, we hardly ever saw him, as he'd turned over his duties to his aide, the supply sergeant, whom we named Gold Tooth for obvious reasons.

Gold Tooth was slim and tough, and looked as though he had mastered all the martial arts. Surprisingly, he never demonstrated any of these skills when provoked, but preferred the time-honored swagger stick to put his point across. His moods ranged from obnoxious at best to downright sadistic, while his ego exploded beyond the bounds of reality. He loved all the authority he had acquired and treated his guards, and us, with equal contempt. The young guards feared him. We despised him. Especially the taipans of Chase Manhattan, Jardines, Standard Oil, British-American Tobacco, and the various huge multi-national banks and corporations, who had been assigned to haul and distribute most of the camp supplies. It was not an easy job. It was backbreaking, and sometimes heartbreaking, when there wasn't enough food to go around, but they treated it lightly, singing bawdy ballads when it got close to being unbearable. And it was just that attitude that drove Gold Tooth into a frenzy. That's when he shouted and shoved and used his swagger stick. He never did learn though: the lousier the job, the more the men sang and made fun of it…and the madder he got.

I couldn't help thinking that Gold Tooth and Guy were cut out of the same cloth: both despised prosperous *taipans*. Possibly for different reasons, but the intensity of their loathing seemed equal. Then it struck me that I hadn't seen Guy in a while. He was still very much in my life—not that I saw him, but I couldn't help feeling his presence. I'd find myself wanting to bump into him, then getting a horrible bout of shakes when I realized I'd probably make an ass of myself if I did. I wished I had the guts to ask him why he was so contemptuous of successful businessmen, and why he believed all their gains were ill-gotten, but I was afraid I'd learn more about him than I really wanted to know. Then again, even if I'd had the courage to ask, the chance of him volunteering anything intimate about himself was almost nil. I knew I didn't have the nerve to ask Nico about him: it would show I was interested in him, and I cringed at the thought that anyone might find out I cared one way or the other.

I had learned from Dan that Guy was a stoker in the camp bakery with Nico; it was not surprising, as Nico's father had been made a shift captain in the bakery. I smiled at the thought of his "culture" coming into its own. It didn't take us long to realize that, if it hadn't been for the steady supply of great bread the bakery made we would have all been on starvation rations.

I made up for not seeing much of Guy or Nico by making quite a lot of new friends. And that was just as well, as Ursula had joined a clique, most her own age or older, and I was not invited into their little circle. It really hurt. She had been the closest person in my life since my toddling days. We had done everything and gone everywhere together, and now I was being tossed out like an old shoe. It took me a while to realize that, until the camp, I had not only been her shadow, I had tried to overshadow her every chance I got. My precociousness must've really got to her, and now, unintentionally, she was evening up the score.

Margo had befriended several other war-brides whose husbands were in military camps, and they helped each other out. She also volunteered to work in the hospital as a nurse's aide and had started pretty rigorous training. She admitted one evening that it was nothing she planned to do for the rest of her life, but it was a change from secretarial work and a great way to help others.

I was restless. Everyone seemed to be finding their niche except me, and although I was getting used to the routine, I was definitely not enjoying it. My idea of nothing was peeling potatoes, or chopping leeks for a couple of hours a day, then tramping around the camp looking for something to do. After a couple of weeks, I complained to the assignment committee, but was told everything would change soon, as they were planning to open school for us in Number Two Kitchen, and we would be too busy studying to have time for any other work.

I didn't know which would be worse, chopping leeks or trying to study in a busy kitchen. I found out soon enough when classes started, and I tried to apply myself with tears running down my cheeks from the fumes of the vegetable prep area.

After a month of students with puffy eyes and allergies stumbling through their studies, the teachers threw up their hands in disgust and said we had to have a better place for our schooling. The committee concurred, and we were moved to the left transept of the overworked church-cum-assembly hall. That wasn't any real improvement, as some days the hall was divided into umpteen different activities, each vying for top honors in the strident category, and my head would be splitting by the end of the day. The only thing that kept me going was knowing that my old nemesis, Claire, was there trying to best me at every turn, and I wasn't about to give her the pleasure.

Claire was about my age, but very worldly. She had been a day scholar at St. Joe, and she and I had fought to be "head of the class", conceding the title back and forth as the months rolled by. Although we were similar in competitive drive, the likeness ended there, as she was a born leader and I was a loner. She had dozens of friends; I had a handful of close ones. No matter what the situation, Claire had to take over. No matter what the event, Claire had to be first. I tried to excel to prove something to myself, Claire did it to prove something to the world. I didn't learn till much later how hard she was on herself the months I was "head of the class". According to her mother, she would stew all month when I had the title, working herself into a frenzy to get it back, then, when she did, she'd get complacent again, and I would take over once more. I guess if I'd known about it, it would have helped explain her behavior towards me on our weekend outings, and her put-downs and caustic remarks wouldn't have gotten to me as much. But I didn't know. I only knew she enjoyed playing court and had to have everyone kowtow to her—something I refused to do.

Well, now, come Christmas and the end of the school year, she would be an item of history.

It wasn't till camp that I found out Claire had a second nemesis; her name was Billie Trainor. She was a true tomboy and a fantastic athlete. Lord, I would've given anything to have her lean, hard build, and almost anything to have her athletic ability.

As captains of opposing hockey teams, Claire and Billie would square off on the roll-call field, and heaven help anyone who got in their way. I played on Billie's team, and after a couple of games, Claire realized she could get rid of a petty nuisance like me by kicking dust up in my face and making me sneeze till I almost passed out; then she'd systematically go after all the other members of Billie's team till the game ended up being completely one-sided. That would make Billie mad, and she would explode on the field till Claire found herself and her precious ego battling for unattainable glory. It always did my heart good to see a vanquished Claire have to show sportsmanship by shaking hands with Billie when it was all over.

Slowly, the chilly spring turned into summer, and as the hot, airless days rolled by, tempers sizzled like overloaded fuses, turning the camp into a powder keg. The chairman of our administration committee, Roger Barton, one of the Kailan's top men, realized if we didn't have some way to vent our steam we would soon be out of control. He discussed it with his committee, and the suggestion was made that what we really needed was entertainment of some kind. Something light and musical to kill the sombre mood of the camp before any *real* killing took place.

Not using quite those words, Roger asked the Commandant for permission to stage a show in the assembly hall. "Thought you'd never ask," he said, smiling, then, on a more serious note, added, "I'll have to get permission from the captain. Hope I catch him in a good mood."

Happily, when the Commandant approached King Kong, he found that he and the guards were as bored of camp life as we were, and all the captain asked was that the first two rows in the hall be reserved for him and his men.

That was all we needed to hear—auditions began on the spot.

It was just as well school was out by then, as the hall was monopolized by rehearsals, and the old piano that had belonged to the university was tuned till it sounded like a Steinway concert grand.

When we weren't listening to Sharon Talati working on Chopin's *Polonaise*, the exquisite notes cascading out of the open windows and climbing the tall pines that surrounded the building, we would peek in and watch Jacqueline de St. Hubert practicing the finale to Tchiakowsky's *Swan Lake*. When, or where, the small band of black nightclub musicians from Peking rehearsed its numbers I couldn't say, but when the show came together a few weeks later, they were superb.

The night of the performance, King Kong made a rare appearance, sitting front-row center, flanked by the Commandant and Gold Tooth, with the rest of the guards filling the first two rows. It's a good thing the camp didn't have a fire marshal, as the remainder of the hall was packed, and the aisles crammed. Even the open windows were jammed with expectant faces.

The program turned out to be a portrayal of all our frustrations, lightened by song, skit, and mime, and punctuated by the *Polonaise* and *Swan Lake* for those who enjoyed classical entertainment.

A complete surprise just before intermission was the appearance of a Trappist monk singing the tragic lament, *If I Had the Wings of an Angel*, the words re-written to reflect our distaste for our new lifestyle. Although the lyrics were humorous and right on target, his voice was so exceptional, I almost missed them. I couldn't help thinking of the MC's short introduction, where he said the priest had just come down from the hills beyond Peking after a twelve year vow of silence! I didn't realize at the time that the vow of silence only covered communication with other people, and erroneously thought, *Even the Lord can't ask that of such a voice...*

When his last notes died away, the applause rang out again and again. There was no way he was going to get off the stage without an encore, but as he had run out of re-written verses, he returned to the original lyrics, and had us all spellbound again by the feeling he wrapped around the words.

No one dared leave their seat at intermission for fear of losing it to the hoards pressing to get in, so the MC cut the break short, and the program resumed with a skit on *The Jerry Trot*.

We were lucky our cell was only a hundred feet from the women's latrines on Main Street; for all those who were blocks away, with umpteen kids or invalids, the "Jerry Trot" several times a day was a must, each person trying to pretend that the object they were carrying draped artfully with a towel was *not* a chamber pot, when it so obviously *was!* The cheery "Hellos", "Nice day, isn't it?" and "How's the family?" as the parties passed back and forth, trying to appear nonchalant, were typically British, and ridiculous, and the skit had us laughing at ourselves till I thought I would cry.

As the evening wound down to a close, it appeared our Japanese captors had enjoyed the program almost as much as we had, even though they hadn't understood a word of it—except, of course, for the Commandant. When it was time for the last number, the MC turned it over to Roy Stone, the leader of the black combo that had given the show such fantastic backup, and he stepped forward and said they would like to dedicate the number to Gold Tooth. The Commandant caught onto the name right away, and standing up, interpreted, as the supply sergeant beamed and hissed in pride at the honor. "And now…we would like to dedicate…to Gold Tooth (here the Commandant obviously put in the sergeant's correct name, as he got up and bowed several times to everyone)…this special number…(in English) *We'll Be Glad When You're Dead You Rascal You!*

The number was a solid hit. Thundering applause rattled the rafters of the old hall as the internees yelled for more, and the encores got louder and louder till the crescendo seemed to break through the walls. It was an ear-splitting success, and Gold Tooth jumped up and yelled and clapped, then climbed up on stage and danced a jig before the ecstatic musicians.

Everything seemed to ease up a lot after that, and ball games on the roll-call field in the evening became a daily occurrence, much to the Puerto Ricans and the "Padres" delight. It didn't take long for me to figure out how Father Windy *really* got his nickname: the fact that his name was an unpronounceable, vowel-less Polish one was secondary to the way he hit home-runs and winged it around the bases. There was only one drawback to his powerful swing— we started to run out of softballs in a hurry.

It must've been around the third or fourth game that the problem resolved itself. After Windy's bat had done its duty and he was sailing around the bases with a look of triumph on his face, and a look of woe on everyone else's, there was a lovely *"Ay-a-a-AH!"* from over the wall, and the ball came flying back in! Our Chinese friends on the outside had decided to join in the fun, even though they couldn't see the action—and whoever pitched those balls back must've had a fantastic arm. Later, when I kidded Windy about his name, he admitted he'd played semi-pro for several years before entering the order.

After the success of the musical and the ball games—the latter also enjoyed by the guards—we had no problem getting permission to put on other group activities and shows. The talent tucked away in that crowd of inmates was nothing short of remarkable. So much of it would never have been found if it hadn't been for the easy-going atmosphere that started to take over in the camp. To break the monotony of the days, people who never thought of performing before would audition just for the heck of it.

That's how Ursula got involved. I remember it so well, as it was right after her eighteenth birthday. Only Dad had had a gift for her on that day—a poem he'd written—and he handed it to her shyly.

> *You're as English as they make them,*
>   *tho' that land you've never seen;*
> *It's a pleasure that awaits you;*
>   *England, with her meadows green;*
> *Sleepy hollows, leafy lanes of oak,*
>   *and elm, and birch;*
> *Grazing cattle, sheep, and lambs,*
>   *and spire of distant church.*
> *And an all-pervading sense of home,*
>   *enveloping, and real;*
> *A heritage that's yours by birth,*
>   *to which you'll e'er be leal.*
>
> *You're as English as they make them,*
>   *with your carriage of a queen;*
> *And the forthright, open, gaze of you,*
>   *purposeful, yet serene.*
> *Placidity sits on your brow,*
>   *no place for troubles there;*
> *Epitome of health, and youth,*
>   *that bides all care beware.*

Long may you thus your best friend be,
and profit by the wealth
Of happiness, and charm, that you
Possess in your dear self. —Daddy

Giving him a big hug, she handed it to Margo and me, and we read it together. It was a simple poem, but I felt my eyes brim. Would I ever see England? I had dreamed of it so often. And of Granny in the big old house on Hale Lane in the Mill Hill district of London. Grandpa was gone now; he had died in '37. I knew Dad worried about his mother, how she spent many a night in the damp, cold cellar, waiting out the terrifying air-raids, and unthinkingly, I stirred up his worries by saying, "Wonder how Granny is getting along."

Ursula gave me a withering look, turned, and marched out of the compound. When she got back, she announced she'd auditioned for a minor role in A. A. Milne's *Mr. Pim Passes By,* and had got the part. It was her way of getting involved and not dwelling on the things she couldn't change. I got her message.

She was all aglow when she came back to the cell after the first rehearsal. She spoke of all the neat, new people she'd met, and in passing, mentioned that a prompter was needed desperately.

Margo perked up, decided that was right up her alley, volunteered, and got the job. It proved to be a happy decision, as the part of Mr. Pim had gone to the Reverend Simms-Lee, the sweet soul who had married her and Jack twenty months earlier, and she thoroughly enjoyed renewing their friendship.

A week into rehearsals, the director said, "We've got to get out some publicity. We need posters—at least one at each kitchen." That's when Margo and Ursula remembered they had a kid sister who was "something of an artist", and I was asked to do the posters. They even supplied art board, and replaced many of my dwindling colors—where they came from I'll never know.

I started out having a ball, at least on the first poster for Number One Kitchen. And I refined it somewhat when I painstakingly re-did it all by hand for Number Two Kitchen. But it became a total drag when I rendered it a third time for Number Three. Everybody *had* to be listed, from the lead to the props, in copy of lessening importance, and heaven help me if I didn't get them in the right pecking order!

The play ran for three nights, Thursday, Friday, and Saturday, so that all could have seats and enjoy it. It was a delightful study in human nature, and the Reverend Simms-Lee seemed a natural for the mixed-up Mr. Pim. When the house lights dimmed for the last time—we didn't have a curtain to drop—I felt a nice cozy glow settle over the audience, reminding them that it was a pretty good old world after all.

About six weeks after the show closed, Margo came off her hospital shift, shaken and depressed. I was reading in the cell when she came in and couldn't help asking what was wrong.

"It's the Reverend Simms-Lee," she said, with a catch in her throat. "They brought him in on a litter. He has terminal cancer… only days to live."

"Do you think he knew it when he did the play?"

"Of course, he knew it!" And then softly, "You know, of all the church people I've known, he's the only one I felt comfortable with. The only one who showed real love and compassion. I was broken up inside when you and Ursula weren't able to be at my wedding, and somehow he was able to turn my mood around and make it the most beautiful day of my life. He loves people, and it shows in everything he does."

He "passed gently by" a few weeks later, and became our fifth loss. The first had been Roy Stone's tall, slim, piano player, who died of a perforated ulcer a week after our arrival, as there were no facilities in the camp to perform the necessary surgery. He was followed by a Belgian priest, a British housewife, and a very young Dutch Father. The last two, like Simms-Lee, died of cancer.

Saturday night dances at K-2 became a regular affair toward the end of summer, and as the guards never checked in on them, we could almost kid ourselves into believing we weren't in a prison camp.

The music was great…and live. It was impossible not to enjoy Roy Stone's band and the two Hawaiian guitarists who teamed up with them. They didn't need amplifiers to send their notes sailing, and although the kitchen windows were open most of the time, no one ever complained about the music.

The dances were also a great place to find out who was going with whom, who had broken up, and who was on the prowl. Lisa and I usually went with a group that fluctuated in number due to work shifts; sometimes I had a date, sometimes not. It was on one of the latter occasions that Guy came in alone. Nico never came to the dances, and I dearly wished he would. If he'd been there, I could have gone over and struck up a conversation without turning into a barb-tongued witch. It happened every time I got near Guy. As I glanced his way, trying not to look obvious, René Francoise, a slim little French girl with flaming hair, went over to him and clung on his arm, looking up at him with her ice-melting eyes. He looked over her head with a bored expression, trying not to make eye contact, but she giggled and finally got him to smile, and they stepped out on the floor. I thought, *Oh Lord, she's nuts over him. Look at the way she's clinging to him,* and I realized, with envy, that I could *never* do that.

I was still quietly fuming over the situation when Norm Shaw, one of the many camp bachelors, and a great dancer, caught my eye. The black mood of the moment was soon forgotten in the enjoyment of dancing with him. When the number came to an end, he asked conversationally if I'd seen King Kong's latest bulletin.

"No. Why?"

"It's a very stern message telling us that we're never to sing *Happy Birthday* on the roll-call field again."

Seeing a twinkle in his eye, I said, "You're pulling my leg."

"Honest—but it did say we could sing *God Bless America.*"

"Now I know you're pulling my leg."

"Come on," he said, grabbing my arm, "it's on the bulletin board. I'll show you." And, sure enough, there it was, emblazoned with King Kong's chop, standing out from all the other notices on the board. I could see the deft hand of the Commandant behind the choice of *God Bless America*. He was obviously trying to soften the blow, all the while making King Kong take full blame—and making him look like a total ass in the process!

The singing of that childish song had started innocently a couple of months after we were in camp. Our kooky block-mate, Gladys Tabor, wearing her usual floppy shorts, ruffled blouse, gobs of make-up, and a big Betty Boop bow, pranced up to Jock Allan one morning while we were waiting in line for roll-call, and said, "Today's my birthday, whatcha got for me?" then she leant over and puckered up. Jock obligingly gave her a resounding smooch on the lips, while his wife, Emma, grinned, and Mark Tabor looked like thunder. Then Gladys, pretending to get all flustered, batted her heavily mascaraed eyes, and simpered, "Oh, Jock, you *shouldn't* have!"

Dad called out meanly, "How old are you Glad-Eyes?"

"Twenty-nine and counting," she quipped, turning her back on him and flipping her shorts in his face as she can-canned back to her place in line.

"Hey, let's all sing *Happy Birthday* to Gladys," Jock called down the line, and as he gave the downbeat, we all broke into the happy refrain.

The idea took off like wildfire. With almost two thousand people in the camp, and only three-hundred-and-sixty-five days in the year, there was no way a day could pass without *someone* having a birthday. Each morning after that, the block wardens would check their lines for "birthday babies" and the song would go up and down the ranks as each celebrant was honored, from the tiniest toddler to the oldest inmate. It was infectious, and it made the days start out on a happier note.

I looked at the incredible bulletin again and said, "Whatever brought that on?"

"I understand that every time the guards stepped onto the ball field with their clipboards, we broke into the darn song, and they thought it was something ridiculing them."

"Couldn't the Commandant explain what the song was about?" I asked incredulously.

"He probably did—but I think King Kong's got his number!"

*****

At the close of a sweltering summer, some of the Catholic priests, and most of the nuns, were told they could return to their monasteries and convents. They had all become such an integral part of camp life, I hated to see them go. Their hard work, and the humor they brought to all their jobs, put us to shame, and I knew I would miss the Sisters most of all. As I started down to the main gates to see them off, I thought of all the hell I'd put them through at St. Joseph after we'd returned from the States, and wondered how all of them—especially Mother Montana—had put up with me.

As boarders, we always went from dorm to chapel, study hall, or refectory, in crocodiles, like fabled Madeline, only the Sisters made us also walk in complete silence. That hadn't bothered me much before going to the States, and still didn't seem to get to serene Ursula, but now it drove me wild.

One afternoon, a couple of weeks after we'd been back, I got caught misbehaving in line on the way to Benediction, and my punishment was to kneel outside the closed chapel doors on the hard black-and-white marble tiles of the corridor, and follow the service from there. My knees hurt, my mind wandered, and on top of it all, the French priest from St. Louis College, who gave the benediction, was late.

I got up and looked down the long, narrow, highly polished hallway, which was kept immaculate by two little Chinese boys, Andrew and Bartholomew. They were a couple of little urchins who had been taken off the streets by the Sisters and fed and clothed. In the course of time they were instructed in Catholicism, became altar boys, and did sundry other light chores around the school, one of which was to keep all the corridors mopped and polished. The latter was done in a way only nuns would think of. Mother Jeanne Hélène, who handled our wardrobe and linens, had made two pairs of "shoe-mops" for the boys, which they wore as they shuffled up and down the hallways, buffing the tile as they went. It was time-consuming, and had to be tiring on their skinny little legs, but they seemed to enjoy doing it and the results were amazing.

I studied the gleaming tile for a while longer, and then I eyed all the neat rows of heavy oak student lockers. As St. Joseph's used the honor system, and as the Sisters were all quite snoopy, there were no locks on the lockers—they were just used to store unneeded books during class.

As I looked at them, a fiendish idea came to mind.

I quietly walked up the corridor, opening all the lockers at arms' level, then when I got to the far end, I turned and ran, arm extended, the full length of the corridor, the doors slamming shut like a continuous burst of machine-gun fire. The tiles were so beautifully slick I slid the final twenty feet, right through the chapel doors that the Sisters had hurriedly opened, into the waiting arms of a furious Mother Superior.

That was it! I was expelled! There was no way they were going to tolerate my rude, disruptive behavior. Mother Montana dragged me off to her office and asked, "What has happened to that beautiful, well-mannered child who left for the States a year ago?"

I was all contrite under her blazing eyes and could only mumble, "I don't know. I don't know."

"I will have to write your parents and tell them to pick you up—you're more than St. Joseph bargained for, and I'll not let you corrupt the rest of the boarders."

I begged and cajoled and wheedled, and when that didn't work, I lost all my stubborn pride and wailed outright, "I can't go home! I can't go home! There's no school in Chinwangtao, and there's no other school in Tientsin that will take boarders. You are not just punishing me, you're punishing my parents. It's not *their* fault. I promise I'll never do it again!"

It worked. Not instantly, but I could see her weakening, and I promised the moon: no more talking in line, no more messy bed in the dorm, no more sassing back, no more being late for class, and when I got through with the "no mores", I realized I really had been putting the sweet Sisters through undeserved hell. Mother Montana finally acknowledged that I was contrite enough to be given a second chance. And she added, "A second and *only* chance." My parents would not be told, or made to suffer, if I stood by my promise.

She was a wise lady, and she knew human nature very well. She recognized in me a person who would die rather than break a promise, even one made under duress, so she patted me on the head, told me I could stay in her office and "cry my sins away", and when I felt composed, I could join the boarders in the recreation hall, then she gave me her beautiful smile and left the room.

When I got to the main gates of the camp she was wearing that same beautiful smile. "You look happy," I said, giving her a hug.

"I am. We all are."

The remark was redundant, as the Sisters were beaming as though they'd just witnessed the Second Coming. It turned out, I wasn't far off the mark: Mother Montana kept insisting that their return to the convent was a minor miracle. "Do you realize," she said, "that because someone was kind to *one* Japanese civilian in a prison camp in the States, their kindness spread like ripples across thousands of miles of ocean, and that Japanese returned it almost two-thousand-fold to the people in this camp?" I knew she was referring to the Commandant.

Soon after the Sisters left, over two hundred Americans were repatriated on a Swedish vessel, the *Gripsholm*—among them the "Peking Padres". I knew they were going to be missed, not only for their ball-playing ability, but for their never-failing good spirits and willingness to pitch in no matter how lousy the job. I also knew Ursula and Father Patrick had learned acceptance in the camp, and had both come out stronger for their friendship. I felt a tug of loneliness as I watched the priests climb up onto one of the old trucks that was rolling out of the gates, and I joined in the shouts of goodbye, good luck, and keep in touch.

Then, as the last few trucks were pulling out, I got a horrible pang of envy. Envy for a country that could grab it's people from an actual battle-zone and take them home, while the rest of us Allies had to sit it out for the duration. Even if the International Red Cross could have arranged for our repatriation, and neutral countries had sent us ships, there was nowhere for us to go; our homelands were being ravaged, and our colonies had either fallen or were being used for staging areas.

I turned to Dan, who was standing behind me, and asked with sudden realization, "Why aren't you and your mother on one of those trucks?"

He stared off in the distance and said, "It's a long story..." and left it at that. I didn't press him.

Finally, as the last truck rolled out through the gates, the Salvation Army band, which had been playing a jubilant *God Bless America,* broke into *Auld Lang Syne.*

Dan and I waved goodbye, and like most of us there, there were tears in our eyes. As we turned to leave, he said, "I thought Gladys was going with Mark."

"What do you mean?"

"Well, that was Mark Tabor sitting in the back of that last truck, but Gladys wasn't with him."

"Are you sure she wasn't sitting up front?"

"Nope. She didn't get on. I know it."

I broke away from him and rushed back to the cellblock in disbelief—and, sure enough, there was Gladys sitting on her doorstep, staring off into the blue. Margo had just come off duty and was sitting beside her, and I heard her say, "What happened, Gladys?"

"Nothing. This is just a setback. Mark says he doesn't know how it happened, except that we must've gotten married too late for it to be recorded. As soon as he hits the States, he'll take care of it and send for me."

The monsoon rains were late that year. As soon as they had come and gone, cold seeped into the camp and chilled the soggy ground and buildings. We hardly had an autumn before winter grabbed hold. The days weren't bad, especially when the sun shone, but the nights were miserable. No matter how we tried, we couldn't seal up our cells to keep them warm, let alone liveable. There was no doubt we would have to have stoves if we were to survive the bone-chilling nights, but the Japs were in no hurry to oblige.

As it was, I spent most evenings in bed, bundled up in my clothes—including my fur coat—doing homework. When the breaker was pulled at ten o'clock and all the lights in camp went out, I would light a little wick floating in my precious ration of peanut oil, and keep on studying while my teeth chattered and my numb fingers could barely write. Ursula was no better off, and I would listen to her sniff as she quietly worked on her assignments. When I finally snuffed out the wick and settled down for the night, I'd pull my covers over my head and breath deeply down into the bed, trying to trap the last ounce of body heat before suffocation set in.

It wasn't until early November that a carload of stoves arrived. They were heavy monsters, and the three of us went down to the canteen to pick up the two for our cells. Even disassembled, it took us a couple of trips. After setting up one in Mother and Dad's cell, we placed ours between the beds at the back of our cell, with the stove pipe angled out through a pane of the clerestory window. A tin plate with a snug-fitting hole for the pipe had been provided to replace the glass pane, and with a lot of cussing and kidding, we ultimately installed the darn thing. Dumbly, we thought with the arrival of the stoves our troubles would be over, but they weren't.

There was no fuel!

It wasn't until several weeks later that a load of coal came in for us, and when we went to get our ration, we found it wasn't coal, but coal-dust. Recalling the lovely big chunks of coal we used to get from the Kailan, I asked in disgust, "What the heck are we supposed to do with this?"

"Make coal balls," I was told.

"How?"

"You mix the coal-dust with mud, and compact it well, and it should burn very nicely."

"How much?" I asked.

"How much what?"

"How much mud and how much coal-dust?"

"You'll have to experiment."

"Thanks a heap!"

"Don't be sarcastic, Bobby, he's trying to help," Ursula said, as she helped carry the bucket of coal-dust back to the cell.

"Well," I said slowly, "If we mix one bucket of dust with one bucket of mud, we might get two buckets of coal balls. That should last us a day, *then* what do we do?"

"It's obvious we can't light a fire till evening, and then only if we are really freezing, as they're not going to give us a ration of coal-dust on a daily basis. Maybe not even weekly."

We soon found out Ursula was right. We also found out how to make coal balls, and after a while, we learned there were different types of soil in different parts of the camp that bound better, and burned longer, and we kept these little caches of special clay a secret from the others.

I'll never forget the day we made our first batch of coal balls. We got filthy, and our hands turned numb as we had to make them outdoors. Then, when they were done, we found we still couldn't burn them as they were wet through.

"Lord, how long will it take these darn things to dry out?" Margo asked.

"The Adams got their coal-dust a week ago, because their name starts with an 'A'," Ursula said, "And they told me their coal balls are only now dried through."

"You mean, after all this, we've got to wait another *week* before we can have a fire?" I wailed.

"Just think how wonderful spring's going to be when it comes around," Margo said facetiously.

It was a good two weeks later, after a gloriously wicked evening of warmth and happy-talk, almost like old times, that I fell asleep to be woken later by the sound of soft crackling. I immediately thought the banked fire had started up again, so I furtively put my hand near the stove. No heat. I touched it. It was cold, but I could still hear the crackling.

I reached for some matches, and lighting the oil wick, carefully peered around the room. Then I saw it, not two inches from Ursula's face—a horrible scorpion, poised to strike!

It was the first scorpion I had seen in our cell, although I'd heard some had been found in the camp. This one had come out of the cracked plaster on the walls to enjoy the warmth of the fire, and when the fire had gone out, it had decided to get some more heat from a human body—Ursula's.

I didn't dare make a sound, in case she woke up and moved. I fumbled quietly trying to find a scrap of paper in the dimly lit room, so I could pick up the creature and kill it.

"What's up?" Margo whispered.

"Sssh! Scorpion!" I said softly.

Finally, finding some Japanese newsprint that we'd used to start the fire, I crept over to Ursula's bed and carefully grabbed the menacing creature; then dropping it on the floor, I proceeded to pound the life out of it with my shoe.

"Hey! What's going on!?" Ursula yelled, sitting bolt-upright in bed.

"You had a visitor. A scorpion. I killed him."

"Oh, my God!"

None of us slept the rest of the night, as we were too scared the scorpion's mate would come to avenge its death.

10

BLACK MARKETS AND BLACKER MOMENTS

A volley of gunfire made me jump. We were sitting for our finals in the assembly hall when it ripped through the cold winter air, completely shattering the feeling of euphoria that had carried me through the morning. *Oh, God, NO!* I thought, completely losing my sense of time and place. It was "The Fatal Eighth" all over again, and Mr. Foxlee, who was now camp headmaster, must have realized the thoughts that were running through our minds, as he said quietly, "It's okay. That was outside the camp. Nothings's going to happen to us. Concentrate. Get back to your exams." That was easy for him to say, but darn hard for any of us to do, and as soon as he had collected our completed papers, we jumped up and ran from the assembly hall.

I headed straight for our cellblock. If anyone knew what was going on, it would be Dad.

He was just returning to the compound when I rushed up, and before I could utter a word, he said, "Damn, I knew it was too good to last."

"What happened? What happened?" I felt like a fish in a barrel. If the camp were attacked, where could we go, what could we do? We had no way to defend ourselves. I guess my voice echoed my fears.

"Don't panic. It was just the lousy Japs. Gold Tooth caught two of the sump coolies with eggs hidden on them, and on King Kong's orders, had them put before a firing squad."

My mind's eye pictured the whole bloody scene, and I felt sick. I knew that the black market had been flourishing almost since the day we arrived, but to die for smuggling a dozen eggs to the parents of some malnourished kids went way beyond the pale of justice.

"King Kong is furious at our defiance of his orders," Dad went on. "He thought when that Trappist monk was caught red-handed and put in solitary for three months, we would learn. When he found that hadn't worked, I guess he felt he had to convince us that he meant business, and those two poor buggers were a perfect scapegoat for his anger."

The sump coolies were only one source of our black marketing enterprise. We had a much bigger operation run on our side of the wall by a zany order of Belgian priests and Brother O'Hanlon, the American Trappist monk. They had honed their smuggling operation into a precision instrument. Their cover was unique. In the twilight hours at the end of each day, they'd say their office pacing along the wall beyond the hospital, gliding back and forth in their long white robes directly under the eyes of the tower guards. This happened day in and day out, and before long, the guards lost interest in the whole charade. That was the priests' master stroke— and the guards' one mistake. The fathers were housed in dormitories on the top floor of the hospital, and from that great vantage point, they could see almost to the horizon in all directions. It was a perfect set-up for smuggling. While they paced the wall saying their office, a lookout would be scanning the fields. When he saw farmers cautiously approaching with their wares, he'd signal to his pious colleagues below, and they'd slip out of their light robes, tucking them into the copious folds of the dark scapulas they wore under them, then melt into the deep shadows along the wall.

With the first timid rap from the outside, they'd start haggling with the farmers over eggs, bacon, nuts, honey and sometimes *baigar*, a potent Chinese whiskey—with money and goods moving back and forth through loose brick pass-throughs in the wall.

Brother O'Hanlon, with the glorious voice, was the one who had been caught earlier, before they'd concocted this sophisticated scheme, and King Kong couldn't understand why we all roared with laughter when he sentenced "a Trappist" to three months in solitary!

Not long after the shooting of the two coolies, we learned the real reason behind the incident: King Kong wanted a slice of the lucrative black market. He had Gold Tooth and the young guards contact the Chinese, who were now too scared *not* to comply, and smuggling flourished once more, just as it had done in North China through the Great Wall at Shanhaikwan. That time the Japanese military had used the subjugated Koreans. Bolder now, King Kong used his own men, with some of the internees doing the actual handing over of the goods, so that he would never be tainted.

As in all cases of smuggling, turf wars soon sprang up between the Jap guards, turning the scenario into a rather comical B-grade Hollywood gangster movie. If it hadn't been for the disgust most of us felt for the internees who aided and abetted our captor's in exchange for a few minor luxuries, we would have laughed at the whole convoluted caper.

I had no trouble getting a job as breakfast cook in the hospital diet kitchen the week after I took my finals, as the committee was still looking for people to fill positions that had been vacated by the repatriated Americans. Although some had been taken over by a contingent of missionaries from Chefoo, who came in after the Americans left, there were still a few gaping holes to be filled, and one was the unpopular early morning shift I applied for. I'd had a yen for that job ever since Margo had told me she hated her early stint at the hospital because, when she sent orderlies down to get the patients' breakfast trays, more often than not she'd find that no one had bothered to turn up to prepare breakfast!

I couldn't help thinking, *what a glorious out!* I loathed roll-call. It was so demeaning. If I could get the breakfast shift for the duration, I would never have to stand roll-call again! I was wrong, of course, as I was told I would get one day off in four, and a captain from another shift would take my place on that day. I got philosophical: One roll-call out of four wasn't as demeaning as four out of four! And then, there was an extra plus. As I was the only one on the early morning stint, I figured I was considered a shift "captain"; of course, I never let it go to my head!

I must have been on the job for about three weeks, and the new year was just around the corner, when I got up at my usual ungodly hour and reached for the basin of water we kept on top of the stove; I didn't expect it to be warm, but I didn't expect it to have half-an-inch of ice on it either! *Well, I'm not going to wash myself today, at least not at this hour,* I thought, as I brushed my hair and teeth, the latter without toothpaste and chattering so badly the toothbrush couldn't keep up with them. Cramming on the clothes I'd worn the day before, some of which I'd slept in, I reached for my old fur coat, which was beginning to look mangy and very worse for wear, and slipped out of the cell.

With luck, the kitchen would be warm, as the stoker got there half an hour ahead of me and got the fires under the *kwas* going. The cook-stoves, or *kwas*, were made of brick and were topped either with huge metal tubs, like gigantic *woks*, or heavy cast-iron plates. The *woks* were used for boiling water and steaming food, the heavy metal cooking surface for everything else. We had ovens, also made of brick, but they were seldom used, as they required a separate firing, and we didn't have enough fuel.

When I got to the kitchen—I had run all the way—my throat hurt from gulping in the freezing air, and I could hardly speak. Dan was the stoker on duty that morning, and although he was as new to the job as I was, he had a beautiful fire going.

"Cold?" he asked.

"Uh-uh. I always wheeze when I talk," I cracked.

"Guess it was a dumb question."

"That's okay, I *am* dumb. Who, but I, would volunteer for this blinkerty-blank shift for the duration."

I remembered being tickled when Dan told me he was going to be a stoker at the hospital kitchen; although stokers were on a three-on-one-off schedule like mine, when they came back on duty, they moved up to the next shift, so I only got to see Dan every third rotation.

As he went off down the hall, I hung my old coat on a hook by the door and started to wrestle with the tub of soaking *hsiao-mi* that in happier years we had fed to our dogs. Owing to mice and rats, the evening crew who had prepared the millet covered it with a wooden lid held down with heavy weights. When Dan got back from checking the boiler-room fire for the hospital's hot water, he saw me struggling with the old tub.

"Hey, let me do that. Where do you want it?"

When I told him, he manhandled it over to the cooking area as I pulled the lid off a huge iron kettle, then, carefully hoisting and tipping the tub, he slowly added the soaking millet to the scalding water while I stirred like crazy so that it wouldn't lump up. When I had to do the job by myself, I bailed the millet out with a smaller pan, and did both the ladling and stirring at the same time. It was a tricky operation, and I already had a nasty steam burn on my right forearm to show for it.

Later in the morning, when breakfast was through and the wash-up done, I started to set up for the lunch crew. As I double-checked the different items I had to put out, Dan came in and asked if I would like to go to the New Year's dance with him.

"Love to."

"I'll pick you up around seven-thirty then."

New Year's Eve arrived bitter and raw, boding no promise for the winter ahead. The cell was like ice as I changed for the dance, and I was still shivering when Dan came to pick me up. His warm smile did wonders for my heart, but nothing for my frozen feet—and I told him so.

"So let's get over to the kitchen and thaw out," he said, propelling me through the door and out into the freezing night.

As we skirted the frozen puddles on Main Street, we were joined by Lisa and her boyfriend, Ian, on their way to the dance.

The kitchen was warm and steamy, smelling romantically of the leak soup we'd had earlier in the evening. The tables had been shoved up against the walls, and the trestles either stacked on top of them, or pushed up against them for us to sit on. The members of the dance combo were tuning up their instruments when we arrived, and Roy Stone was talking to Deirdre Carver, the lovely girl in the last cell in our block. He seemed completely taken by her, and the musicians were getting a boot out of watching him try to make time. Finally Smitty, the bass player, called out, "Come on, Roy, let's *g-o-o-o!*" and with a flustered giggle, he turned to the group and they broke into *My Blue Heaven.*

It was then that I got a passing glimpse of Guy. He looked in, glanced our way, and went back out. I didn't know if he had noticed us, and tried to pretend to myself that I didn't care, but I couldn't help thinking of him and of Dan. Dan always made me feel good about myself, and we had a "thing" going that was clearly more fun than romantic. Sort of a mutual admiration society with a lot of laughs. *Why couldn't Guy be that way?* I knew the answer before I finished the question. It wasn't in his nature—at least not around me. Everything about him was serious, leaving no room for life's little pleasures and fun moments. He came back in a while later with René, and I found myself looking at her red hair, boyish figure, and freckles, and wondering what she had that I didn't have. Dan, who read my moods like a book, looked at Guy, then at me, and back to René, and caught my vibes.

"Did I ever tell you the one about the elephant in the strawberry patch?" he said with a twinkle.

"No, but I know you're going to," I said smiling. Like Nico, he had a knack of defusing bad situations just with his grin, and when he told corny jokes and cut up, his antics were contagious.

Now, when I saw Ian with Lisa, I got the feeling he'd stepped out of the nineteenth century, all stilted phrases, stumbling words, and deep blushes, and I wondered what she saw in him. She was so tall, slim, and striking, she could have had any boy in the camp, but Ian, in his bumbling way, completely monopolized her. And, in an odd way, I felt she enjoyed his attention.

It was a while later, when Dan and I were slow-dancing to *Blue Moon*, that Guy cut in. It was obvious he'd been drinking. As Dan nodded and stepped away, Guy grabbed me and held me tightly, his breath reeking of *bai gar*. The combination was suffocating, and I squirmed to break free. "Hey, cut it out!" I snapped. "Bet you don't squeeze René this way!"

Leering, he held me at arms length, and looking down at my bust-line, said, "Hell no, why would I? Dancing with René is like dancing with Nico!"

It was a crude comment and I found myself blushing furiously. "I've had enough, I'm going to go sit down."

"Uh-uh. No *way!*" he said, as I broke free.

I was just about to turn around and slap him, when the last haunting notes of the number came to a gentle close, and I thankfully dropped onto the nearest bench. When Dan and Lisa joined us a few moments later, I noticed Ian was nowhere in sight.

"Where's Ian?" I asked.

"We had a tiff," Lisa said. "I told him to go cool off."

Turning to Guy, who looked like blazing thunder, I said, "That's an idea. Why don't *you* go and cool off?"

As he spun on his heel and stormed off, Lisa said, "That wasn't very polite."

"Maybe not, but you don't know what led up to it, and I'm not about to tell you. Okay?" I was still mortified by what I'd gone through and wondered how many people had heard his crude remark.

Dan grinned and said, "Lisa, you've got to learn something; when Bobby's around Guy, she's a witch!"

"So I've noticed," she said.

I hadn't realized I was that obvious. Dan might have fathomed my feelings for that drunken, leering Lothario, but not Lisa! *Cool it, gal,* I said to myself, as Ian rejoined us, and with a peck on Lisa's ear and a mumbled apology, we all got back into the mood of the evening.

The band was outdoing itself. Smitty was wound up like a top, and by his raucous ad libs and wild innuendos, I knew the consumption of *bai gar* had not been limited to Guy Woodruff. Roy Stone was following the beat of his heart more than that of the music, while Deirdre glowed with happiness at the boisterous noise.

When midnight rolled around, they broke into a nostalgic *Auld Lang Syne*, and, after everyone kissed and got maudlin and mushy, Dan walked me back to our cell.

I'd just started to invite him in, when I heard Ursula sobbing. I was stunned. I'd never heard her cry in my life—except one time when a crab got her toe—so I hurriedly said good night, and as he gave me a shy kiss and walked away, I whispered, "Happy New Year!".

Taking a deep breath, I walked into the cell.

Ursula looked like the devil. None of us girls cry prettily. Our faces get puffy, blotchy, and blue, and twisted out of shape like a wrung-out sponge.

I tried a little humor, and said, "What happened, crab get your toe?"

That was a mistake.

"Grant and I broke up!" she wailed.

"Bet Alex's happy!"

"He doesn't know about it. It only happened at the dance tonight. Grant said we were through. Just like that. I can't believe it."

"Think there's someone else?" After I said it, I knew I wasn't being tactful. *Damn,* I thought, *I'm really putting my foot in it tonight.*

To my surprise, Ursula said, almost calmly, "I think it's Tessie, only he insists there's no one. He just wants to play the field. God, it hurts!" She started to cry all over again.

"Hey, Grant's not worth it. He's a schnook!"

"Why don't you like him?"

"Because he likes himself too much. He doesn't leave room for anyone else's feelings. Forget him!"

"I can't, even if I wanted to—I'll see him every day. I can't get away from him…" and then with a sob, "…and I don't *want* to!"

"Wait till you see him out with someone else, and you will be so mad you'll wish you never wasted a tear on him." I could be so objective, it wasn't my heart that was broken.

She started to cry uncontrollably, and I made a mental note before I went to sleep to tell Alex that the coast was clear. I always liked Alex better than Grant, because he was so down-to-earth and treated Ursula like a princess, something Grant never did. As it turned out, my good intentions weren't necessary. Alex had seen the blow-up at the dance and was waiting the next day to pick up all the pretty pieces.

At work that morning, I found myself comparing the two of us. I knew I was impatient, and if life didn't move fast enough, I gave it a kick in the pants to get it rolling, but I wasn't uncaring, and had to fight to hide every emotion I felt. Ursula was different. Justly or not, I felt her aura of quiet poise covered unconcern, and that to her, life could be plumbed or she could walk away from it, depending on how much she wanted to get involved. Unlike me, the only emotion I'd ever seen pass over her face was an occasional one of happy surprise.

I had a hard time adjusting to this new Ursula who really did have feelings, even though I felt they were misplaced. I got to wondering what she would do if she saw Grant out with Tessie, who was her best friend. Would she blow up? Would she cry? Would she play up to Alex to see if she could get a rise out of Grant? I really didn't know. I soon found out.

With her usual quiet aplomb, she ignored Grant. When they met at get-togethers and dances, she treated him with her usual reserve, and if her guts were being twisted, no one knew, least of all me. Then I realized that's why she had turned into such a great actress, she could be living one thing, and acting out something totally opposite.

It was a gusty afternoon just before my seventeenth birthday; Dan and I were strolling up Main Street, and he said something about having to stop by the cell to check on his mother, who had a lousy cold. I went into the cellblock with him and waited outside while he spoke to her.

The compounds weren't enclosed any more. The pretty latticed end walls and decorative gates were gone, and with them, any modicum of privacy we'd ever had. The Japs had made us pull the walls down, as the bricks were needed to enclose a considerable section of housing to the north of the main gates. The new wall was the height of the camp's outer walls and topped with ugly barbed wire.

The people still inside the compound laughed and said they felt they were in quarantine and must have some horrible, contagious disease they didn't know anything about. We laughed with them as we watched the work progress, and when it was completed, we couldn't help wondering what the Japanese were up to. One thing we'd learned: they never did anything without a reason.

It was while I was standing there, considering many possibilities and discarding them one by one, that I saw Dad slip furtively out of the Woodruff's cell and walk off in the opposite direction.

I almost choked: my worst fears had been realized. *Dammit, what was I going to do?*

I started to think how Guy must be enjoying the situation and getting a boot out of Dad's shenanigans. How could I face him?

And Mother...*she must never find out!*

I didn't hear or see Dan come out of his cell. I was completely lost in the enormity of the situation.

"What's up?" he said, breaking into my searing thoughts.

"How long has my Dad been seeing Guy's mother?"

"Oh, I don't know. For about a month, I guess."

"Why didn't you tell me?"

"What good would it have done?"

He was right. I shrugged and said, "Let's get out of here," completely forgetting why we were there in the first place.

"Yeah, let's go to the library. Mother's cold doesn't seem to be clearing up, and she asked me to get her a book. A mystery, or a love story—something light. Maybe you can help me pick one out."

I didn't know if I could do anything as simple as picking out a book right then; I only knew I had to get out of that compound fast and try to sort out my thoughts.

Surprisingly, as we headed for the library, my dark thoughts were replaced by memories of the camp's second "minor miracle"—the arrival of several cartloads of books during the sweltering heat of the previous summer.

When they were uncrated, most were found to be in deplorable condition, and the assignment committee requested that if anyone knew anything about bookbinding would they please step forward. Dad, who had had a fine collection of books, some rare first editions, had taken up binding as a hobby in the port, but had never done much with it. He told the committee he would gladly do the job.

His workshop was a partially isolated little cell near the hospital area. And that was just as well, as the fish glue he heated up to tip in the pages and mend the spines had a stench that made me gag. I once asked him how he could stand it, and he said, "Oh, like everything, you get used to it."

I had to admit he did a lovely job on the books; especially the spines that always got the worst beating. He not only repaired them so that they were stronger than before, but would painstakingly letter the titles and authors, so that they looked like the original bindery job. You could tell he was happy in his work. And, as he was also his own boss, I knew he read most of the books before, or after, he bound them. Dad, like me, loved to read, only he had a photographic memory. He could scan pages so fast it was impossible to believe he had read them. He used to read a book a day on tiffin break in Chinwangtao. He not only read the books, he devoured them; and from them he got a vocabulary that was second to none. I never recall opening a dictionary until I went away to the convent; if I got stumped, I always asked him for the meaning of a word. He would not only give it to me, but he would give me the root, the usage, and all the derivatives. *He* was my dictionary.

Oh, hell, Dad, how can you be so nice—and such a dirty bounder at the same time?

11

CAPTIVITY AND ESCAPE

When I got off shift one afternoon, I noticed something was up. All the internees in the high-walled, barbed-wired "quarantine compound" were being moved to other parts of the camp. I found Dad's rotten affair with Mrs. Woodruff quickly taking a back seat to the intrigue of the moment. What the heck was going on?

Speculation was rife. The Japs, as usual, were tight lipped and sullen, and if the housing committee was privy to the upcoming influx—and it was obvious we were making room for more internees—they were mum to a man.

I was sorry for those who were being relocated. Most had done wonders perking up their little corner of the world, a limited and frustrating job at best. Now they were having to give up the little they had, to be dispersed throughout the camp and crowded into whatever space could be found. They took it all with "amazing grace", and I saw many of them down by the gates waiting with the curious, like me, to see who had usurped their place.

Rampant rumors did nothing to quell my impatience, and time dragged as we stood under the pines surrounding the assembly hall, looking down on the massive main gates. The guard shack across the street from us was a hive of activity. Even King Kong had put in an appearance.

While I was thinking, *God, if we only had some real news we would know what to expect,* Peter Fox elbowed his way through the crowd and stood beside me. He was sweaty and smelly, and had obviously just got off his shift. He looked at me as he mopped his brow and said, "You part of the welcoming committee?"

"I'll let you know when I find out who the heck I'm supposed to be welcoming."

"That won't take long, they're here," Pete said. And he was right. We heard trucks snorting and grinding as they rolled up to the gates. When the guards threw them open, and the new arrivals started to climb down off the vehicles, Pete said, "I hope you speak Italian."

"Why?"

"If you look closely and listen you'll know."

"What are *they* doing here?"

"Rumor has it that Benito Mussolini was ousted last year, and was replaced by a Marshall Badoglio. The Germans tried to save his arse, and he's their puppet, heading a Fascist Republic in northern Italy behind German lines. So much for *Il Duce.* Then, last October, Badoglio had the unmitigated gall to declare war on Germany! Remember the Axis Alliance—Germany, Italy and Japan? Well, to the Japanese, when the Italians declared war on Germany, they became traitors to the Alliance. There wasn't much the Japs could do on the other side of the world, but they did put all Italians in China under house arrest. And now they've interned them, as 'Dishonorable Prisoners of War'!"

I smiled at the distinction, and the Japanese mind set: *Honorable Prisoners must not be contaminated by* Dis*honorable Prisoners!* Hence the "quarantine compound". The only people I recognized in the whole group were Mario and Carlotta Maccini. And with recognition came the realization that I hadn't seen them since the fall of 1940, following our fun-filled summer with Anne Newmarch.

Anne had not really helped our friendship with Carlotta much. We had known her since the spring of 1937 when Mario, Elena, and a then eleven-year-old Carlotta had arrived in the Treaty Port amid preparations for the coronation, an event that upstaged everyone and everything for many months. To our surprise, Mario, the new Commissioner of Customs, didn't mind his arrival playing second fiddle to all the royal preparations, as he was a complete monarchist himself who loathed the turn of events in Italy.

I remember Coronation Day, and all the men in their dress whites, and Mario being the only one to turn up in pinstripes, a morning coat, and high silk hat, with Elena draped over his arm. Carlotta was with them, looking like a Gainsborough painting, in an extravagant straw hat with streamers cascading down her long blonde hair. I recall looking at the trio and back at Mother and Margo in their pretty voiles, with floppy hats and short gloves, and deciding *no one* looked as lovely as they did.

Now, seven years later, here were Carlotta and Mario coming up the hill from the main gates. I caught myself thinking smugly that she certainly wasn't making any fashion statement this time. She was disheveled, and her pretty but sulky mouth looked grim. Mario, trudging beside her, carried both their suitcases. He looked embarrassed, as did all the Italians, their pride crushed. I knew most of them had come to China in the early thirties, because they *weren't* fascists, and their loyalty to King Victor Emmanuel had been suspect. Now they were being branded unjustly by the Japanese because a deposed dictator had got his just deserts.

Before any of us could make contact with them, they were unceremoniously herded into the "quarantine quarters".

As I turned and slowly walked back to our cell, my mind went back to the coronation, to Henry whisking us off to Eric Arnold's, and to watching Carlotta wave to her parents from her car window as she was driven home. We didn't know her well then, but I couldn't help thinking anything would have been better than being with Eric Arnold that day.

The following day Carlotta was at the gymkhana, and we all had a great time together. After that, she became a big part of our lives, even attending St. Joseph's when the fall term began. And of course, with our new friendship, Carlotta spent the summers from thereon out mostly at our house, and Mario and Elena became "Uncle

Mario" and "Aunt Elena."

It seems to me, it was the following summer that Dad and Mario decided we should go on a picnic. Joyce Marsh and her parents joined us. Our three cars, with the Maccinis in the lead, made an interesting little caravan, as we all happily took off through the native city and struck out on a dusty road that Henry insisted led to a big, walled city with a beautiful pagoda.

All the little walled villages we passed through straddled the road with sturdy gates at each end to seal off each hamlet.

"Why do they have gates? If they closed them, there'd be an unpassable roadblock."

"That's the general idea," Dad said, catching my comment. "Did you notice huge iron bells hanging from oak trees well outside each gate? When farmers sight marauding bandits, they ring the bell to warn the other field workers, then high-tail it for the village. When they're all safe inside, the gates are closed and the village turns into a small fort."

We passed through several such hamlets before coming to a long, wide, straight strip of road teaming with people hauling carts full of produce and squawking chickens. Every once in a while a pig, led by a child, would break loose and run squealing through the mob. Pandemonium would follow, and children would chase after it, darting in and out among pushcarts and people till it was finally corralled.

All this activity kept us crawling at a snail's pace, with horns tooting and chauffeurs cussing. Henry finally calmed down when we saw a high-walled city looming up in the distance, the spire of a pagoda stabbing the clear blue sky.

"See, Master, see!" he said, pointing proudly.

"Hey, Henry, you were right!," Dad said, pounding him on the back. Turning to us, he added, "I bet there is a pretty little park around the pagoda where we can eat our lunch."

As we began to relax and look forward to breaking into the tantalizing picnic basket Jung-ya had helped Cook prepare, the Maccinis' car stopped, and Mario came back and said, "If you look up ahead, you'll see the road is lined on both sides with beggars.

Our chauffeur says there is a fair going on, and we have to toss coppers to them or we'll have bad joss. George, you take the right side, I'll take the left, and I'll suggest to Fred Marsh that he look out for any disgruntled beggars and take up the slack."

"This is too much…" Mother started.

"Come on, Gee, let's face it, we'll be heroes," Mario said with a smile and went on back to talk to Fred Marsh.

Starting up again, we slowly ran the gantlet, while miserable, stunted bodies thrashed out in the dust for the coins we tossed. Some were totally crusted with sores that crawled with filthy flies, other were maimed and grotesque, while the blind cried out in anguish, grabbing vainly for unseen coppers. It was sickening, and I began to feel nauseated.

"Lord, what's happened up ahead!" Dad said, as Henry suddenly stopped dead behind the Maccinis' car. Mario and his chauffeur jumped out and ran to the front of the vehicle, as we all piled out to see what had happened.

A boy of about twelve was lying under the car, having been run over by the right front wheel. It had gone over his mid-section, and he looked ghastly. All this because we'd been so busy tossing coins to the beggars, we hadn't noticed him darting out after a pig that had run oinking across the street in front of our caravan.

Within minutes, police appeared from nowhere, and the scene started to get ugly. Dad and Mario tried to explain that it was an accident and that we would turn right around and take the boy back to the hospital in Chinwangtao for care and treatment.

They were told quite bluntly that they weren't going anywhere, neither was Fred Marsh. All three men were arrested and taken to jail. The rest of us, meanwhile, were allowed to return home with our chauffeurs. Margo rode in the Marshes' car with Joyce, as she had going out. As Elena and Carlotta were on the verge of hysteria, the boy was put into the back seat of our car. A mean-looking gendarme climbed in beside him, leaving Mother to sit up front with Henry, and Ursula and I scrunched into the back seat with our two passengers. Every time we hit a bump or chuck-hole, the police-man's gun jabbed into the side of my leg and I thought it would be blown off. Lord, what a trip!

"Why did they arrest Daddy, Uncle Mario and Mr. Marsh?" I asked, as we crashed along.

"They were afraid, if we took the boy, we would dump him along the roadside and leave him to die. This way the gendarme gets to see we deliver him to the hospital; then he'll return with Henry, and Daddy, and the others will be released and allowed to come home."

"We would *never* throw him out of the car!" I said angrily.

"They don't know that. Maybe that's what they'd do, so they think we would too."

A week later, after every imaginable x-ray and test had been given him, a healthy little boy, without a single broken bone or internal injury, was sent home on a bus with five dollars in his pocket—and a story worth telling for the rest of his life!

Whenever Mario talked about the incident, he always insisted that it was his new pneumatic tires that had saved the little fellow's life.

After that picnic, which really never was, we lost our yen for field trips away from home and spent the rest of our summers enjoying the simple pleasures of the little Treaty Port, especially the summer Anne Newmarch was our guest.

I remember when we got back from seeing her off at the station, Ursula suggested we had better visit Carlotta. It was not surprising that the gesture was met with disdain. "Now that your wonderful Anne is gone, you think you can come over here? Forget it!" she had snapped. A few days later, she took off for a shopping spree in Tientsin with her parents before returning to St. Joseph's. That was the last time we saw Aunt Elena alive.

When we arrived at the Astor House a couple of days before school started, we were met by a distraught Mario with the horrible news of Elena's death. As he came into our room, he kept saying, "Oh, Gee, what am I going to do? My Elena! My Elena! I can't live without her."

Mother gently led him to an easy-chair and suggested he tell her everything, then signaled Ursula to ring for the room boy. While he was softly sobbing, she ordered stiff brandies for them both, then sat in the window seat and said quietly, "I'm listening…"

I couldn't help feeling Mario's anguish, as he blurted out the tragic story.

The previous day, the three of them had been shopping on a grand scale, and when they got back to their rooms, Carlotta said she wanted to see a movie. Elena was exhausted and told them to go on without her; she was going to bed. Hours later, when Carlotta and Mario had quietly slipped into the room, he heard a strange sound like a death rattle, and rushed to Elena's bed. It was too late; she slipped away before he could summon help.

He'd found an empty pill bottle by her bed and was terrified that she had taken her life and that it would all come out in the autopsy that would have to be performed. Mother could see that guilt was killing him, and said kindly, "Do you know how many pills there were in that bottle?"

"No."

"Wasn't Elena taking medication for a heart condition? Maybe it was because she was out of pills that this tragedy happened."

"We should never have left her alone when she was so exhausted."

"Mario, you can't blame yourself."

Carlotta was as cool as ice through the whole thing, and when Mother tried to put her arms around her, she shrugged her off and left the room.

"The full impact of what's happened hasn't hit her yet," Mother said softly to us, "and it's just as well, as Mario's grief is so overwhelming, he'll need her calming influence."

Ursula and I slipped out of the room a few minutes later and went downstairs to look for Carlotta. She was sitting by a huge potted palm in the high-ceilinged lobby, staring with unseeing eyes at bustling Victoria Road and the endlessly flowing traffic as it streamed back and forth.

"Carlotta, your father needs you," Ursula said gently, tapping her on the shoulder. She got up without a comment and followed us blindly back up to the room.

That was the last time we saw her, as she didn't go back to St.

Joseph's that semester.

Mother wrote us a while later that the autopsy revealed Elena had died of heart failure. Her second letter ended with, "Mario has been transferred to Shanghai. I hope he and Carlotta can rise above their tragedy and start a new life for themselves."

Now here they were…in a prison camp.

Not long after their arrival, the weather turned bitter, and the long, cold evenings started to get to us. None of us could afford to fire up a stove; we found ourselves keeping our little stashes of coal-balls for emergencies, or a possible illness requiring heat for recovery. Even when we huddled in each others' cells, the cold dampened our mood and stunted conversation. The only night we all looked forward to was Saturday, where the dances in old K-2 really warmed us up. It didn't matter that the place stank of rancid stew, or pungent leeks; it was warm, and that's all we cared about.

The Saturday following my seventeenth birthday, Dan had the evening shift, so I went to the dance with Lisa and Ian and the rest of our little group, most of whom had paired off by now, leaving me feeling rather like the proverbial "crowd". When we got to the kitchen, Ursula was there with Alex. And I saw Grant come in with Tessie. *Well*, I thought, *just to round it out nicely, Guy should arrive with René.* But he didn't.

Tom Hazlett and I had just finished a number and were waiting for the next piece to start, when Guy came up and asked if he could have the next dance.

"You asking me or Bobby?" Tom said with a grin.

Guy gave Tom a friendly shove, then led me out onto the floor. For a person who wasn't very athletic, except for an occasional game of soccer, it always amazed me how strong Guy felt when he held me and we danced. Actually, when he wasn't drunk or obstreperous, he was a pretty good dancer and I found myself enjoying the number immensely. I even dreamed I could feel a friendly thaw taking place, and a pleasant tingle ran through me. When the music stopped, I surprisingly found no barbed remarks waiting to surface;

in fact, for once, I was completely tongue-tied. It was Guy who broke the awkward silence.

"It's stuffy in here, let's go for a walk."

"It's pretty cold outside."

"We don't have to go far…just for a breath of air."

Stepping outside, he closed the door behind us, and turning, held me close and kissed me long and hard.

It was so sudden, and unexpected, it left me shaking all over. "What was *that* for?" I stuttered as I broke away, with what was left of my senses spinning in a whirl of mixed emotions.

"I heard you had your seventeenth birthday on Tuesday; that's a belated birthday kiss. I haven't got anything else to give you." His eyes were twinkling, and a weak smile crept into mine. Then that evil imp on my shoulder whispered in my ear, *"For God's sake, don't let him know how you feel!"* , and I quickly snapped, "Aren't you afraid you might get contaminated—kissing a capitalist?"

He ignored my biting tone, and said, "That could work both ways, you know." His grin still a mile wide.

"Not a blithering chance!"

He thrust out his chin, and looking down with a smug look, said slowly, "Talking about capitalists—I've met your father."

I felt my skin creep.

"And…?"

"And nothing."

"You can do better than that…he's seeing your mother, isn't he?"

"So what?"

There was no polite way I could tell him what the camp was saying about his voluptuous mother, so I shrugged and suggested we go back inside.

"Not yet. Do you realize we've been together and talking for several minutes without fighting? That's a first, and I don't want it to end."

Surprisingly, I found I didn't either.

"Do you play bridge?" he asked.

"Yes, but I'm no whiz."

"How about joining Nico and me in the afternoons in Number

One Kitchen? We'll pick up a fourth."

"Okay."

A thaw had definitely set in, and I thought, *Great! Things* are *looking up, and just maybe, if I can see Guy away from* his *place, and* our *cell, Dad won't find out.* A shiver of anticipation ran through me, and Guy, thinking I was cold, put his arm around me and steered me back into the noisy kitchen. We chatted lightly for a few minutes, and I felt the walls of Jericho tumbling down. As the music started again and Guy turned to ask me to dance, Claire Blessing barged over and said, "Hey, this is my number!"

I knew the look I gave her could have killed a rhino, and I waited for Guy to turn her down, but he didn't. Instead, he grinned and stepped out onto the floor with her, leaving me to stew quietly.

Claire spent the rest of the evening fawning over Guy and completely ignoring me, or the fact that she had as good as lifted my date, and he just lapped it up. *Dammit, what did Claire have that made men go ape over her?* I was so glad I didn't have to put up with her in school any more, but this, *this* was worse. If she'd had a spat with her date, there were umpteen other unattached males she could waltz off with without taking Guy. I knew she didn't give a darn for him. She was either trying to get back at me for some dumb thing I knew nothing about, or she was getting back at Randy, her current beau, who was standing over by the band pretending not to notice her antics.

Lisa came over while I was still steaming and said she'd had it with Ian and was going home. I looked around at the rest of our gang, and seeing them all happily nuzzling on the dance floor, I grabbed my coat and left with her.

As we slipped out of the kitchen, she said, "Hey, you and Guy looked like you were having a good time. What happened?"

"Claire happened!" I snapped.

"Yeah, I heard her and Randy really getting into it earlier in the dance."

"That's no reason for her to grab Guy."

"Jealous?"

"Heck no!" I said quickly, "I just don't want him to get hurt by her. He's too dumb to realize she's trying to get under Randy's skin and that she's using him as a means to an end."

"Oh, yeah?" There was a definite sound of skepticism in Lisa's remark that I decided to ignore.

"What's with you and Ian?" I asked.

"Nothing." She said. "That's the problem. He's dull. He doesn't talk. And he won't do anything. He says he's just happy being with me. Well, I'm not happy just being 'with *him*'. All he does is sit and look at me; it drives me up the wall!"

"He's in love," I said, laughing.

She started to laugh too, and said, "Lordy, what we put up with!" Then giggling, she said goodnight, and huddling down into her thick winter coat, darted off for her cellblock on Rocky Road.

Between my breakfast shifts, the posters I did for the different shows, and the watercolor lessons I took with Pierre Travers-Smith, I had kept pretty busy. But when the weather turned freezing, as it was now, the art lessons had to be dropped, as they were held outdoors, and I found my afternoons turning into a drag like the long, cold evenings. It was then that I remembered Guy's offer of bridge in Number One Kitchen, and one day, screwing up all the courage I could muster, I looked into the big, sunlit room and saw Guy and Nico playing some weird game of cards, while René looked on.

Nico was the first to see me, and grinning widely, waved me over. "Hey, look! We've got a fourth!" he said, as I came over and joined them.

"What took you so long?" Guy asked, not bothering to look up.

"I've been busy," I said defiantly, tossing off my coat and sitting down at the table.

"Yeah?"

René turned and gave me an annoyed look. I could sense my presence wasn't going down well at all, especially as she realized from Guy's terse comment that he must have invited me at some earlier date.

Nico, as usual, refused to acknowledge any tension, and said, like an umpire calling a ball game, "Let's play *c-a-r-d-s!*"

Guy paired off with René, and I with Nico, an arrangement that would follow through all the games we played together. Actually, they turned out to be a lot of fun, with Guy being the only good player—Nico, René, and I muddling happily along.

At first, I thought it must be rather dull for Guy, but then I realized he really enjoyed showing off his skill, and I got to thinking how great it would be if Nico and I could give him a drubbing just once. But it never happened. Oh, we won a hand here and there, but nothing to crow about.

I think the thing that got to me was René's smug look every time Guy made the tricks he bid. I thought meanly, looking at the adoring looks she gave him, *Anyone can play "dummy"*, but deep down inside I knew that great, green-eyed monster was flailing his humongous tail.

And so, one by one, the days went by. Even our anniversary, March twenty-third, slipped into oblivion without a whimper.

April finally arrived with blue skies and scudding clouds. Spring was definitely trying to take over, and I noticed, with a nostalgic nod to the past, that the acacias were beginning to bud. I even smelled a far away scent of violets. "Oh, it's good to be alive," I said out loud, as I stepped into our compound intent on a spending the afternoon reading a long-awaited library book. But it was not to be.

As I reached our cell door, a filthy tirade spewed out of Gladys Tabor's cell. I'd never heard such words in all my life, not even from men. She never slowed down to take a breath. When she ran out of English, she switched to Chinese, her expletives so graphic, I grudgingly found myself admiring her vocabulary. Suddenly, I heard a crash and to my surprise, Margo flew out of Gladys's cell with a look of panic. Chinese then turned to Spanish, and several large objects sailed out the door.

Jock Allan was standing in his doorway, as Margo rushed up to him and said, "Oh, God, this is terrible. I wish she'd cry and get it out of her system."

"Don't worry," he said, "rage is better than tears. I think she's finally realized she is lucky to be rid of that s.o.b."

I stood bewildered, wondering what had happened. There hadn't been so much excitement from the Tabors' cell since Mark had left in early autumn. In fact, the last time had been in August, when I was hanging out a small wash, and Mark had thrown Gladys bodily out of the door, and she'd slammed against a tree. That time I'd watched, too scared to intervene in case I made matters worse. I remember Gladys sitting up stunned, and slowly crawling back to the cell on her hands and knees. When she reached the door, Mark flung it open and shoved her back into the compound; then stepping over her, he strode off. After he left, a very pregnant Emma Allan had rushed over to help her.

We didn't see Mark for several days after that, not even at roll-call. I figured he'd found some corner of a men's dorm to hole up, but Margo was convinced he was playing around.

"Who the heck could put up with him?" I asked disgustedly.

"That type is always nice when they want something. I'll bet he was nice to Gladys once; that's why she married him."

When he finally came back, Gladys tried to keep him at arm's length, but it didn't last. Before long, she was making every excuse for his beastly behavior, and smothering him with love and misplaced understanding.

The more I thought of Mark and Gladys, the more I wondered how they'd ever gotten together. All we knew of them was that they met and married in Peking, just before leaving for camp. She was irrepressible, with a repertoire of wild stories and funnier jokes, and he was a complete introvert, with mood swings that went from black to blacker. Tall, dark, and very good looking, he was at least ten years her junior. It was obvious she saw in him someone who needed mothering and had decided she was just the person to do it. When they moved into our cellblock, Mark was already palled by her ways and was treating her like a bothersome pup. Somehow she never seemed to notice, and gushed over him, waiting on him hand and foot.

When Margo came up to our cell, I asked her what had brought on the lurid tirade, and she said, "That no-good-son-of-a-bitch has just divorced Gladys."

"How could he do that?"

"Easily. He had his attorney in Reno, Nevada, state that if she didn't appear in court on January 4th, she would be divorced by default. That was three months ago!"

I thought back to the previous summer, when Mark led the stampede to sign up for repatriation. Gladys was almost walking on air when she learned she would be leaving with him, and told us happily that Mr. & Mrs. Mark Tabor would soon be kissing us all goodbye! We were thrilled for her, as it was obvious life had dealt her some pretty low blows, and except for Mark, the only other soul she could claim as "family" was a kid brother somewhere in India.

Now this…

As I followed Margo into our cell, I asked her how she'd got involved; she said, when Jock brought the mail, he noticed the Reno postmark on the large manila envelope and asked Margo if she'd mind being with Gladys when she opened it.

"It was horrible. Like Jock, I knew what that louse had done even before the envelope was opened. I tried to get Gladys in a calm mood before I gave it to her, but she was so excited, she grabbed it from me. The attorney who mailed those papers to a prison camp is as rotten as Mark; he should be disbarred." Then she added, "When did you arrive on the scene?"

"Just about the time you came flying out of her cell."

"Well, you heard it all, I guess."

"It's awfully quiet now, do you think she's okay?"

"I'll go see."

"I'm coming with you."

When we got to her cell her rage was spent, and tears were flowing. Her mascara had run, her Betty Boop bow had come untied and was hanging down like limp rabbit's ears, and she looked as if she'd never be able to rise up again. After a while, Margo got

her quieted down and tucked into bed. At last, completely exhausted, she fell asleep.

I was off duty the next morning, and eyeing our bedraggled row
of cell mates on the roll-call field, when I noticed Gladys was not
in line. A horrible fear grabbed me, and I turned to see if Jock was
concerned. He didn't seem to be. In fact, he craned his neck for
a moment, then turned and winked at us. I was just wondering what
was up, when Gladys came around the end of the line. She was at
her outrageous best, in the most god-awful outfit I'd ever seen. She
put her hands on her hips like a drum majorette, pumped her knees,
and strutted up the line singing *I Love a Parade!*

We all got her message, loud and clear.

No one spoke of Mark again...to her, or to anyone else in the
camp. It was as though he had never existed.

That spring brought more than just a seasonal change: Roy Stone
and Deirdre Carver started going steady. They made a really cute
couple, and although they caused quite a few raised eyebrows, with
her being white and him black, on the whole, the camp showed a
tolerance that was not going to reach the rest of the Western world
for decades to come. Of course, Deirdre's mother couldn't say a
word about it, as she had married out of her race a couple of decades
earlier, and had enjoyed a life of luxury and love that many would
have envied. Margo, Ursula, and I couldn't have been happier about
the affair, as Roy and his group started holding jam sessions several
times a week in our cellblock, and the stodgy old place really came
alive!

Gladys was in seventh-heaven. A jam session meant only one
thing to her—a party! And she needed that break. The housing
committee, after learning of Mark's duplicity, had moved a room-
mate in with her. They told her it was to justify her keeping her
cell, as the camp was crowded once more with the arrival of the
Italians, but they had an ulterior motive: they needed her bubbling,
nurturing nature for a little old lady who had to have care around
the clock, something she couldn't get in a raucous women's dorm,

and they knew Gladys was just the person for the job. It was heart-warming to watch the tragic little figure respond to all the loving care Gladys gave her, and old and infirm as she was, she too enjoyed the rambunctious music that cut through the balmy spring evenings.

One evening, in early summer, while I was waiting for Lisa to join me for our evening walk, I found myself thinking about her. I realized that whenever I thought of her it was as a gentle saving grace in a camp that had all too little of that quality to spare. She was always doing things for others, especially her little step-brother and sister. She enjoyed getting down to their level and playing with them, or reading to them, and as she did, I'd watch them light up like candles on a birthday cake. She was the same with everyone, and people used her. I know I did. Her never-ending interest in others made it hard for me not to tell her about my dreams and aspirations—everything, that is, except how I felt about Guy. She reciprocated to a certain extent, but if she had any problems, she never mentioned them. It had been like that from the beginning. That's why, when she joined me that evening, I wasn't prepared for her explosive tirade.

"I hate him! I *hate* him! *I hate him!* And I *know* he hates me!" she burst out.

Although she and Ian were still a twosome, I knew he couldn't evoke such emotion out of her, and I knew he didn't *hate* her, so I asked, in amazement, "Who?!"

"Curtis, of course!"

Curtis was her stepfather.

"Oh, come on, he doesn't hate you." I was still bewildered at her incredible outburst.

"A fat lot you know!"

She was right; I really didn't know a thing. Until this moment, I'd been living in complete ignorance. What's more, I hadn't even *felt* anything amiss, because Lisa and her stepfather kept their emotions so well under wraps.

"What does he do to you? Does he hit you? Cuss you out? What?"

"Oh, nothing like that," she said, "it's just a feeling. He'll be saying one thing to me, but his eyes will be saying something else. Now, with Billy and Jane, it's different. When he hugs them, or takes their hand and walks around the camp, you *know* he loves them. But with me, it's different. Do you know, he's never hugged me in all the years I can remember? It's as though he can never forgive Mummy for having a love before him, and to punish her, he takes it out on me."

"But you just said he doesn't do anything to you!"

"Oh, what's the use? You'll *never* understand! No one does."

I tried to put myself in her shoes, but it was useless. I wanted to help, but I didn't know how.

We walked for a while in silence, then I asked, "When did you find out he wasn't your father?"

"I always knew. Daddy died just before my sixth birthday, and Mummy married Curtis a year or so after." She sniffed, and her pretty mouth trembled. "Everyone said it was not right, her remarrying so soon."

"Maybe she was lonely. It must be horrible to lose someone you love."

"I lost my *DAD!*" There was anguish in her voice. "I loved him very much. Mother replaced him with Curtis. I can *never* replace him!"

I wanted desperately to help her, but I couldn't think of anything to say. I'd never really lost anyone close to me, not so's I could remember. Even my baby brother, Tony, who had died of dysentery at eighteen months, had never left a real dent in my life, because he had come and gone before memory and emotion had been instilled in me. The only hazy recollection I had of his death was of seeing Dad cry.

And then my thoughts reached way back through time and I remembered darling Brewster One, the first of our chowdogs, who had come up from Canton and sired our early litters. He was named after the then-popular movie *Brewster's Millions*, because when he arrived, he had millions of fleas. After Mother and Margo had bathed, groomed, and de-flead him, he was so gorgeous, there was nothing to do but send away for a bitch for him, so that he could really strut his stuff. That's when we got our beloved Jane, and although she was as red as he was black, all their pups turned out black like him. We never really knew his age though, and after a couple of lovely litters, one of which produced Brewster Two, he passed away, and we buried him under the yellow roses that graced our garden wall.

I remember my heart was broken when he died, and I moped around for days. Finally, Mother sat down beside me on the veranda steps and said, "Brewster is gone. He will never come back. But his son needs your love."

"I'll never love him like I loved Brewster," I said stubbornly.

"That's right, you won't. That was special, because he was a special dog. But when Brewster Two grows up, you'll find you love him just as much. You don't stop loving someone, or something, you've once loved; they'll always be a special memory, but you also don't stop loving *other* people, or pets, just because they've gone."

It dawned on me that I never realized what she meant till now, and I tried haltingly to explain it to Lisa. I only succeeded in getting her to cry almost uncontrollably, but the anger was finally gone.

I didn't see her for almost ten days after that. I knew she was avoiding me and was embarrassed at her earlier outburst, but I kept hoping it wouldn't change our friendship.

It took a while for us to get really close again, but when we finally broke the ice, there was a depth to our friendship that hadn't been there before.

It was June nineteenth and head-count time on the roll-call field. I remember the date exactly, because as I was trying to ignore the indignity of the moment and savoring my day off, an outbreak took place that had guards suddenly exploding in all directions like firecrackers. After lots of shouting and yelling, one peeled out of the group and rushed off for King Kong.

We were all standing around stunned, and except for intermittent yelps from the remaining guards, the silence was deadly. Finally, Jock went over to the warden of the men's dorm section, where the eruption had taken place, and asked what had happened. After a while, I saw him nod, and coming back to our line, he whispered to Dad, "Laurie Tipton and Arthur Hummel have escaped, and the guards have just found out. Pass it down the line, but hold the applause."

When King Kong arrived, he was livid with rage and had the nine men who were dorm-mates of the escapees pulled out of line and marched off to the Assembly Hall, where they were put under heavy guard. We didn't like that, but there was nothing we could do about it, except pray that they wouldn't be tortured to give out information about the escape.

The hall was put out of bounds, and they were held for eleven days on starvation rations, while they were interrogated mercilessly, but none of them could tell the Japanese a thing, because they hadn't known of the escape—which took place on the sixth—till after it had happened. The only crime they could be accused of, if it could be considered a crime, was that of covering up the escape by juggling places in the roll-call lineup to confuse the guards and buy time for Tip and Arthur to get well away.

When Gold Tooth couldn't get confessions out of the men, King Kong put out an official press release that was carried in all the local papers. According to Dad, who translated the write-up, it said nine men had escaped, but seven had been recaptured. "That's the Oriental way of saving face, or covering one's arse," he said wryly.

12

THE EDGE OF FOREVER

The climate in camp swung from arctic cold to tropic heat with clock-like precision. And as the summer progressed, with temperatures sizzling well over the hundred mark, I tried to recall the freezing winter and psych myself into cooling down, but my poor brain was so stewed, it was beyond the point of functioning.

The only thing summer had going for it was that, unlike winter, where warmth required next to non-existent fuel to heat our bodies, in summer we could at least cool off from time to time with cold showers. Although they were sheer bliss, I was still so pathetically modest I couldn't get used to the complete lack of privacy. Right or wrong, I just knew everyone was looking at me, and I found myself longing for the convent, where we took our baths in a lavabo with private cubicles. Here there were no cubicles, just open stalls, and I whisked around flipping my towel like some exotic fan-dancer, only exposing myself at the very last minute as I plunged under the cold water. Still, the refreshing result had a way of offsetting any embarrassing moments.

After the shower, when I stepped outside, I always felt guilty when I realized what that brief pleasure cost. I'd be all cool and refreshed, trickles from my damp, slicked-back hair running down my spine, and I'd see some poor internee pumping away, his body bathed in sweat, his brow-band next to useless, as he kept the shower water flowing, and I'd realize for every little moment of enjoyment, someone picked up the tab. We were lucky to have so many good wells in the camp, but they weren't motor-driven, and we had no mules to work them. Manpower was what it took, usually around the clock, so manpower was provided: short, strenuous shifts, with the summer months taking the greatest toll.

But keeping cool was a minor problem compared to that of the Italians in the dishonorable, or quarantine, compound. As the summer progressed, it was easy to see that they hadn't learned roll with the punches, and that their situation was pretty grim. Volatile by temperament, and vulnerable to all the slights and slurs they felt were being hurled at them when they came out for exercise in little guarded groups, they appeared just one step away from straight jackets. We couldn't help feeling sorry for them in their plight, but it wasn't until midsummer that the Commandant was able to talk King Kong into opening up their compound and letting them mingle with the rest of us.

That first afternoon, when the chain and padlock were removed from the gates and they learned that their segregation was over, they came out *en masse,* almost shyly, to see if they would be accepted by the rest of the camp. Their surprise at the roar of delight that went up from all of us was heartwarming, leaving the Japanese completely baffled. *How could honorable prisoners of war accept the company of such disgraceful turncoats?!*

Margo told me that the action hadn't come any too soon, as there'd been several attempted suicides. None had been fatal, and after the Italians had been cut down by fellow internees, the guards had been told they were ill, and they were rushed to the hospital. There, the overworked medical staff covered up the real reason for their hospitalization, so that the Japanese would never have the pleasure of knowing they had driven anyone to such lengths.

Right after their gates were opened, there had been another suicide attempt, only this time it had been from our side, and it made Margo seething mad. That would-be suicide was Pete Fox's brother, Mike.

I'll never forget the first time I met him. He came into our compound, supposedly looking for Peter, and while Margo and I, both looking dirty and scruffy, were chatting on the cell step, he said, clear out of the blue, "Next to Ursula, you two are a couple of also-rans."

I didn't comment at the callous remark, but Margo did. "Great!" she snapped, "if you can't say anything nice, try an insult!"

"I believe in calling them the way I see them," Mike said smugly.

Margo grinned, "Next to Pete, you were left at the gate!"

"Touché!" he said, surprised at her comeback.

Now, here was Margo, venting off steam again. This time cussing out spineless suicidal idiots in general and Mike Fox in particular.

"Damn, Mike," she hissed, "he not only took the last of the morphine and aspirin...he muffed it!"

"Margo!" I said in horror.

"I mean it. We have people dying of cancer, in extreme agony, people who want to live so badly, they're fighting on when all hope is lost, and this creep has to finish off our only pain killers and take the last moments of peace they may ever know!"

"How did he get hold of them?" I asked.

"Hell, he's a hospital orderly!"

"You're tired," Ursula said, putting her arms around her.

Margo wasn't to be soothed: her nostrils flared and her eyes flashed. "You bet I'm tired! I'm tired of helping them pump his stomach to save his life. Dammit, it's not fair! Like that witch who ate a box of match-heads and got violently ill. We worked around the clock on her. And the one who slashed her wrists, but not deep enough to make it work. Or the umpteen Italians, begging for attention and a way out of their prison compound, who never hang themselves high enough to get anything more than a crick in the neck and a week in the hospital! They don't *mean* to commit suicide; all they want is sympathy, and I'm fed up! They don't deserve it. I'm going to talk to Roger Barton. I think, if they care so damned little for their lives, we should make them into a suicide squad, and if we're attacked, we'll send them out as the first wave!"

I'd never heard Margo so hot on anything before, but then, I hadn't worked upstairs with her in the sadly-wanting hospital and seen all the suffering. When Ursula and I finally got her calmed down, I sensed she wanted to be alone, so after Alex picked up Ursula for their bridge game with Claire and Randy, I went for a walk.

As I aimlessly walked, some of her frustration rubbed off on me, and try as I might, I couldn't get her explosive tirade out of my mind. Looking back on all of the attempted suicides, there seemed to be a common denominator: each person had, at some time, been a "somebody" in a once exciting world.

The woman who swallowed the box of match heads had been a famous fashion model in the States back in the thirties. She was still very beautiful, with a doting husband—and no children, as she didn't want to ruin her figure. She was living in the past and couldn't stand the anonymity of being just another lost soul in a prison camp.

The girl who slashed her wrists was also extremely beautiful. Her mother had been the most famous madame in Peking, and she the toast of the nightlife of that cosmopolitan city. When they landed in the camp, the old lady decided to make the best of a bad deal and forced her daughter to get involved with a very successful American businessman with a wife and family in the States. The dutiful daughter got herself pregnant by him, so that they could bleed him for all he was worth when they got out of the camp. She hit a snag though; she fell in love with him and knew she couldn't go through with the scheme. She wanted his child and him too.

I found my blind wandering had taken me down to the roll-call field, and for once, it was almost void of people. There was a Belgian priest saying his office in the lowering shadows of the southern boundary and a couple of kids playing toss in a corner; I didn't see a guard at the tower rail and decided he must be inside drowsing. I liked the solitariness. *Everyone must be in their cells or in the kitchen, winding down the last meal of the day,* I thought.

The feeling of being alone was great, and I enjoyed it.

Lately, our cell seemed to be getting smaller and smaller, and I tried to stay out of it as much as possible. I felt our tempers wearing thin, and as much as Margo and Ursula got on *my* nerves, I knew I was driving *them* up the wall. Sometimes I'd come in after my shift, just wanting to relax, and I'd see their reproving looks, and I'd stomp out, and as the door slammed, I'd hear, "What the hell's got into her?" And for the life of me, I didn't know.

I needed desperately to be alone, but there was nowhere I could go where I wasn't reminded I was a prisoner...or underfoot...or a pain in the neck.

It was getting harder and harder for me to enter into my old world of make-believe, and I'd find imagined hurts crowding out my old avenues of escape. I'd dwell on the hurts, instead of dropping them by the wayside, as I'd learned to do in "my other life". It was true, sometimes I felt I'd been reincarnated into another world—another time—and that nothing before had ever been.

This blessed moment of solitude was making up for it though, and my thoughts turned to all the teeming, driving people in the camp, like so many ants in an ant hill, each with their own problems and idiosyncrasies, and inevitably, my thoughts turned to my family. To Dad, with his damn affair that he so adroitly kept concealed. To Mother, who had built a little cocoon around herself, quietly meditating and pinning her hopes on a future that, to her, was just around the corner. Margo wasn't much better: she hadn't built a cocoon, but between the war-brides she had chummed up with and her friendship with giggle-a-minute Pete, we hardly ever spoke to each other.

Then, there was Ursula.

And with the thought of her came the horrible realization that we were now sisters in name only. There was no sharing any more...or caring. I didn't believe she thought about me for a moment, and it hurt like hell.

I found myself thinking of Mike Fox again, whose Indian mother had been of extremely high caste. She had debased herself by marrying a British taipan, and because of this tragic alliance, both she and his father had lost their social standing—they were without a niche in either world. When Mike became a celebrated correspondent, all this was swept under the rug, and he was welcomed into the society that had once blackballed him. Now, in the prison camp, he was back at square one: a nobody in an uncaring world.

And the Italians. Many were titled and came from some of Italy's oldest families. None of them could stand the fascism of Mussolini, or the Axis Alliance; now they were being called traitors and incarcerated for a war they couldn't stomach.

My mind was swirling with half-formed thoughts all starting with "Why?". Why aren't people satisfied with what, or who, they are? Why do they feel they need status…understanding…sympathy? Why are their feelings the only ones that count? Everyone has to face their dragon sometime. No one's immune.

They're all nuts! I thought. *If they really feel they can't face the future, they don't have to hang themselves, swallow match-heads, slash their wrists, or overdose on pain killer—all they have to do is walk up a ramp along the wall and grab the wires. It's that simple!*

I hadn't realized how far my thoughts had carried me, or that I had walked over to the forbidding grey walls; all I felt was an overwhelming urge to show those dumb fools how easy it was to do the job right! The precocious kid had turned into an unthinking adult. As I reached up for the wires, I was struck by what felt like a roaring express train. It wasn't the jolt of electricity I had subconsciously expected, but a hurtling body, panting from exertion, that knocked me down into the dust, rolling over and over with me to the bottom of the ramp.

Groggily getting to my feet, shaking so badly I thought my legs would give way, I looked at my savior. It was the priest, his long black robes filthy with dust and dried leaves, his face ashen with what he had just witnessed. He grabbed me by the shoulders and shook me till my teeth rattled.

"What you do? What you do?" he shouted in broken English, over and over again.

"I don't know," I wailed, starting to cry uncontrollably.

I was scared. It had happened so fast. If he hadn't been there I would have been dead. I shuddered. That was *real* suicide. It came in a moment of pure insanity when one stepped over the line.

It was a long time before I got over that incident. I had nightmares of terror. I couldn't talk to anyone about it, especially the priest, as all he could think of was the mortal sin he had averted. I knew if I mentioned it to Lisa or Dan, I would only have scared them. Margo had already let me know how she felt on the subject in no uncertain terms, and Ursula was out of the question. I never even considered talking about it to Mother or Dad.

Through it all, I tried to figure out *why* I'd done it—recalling, with a squirm, the smug way I had been able to analyze all the other attempted suicides. One thing, it hadn't been for sympathy; sympathy predicated that one would be around to be consoled after the act, and what I had attempted left no room for *that*.

I didn't feel depressed. I might've felt a little sorry for myself for losing touch with Ursula and Margo, but certainly not to the extent that I wanted to take my life. Was it curiosity? No, because I hadn't thought that far ahead. Was it just blind stupidity—without any thought of the consequences? *God, I hope not!* Was it Guy? The Ch'ing princess syndrome, unrequited love? Never! When Grant ditched Urs, she didn't go grab a wire.

I skirted around the only thing it could've been, trying desperately not to admit it to myself. Finally, there was no alternative. For one mad, terrifying moment, I hadn't been responsible for my actions and had stepped over the edge.

Into what? Insanity?

The feeling of terror would grip me again, the fear that I might try once more and this time be successful. The horror of these living nightmares would come to me in the wee hours, and my rickety canvas cot would groan and grind with my every frantic toss.

Was I mad? That thought accompanied me through the days too...

"Where are you Bobby? You're not in the camp, that's for sure."

Lisa's words cut into my thoughts like a buzz-saw. "Frankly," she was saying, "you haven't been here for weeks—it's as though you've escaped into a world of your own."

I hadn't realized I'd been acting differently. "Oh, I'm here all right," I said shakily.

"Good. Any time you think you can forget *that,* all you have to do is look around you," she said, pointing to the walls with their hot wires silhouetted against the sunset. "They have a lovely way of jolting you back to the present."

The words were uncanny. My heart almost stopped, and I started shuddering uncontrollably.

"What's up?!" Lisa looked scared.

I took a deep breath. "I'm okay. I must have a bug or something. I'll get over it." I hadn't dared take an evening walk alone since the incident.

We'd just come down Rocky Road onto the roll-call field, and the dying sun was throwing an eerie light on the guard tower, highlighting the young soldier on duty. Following my line of sight, Lisa said musingly, "Have you ever wondered what it would be like if the Japs won?"

I looked at her for a long moment, and suddenly everything was clear.

Son-of-a-bitch, I thought, *the little buggers almost DID!*

While I had been slowly slaying my personal dragon, the Sports Committee had been toying with the idea of a track meet. Nothing that would really tax our stamina, as our diet was so limited, but something that would give us a lift and let athletes show off their ability, just as our stage performers were doing.

The race was to start at the Assembly Hall, turn and go the length of Main Street, around the bell tower and the women's dorm, and back down Rocky Road to the roll-call field.

One day, while I was making posters for the event, Nico came up and told me proudly he would be entering for Greece. I hadn't realized this was to be an "Olympic" event, and I smiled at his excitement. I knew he was athletic, but I didn't know he was good in track. As he jogged off with a grin a mile wide, I said, "Good luck, Nico. Knock 'em dead!"

When the great day arrived, I wasn't to be disappointed. Nico won most of the junior men's events, his short, muscular legs pounding like pistons on the dusty road. He raced so hard, and with such a look of elation, he had us cheering for his spirit more than his prowess.

Then, to my surprise, Eric Liddell, a quiet-spoken Scottish missionary, won a grueling senior event. He was so unassuming that few in the camp knew he was an Olympic runner, who twenty years earlier, had won the Gold for Great Britain at the Paris Olympics. That time, it had been the four-hundred meters; this time, no one had measured the track; it was more or less an endurance race, but figured so that no one would overtax his limited strength.

Then the girls' meet was called, and I watched Claire stroll up to the starting line and eye the ragged runners. Her eyes passed over all of them without a hint of recognition till she got to Billie Trainor; then, they locked in a challenging stare. *This should be a doozy,* I thought, as they toed the line.

It only took a couple of laps to eliminate the other runners, and the finish was left to Billie and Claire. As they kept plodding along, I noticed our very deficient diet taking its toll. On the last lap, even robust Billie was beginning to flag, but she still led, her long strides slowly stretching the lead. Then, just as I was conceding the victory to her, Claire made a superhuman spurt and broke the finish line a split second ahead, only to collapse writhing in the dust.

As I stood dumbfounded, looking down on her ashen face and racked body, someone cried, "Get a doctor! Get a doctor!"

It was weeks before Claire was up and about again. Everyone said it was malnutrition that was the real culprit—but I knew better.

Ursula's drama group put on Noel Coward's *Hayfever*, and she landed the part of Sorrel Bliss. I also got involved, this time as a stagehand, helping with the challenging sets. "Challenging" here actually meant ingenious: How to depict a typical English home with next to nothing to furnish it with. Pleas went out on bulletin boards for all sorts of odds and ends, and surprisingly, people came forth with just about everything we needed. Why anyone would bring andirons to a prison camp…or vases…or a cuckoo clock…or any of the other myriad things we "borrowed"…was beyond me. We never questioned the donors though, accepting their offerings with thanks, and promising to return them in the same condition in which they were received.

To me, the greatest challenge, and enjoyment, came with painting the sets: depicting a paneled room and ornate fireplace with nothing but odds and ends of paint, a brush, and a ragged backdrop; working in highlight and shadow to give a three-dimensional effect, adding fake windows with beautiful pastoral scenes, painting foreshortened wings to give a feeling of depth, and then sitting in the back of the hall to admire the effect.

It was while I was eyeing the set from a distance that the cast trooped onto the stage and started rehearsing. Ursula was completely wrapped in her part, and I watched enchanted. Suddenly, I had a flashback: I was five, maybe six, and I asked Mother, "What's it like to be Ursula?"

After a rather long pause, Mother said, "That's something you'll never know."

"Why?"

"That's the way it is. You'll never know what it's like to be Ursula, and she'll never know what it's like to be you."

"That's not fair!" When I was five, nothing was "fair" to me.

"What's unfair about it?"

"I *must* know!"

"Well, God didn't make any two of us just alike; not even twins. They may look alike, but inside they are different."

"Where inside?"

I saw a frown on Mother's face, and I got impatient. "Where is *me*?" I asked.

"You mean, where am I?"

"No! Where is *ME?*" I slapped my arm, my head, my leg, and

said, exasperated, "That's not *me*! Where is *ME?*"

"You mean the "me" that feels hurt, or happy, or wants to laugh or cry?"

"Yeah!"

"That's the thing that God made different in all of us. The thing that makes you different from Ursula. That's your soul, Bobby. The part of you that goes to heaven when you die. The part of you that lives forever."

I could see she thought she had answered my question and that now I should be entirely happy and enlightened. I wasn't.

"But, where is it. In my foot? In my head? In my..."

"That's God's secret." She sounded smug to me, and it only made me madder.

"That's not *fair!*"

I'd never really forgotten that incident, and here I was, over a decade later, still haunted by it. Watching Ursula move gracefully about the stage, totally engrossed in her part, I realized that, for once, Mother had been wrong. *Ursula knows what it's like to be someone else,* I thought, *or she couldn't act the way she does. That's how she escapes the monotony of the prison camp.*

"Let's stop and see Claire," Lisa said, on our daily evening stroll, "she borrowed a sweater of mine months ago, and I want it back."

When we got to the cell, I noticed Claire looked great and appeared completely over her collapse. Ursula and Alex were also there, playing bridge, Randy making up the fourth.

I found myself thinking of her popularity that seemed to break all the rules of friendship. I'd been told that friendship was based on a genuine interest in others. Claire had only one genuine interest: herself. Friendship was "doing" for others: Claire never did anything for anyone unless she had more to gain than they did. Was it charisma, that elusive something that held her little coterie of followers around her—Ursula and Alex among them—waiting on her beck and call? I couldn't fathom it, but whatever it was, she had it in spades.

A few moments later, Lisa, cardigan in hand, came out of the cell. Noticing the look on my face, she asked what was up.

"Nothing," I said rather curtly.

Then she looked pensive. "I don't know why I keep loaning things to Claire, she never returns them." Then, as if she were travelling my troubled wavelength, she said, "I really don't know why I like her."

"I guess that's as good a definition of "popularity" as you can get; you like her because everyone else does. It's contagious." I could hear the envy in my voice.

"I don't know if that's it or not. It's as though I can't help following her, even when I don't care for what she's doing."

"For instance?"

"Oh, nothing in particular. Just, when she ridicules someone— like René, for instance—I find myself laughing, instead of telling her to shut up."

"What about me?"

"What *about* you?"

"I mean, does she talk about me?"

Lisa was thoughtful for a moment, then said, "You know, she never has...not in front of me. But you've got me thinking. I wonder what she says about *me* behind my back?"

"Oh, forget Claire!" I said in disgust. Then, out of the misty reaches of the past, a craving hit me, and I felt saliva rising in my mouth, and a rush of delectable aromas flooded my memory. "God, I'd give anything for a piece of candy!"

"Me too."

"Can't you just *smell* Keissling and Bader?"

"Shut up! Don't talk about it."

But that was impossible. Talk wandered from the legendary desserts and sweets of the aromatic coffee-house to the crab-apple hawker who came up to our back door in Chinwangtao with his little portable charcoal brazier. He was a quaint old man who'd let Ursula and me pick out crab-apples from his basket, then he'd thread them onto a bamboo skewer, dip them into molten syrup, and while the glaze was cooling, decorate them with flowers of dried fruit, blanched almonds, and coconut flakes. As I described them, my complaining stomach started to cry out, and Lisa wailed once more, *"Shut up!"*

I looked at the anguish on her face and switched hawkers in a hurry. "Have you ever seen a rice-doll maker sculpt a devil dancer?"

"A *what?*"

"A devil dancer."

Walking by the basketball court nestled in the L-shape of the hospital, I told her about the doll maker who also came to our back door in Chinwangtao, modeling rice paste over a delicate armature to make the graceful body of a male dancer, with waving arms and stamping feet. How he would take tiny rolls of vibrantly colored rice paste and place them around a slightly larger core of white, and with a quick twist of his spatulate thumb and forefinger, flatten out the paste into a piece of intricate striped "fabric" that he'd drape into a skirt. Then he'd add a black jacket, a bamboo spear with flying tassels of scarlet paste, and finish off the face with flared eyebrows, piercing eyes, and scowling lips. I found myself smelling the strange, sour odor of the paste that dried to a hard, porcelain-like finish and wondering what had happened to those beautiful works of art, lost now somewhere in our home in the little Treaty Port.

We found ourselves back on Main Street just as the last hint of daylight faded into night, and dark shadows filled the corners of the camp. It would soon be curfew. Damn curfew, I wasn't ready to call it a day! As I reluctantly said goodnight to Lisa and turned into our cellblock, the lights dipped and went out.

Still defiant, I sat down on an old stump we used for a stool, and let the night breeze play around my shoulders. It was such a beautiful night I hated to go into the musty cell.

Ursula came into the compound a while later, and remembering her evening of bridge, I said nosily, "Who won?"

"Who do you think?" she countered.

I smiled inwardly, and found myself thinking, *Why aren't I surprised...?*

*****

Not long after the "dishonorable quarantine" had been lifted, Mario started coming over to visit Mother. They would talk for hours about the good old days, and hash over the mess in Europe, especially how it had reached out and ruined so many lives all over the world.

One evening, when torrential rains were turning the camp into a sluice box, I lay on my bed reading an exciting mystery; during a lull in the pounding downpour, I overheard Mother and Mario's voices in the next cell.

"You don't know what it's like to be in jail for something you didn't do," Mario was saying, his voice throbbing with self-pity.

"What the heck do you mean—*I don't know!*? There are around fifteen hundred people here, who are all in the same boat as you. Come on, you're not going to get any sympathy out of me!"

I tried to get back to my reading, but it was useless.

"Gee, you know what I'm talking about. I'm not talking about *here*. It was when I was in Ward Road Jail in Shanghai. I was in solitary. I was accused of everything the little bastards could throw at me. I was despised!"

"Well, you survived and you can be philosophical now. It was *because* you were despised that they threw everything at you. The Japs are strange: to them, there is honor in war. Italy was dishonorable—at least to them—ergo, *you* were dishonorable. They didn't care whether you had a stomach for the fight, or whether you had been Axis or Ally; all they knew was that you were Italian, and Italians were turncoats."

"Thanks a lot!"

"Sorry, but they were. That they've joined the right side now,"—I could hear the wicked chuckle in her voice, and visualize her disarming smile—"goes to show even Italians can't stay dumb forever!"

"Damn, Gee, you're a tonic!"

I smiled. Only Mother could get away with such dastardly remarks. Bill Chilton liked to call her a "diplomat without portfolio", and I found myself chuckling along with her, as I recalled incidents where she'd defused situations, and people, with simple understanding and delightful finesse. Somewhere she'd learned all about human nature, and how to get people to tick in unison. When she entertained, all she had to be told was that a certain individual was having trouble with someone, and she would wrangle a way to get them together, possibly seat them at the same table, or pick them to judge an event, or have them assist her with a troublesome situation. Whatever it was, she completely ignored any coolness they showed toward one another, and before they knew where they were heading, they'd find they were going there together...and enjoying the trip.

As I turned back to my intriguing book, I couldn't help thinking that the Foreign Office would have done well in appointing Mother to some top position.

After the rainy season had stormed out of the camp, we had one final short splurge of Indian summer. Not hot and unbearable, but sweet and clean-smelling, and I found myself spending every moment I could outdoors.

I was hanging up a small wash in our compound one day, when Mother and Dad came out of their cell and stood watching me. I turned with a strange feeling, and noticed they were smiling broadly and holding hands.

"What's up?"

"It's our anniversary. We've been married twenty years today!" Mother said with a smile.

"Twenty wonderful years," Dad elaborated.

"Congratulations!" I said smiling, as I hung up my last shirt. Then, something sounded wrong, and I turned around and said slowly, "*Twenty* years?"

"That's right."

"And Margo?" I asked. She had been twenty-two when she married Jack in December '41; she was twenty-four now.

Without batting an eye, Mother said, "Oh, she's your half-sister."

Dad must've realized that wasn't quite the way one broke such news and ducked quickly back into the cell, waiting for the fireworks and, as usual, leaving Mother to face them.

I thought for a moment before I spoke. "Her last name is Moore, not Simmons, isn't it?" I could barely hide my anger.

"That's right." she said, seemingly surprised that I should know. "Her father was an Australian I met in the first World War."

"Where's he now?" I asked.

"I don't know," she said, ending the discussion by stepping back into the cell.

Just like that!

I stood unblinking for a moment, and it all came rushing back to me. *Margo was my half-sister.* That explained all the sly cracks we'd put up with through school. Kids can be so smug and mean. We were so naïve, and completely in the dark, we didn't know what they were driving at. It was obvious now that they had heard their parents talking and had been told not to tell us "the secret", so they just hinted and giggled, making us mad. I'd always believed it wasn't true, but now I knew it was.

Then, slowly, remembering Lisa's outburst about her stepfather, the signs that I had totally ignored stood out like lighted signposts on a murky road, and it dawned on me that never once had I seen Dad put his arm around Margo and give her a hug, and definitely not a kiss. He never spoke of her when she was away at school, unless it was in rage over the cost of her board and tuition. I remembered the horrible fights Dad would have with Mother when Margo was attending Tientsin Grammar School: any time he was ever mad about *anything*, it always came around to something Margo had done, or hadn't done.

I guess it all began to finally sink in when I thought of how he introduced Ursula and me: he would always preface our names by saying, "I would like you to meet *my two daughters...*" never "*...two of* my daughters!" And, as far back as I could remember, every time Margo made some money, even before she was a secretary, part of it always had to go to Dad for "room and board". I recalled times when she'd taken care of someone's horse or pet while they were away, and I'd hear Mother say, conspiratorially, "Don't let Daddy know what you're doing, and keep any money you might get; you need new clothes"…or whatever. Come to think of it, the biggest fights Mother and Dad ever had were always over Mother's budget. Now I realized why. It was not the spending of money, *per se*, that Dad wanted to know about, it was the item, or person, on whom the money was spent.

When we were in Chinwangtao, costs like boarding horses were absorbed through the Kailan's dairy account, and Margo's precious Darby, a gift from Bill Chilton, had been stabled down by the cow pens, the dairy workers only too happy to double as handlers, or *mahfus*. But when we were in Tientsin, Darby had been boarded out at the Race Course stables, and hauled to and from the steeple chases and hunts at the French Arsenal with all the other mounts, with Dad always exploding when he had to pick up the tab.

Oh…my…G-o-d! I thought, as the memory struck me.

That evening, after we three had all hugged each other, and discussed what, to me, was earth-shattering news (although I got the definite feeling Ursula had figured it all out when we read the wedding blurb), I asked Margo, "What happened to Darby?"

She frowned for a moment, and then a look of the deepest hurt clouded her lovely dark eyes.

"Dad had him put down, because his board and grooming bill were too high."

"It wasn't pneumonia?" I asked in horror.

"No."

I didn't know what to say. I knew Dad was no saint and had done a lot of things I didn't fully like or understand, but I would never have believed him capable of such cruelty.

13

LIFE GOES ON

The delightful Indian summer ended all too soon. Cold crept into the camp once more, and the lovely chore of making coal-balls was a drudge that none of us looked forward to. I hadn't realized how rough it was on Dad, till he read me his *Ode to a Coal Ball*, trying to make light of the slimy, back-breaking job.

> *Thou scurvy substitute for coal,*
> > *Menace to my immortal soul.*
> *Thou nursery for thoughts unclean.*
> > *Thou trollop! Oh, thou child of spleen,*
> *Which doth my weekend rest benight.*
> > *Thou noxious, noisome parasite—*
> *Offspring of muck, and refuse spoil,*
> > *Drawn up from mine by honest toil.*
> *Thou sneering, jeering, loathsome mess,*
> > *Which I must mould by hand, alas,*
> *With creaking knees, and aching spine,*
> > *Then lay thee out, line after line,*
> *To dry at leisure, as ye may—*
> > *My rosary of coal and clay!*

I grinned at the last line, asking if he said a Hail Mary as he laid each one down.

"Hardly. It's usually an expletive from a much darker side of the hereafter."

Once again, I found myself wistfully thinking of the blistering summer, the sun-dappled shade of the acacias, and the cold showers taken to cool us off. Why did the weather have to be so extreme? The cold of winter exacerbated conditions in the camp: the wood around our windows was splitting, plaster on the grey brick walls was dropping off in ever-larger chunks, and cold was seeping back into every corner of our cell. In desperation, we swiped some flour from the bakery and made a paste, taping strips of newsprint around the windows. That helped stem some of the drafts, but it did nothing to hold in the little heat our bodies, and the seldom-used stove, gave out. Except for the morning hours, when I worked in the diet kitchen, I can't remember having warm feet or fingers from October through to March. It was ironic that the job I had begun to loathe turned out to be the one warm spot in my day.

One frigid afternoon, while our bridge four was trying to find a corner of Number One Kitchen that didn't have a draft, Nico said, with his usual happy smile, "Eric Liddell says I've got what it takes to be a great runner, if I really work at it. He's coaching me almost daily. He's wonderful. There's so much more to running than just pounding round the course."

"Oh, I didn't know he was coaching you; when did you start?" I asked.

"After the track meet last summer."

"No kidding? That's great! Where do you run?"

"On the roll-call field before head count," he said, adding, "You know, the guards always cheer me on when they see Eric eyeing his stopwatch. I think they like me."

I looked at Nico. His stocky little figure was much like that of our young captors; maybe that made them feel he was one of them. They were the same age, that was for sure. And they had to be lonely for camaraderie, especially in their despised role as jailer.

That was the year the words of the Commandant came back to

haunt us, as we looked at our bedraggled clothes and barely-shod feet, and saw our reflections in the young, forgotten guards. They had put newsprint in their boots to keep their feet warm, and wrapped their legs in whatever rags they could find, as they, like us, had no socks to wear. Their uniforms were in shreds, and their bare hands, as they checked off the roll, were cracked and bleeding from the cold.

"Here's a spot," Guy said, finally finding a snug corner of the kitchen, and he and Nico hefted a couple of upturned benches off a table, broke out a badly scuffed deck of cards, and we sat down to play.

As much as I wanted to be near Guy, I couldn't help feeling I was being a total ass putting up with this type of self-torture several times a week. It wasn't as if the games were exciting: they were so one-sided, all they did was build up Guy's ego and give René a chance to drape herself all over him. The only thing that made them slightly bearable was that Guy seemed totally oblivious of her fingers running through his hair and of her adoring looks. But, that day, after Nico told us of Eric Liddell's coaching, something snapped in Guy: it was as though he couldn't face the fact that Nico could be better than him in any way. He changed from an easy-going show-off to someone obsessed, and the game became utterly cutthroat. I felt Nico's hurt at his friend's frantic play, and suggested quietly when we left the kitchen that he and I should either bone up, or give up. I didn't add I hated losing to *anyone* this way.

The days weren't all divided between the diet kitchen and bridge. I found another terrific art instructor: Lena Tavella, an Italian from Shanghai. She was a very distinguished lady with beautiful white hair and exotic makeup that included royal blue mascara, something that totally blew me away. She always had an entourage of young men following her around, kidding and teasing and paying her court, and I marveled at her repartée and outlook on life. Age meant nothing to her. I knew she would always be outrageous and young-at-heart.

I'd met her when she offered to help design our stage sets. Where our old sets had always received loud applause, more for the nostalgia they evoked than their grand design, when Lena took over, they became unique. It wasn't that she had anything more to work with, but it was how she used what she had. It was a lesson in complete ingenuity, and I never stopped learning.

She could tell I enjoyed this new field of art and encouraged me to become a designer. When we weren't working on sets, she had me doing book jackets. It had started one day when I told her I was reading a compelling novel of mystery and mayhem, and she said, "How about making a dust-cover for the book?"

I didn't know what she meant, and said, "Come again?"

"Design me a book jacket."

The assignment was pure bliss. As I arranged, and rearranged, my elements, and worked on the lettering, I kept hearing Mother Hèribert, my little French-Canadian art teacher in the convent, saying *"Stylisé! Stylisé!"* as she looked over my shoulder at my early crude attempts at floral design. Now, when I said the same words to myself in English, "Stylize! Stylize!", they meant so much more.

Before long, I turned to designing clothes—beautiful gowns, suits, shoes, hats, and jewelry. They looked like nothing I'd ever seen before. I couldn't figure where all the ideas were coming from; one seemed to bring on the next, in an unending succession of extravagant creations. The ideas transported me into the outside world, and I couldn't wait to become a part of it again.

I had always enjoyed my fine art instruction: the charcoals, pastels, oils, and water colors. But they were all from life, or still-life, and now seemed very structured. I remember Pierre Travers-Smith, whose work hung in the Royal Academy, lecturing on shadows and shadow play, and explaining how paintings were judged by their accuracy and plausibility. Even when I studied under Mary Augusta Milliken, an American who taught me how to work with mixed media, we still only worked on portraiture, bringing in beggars from the street and paying them a few coppers to sit quietly while we sketched.

This new field of design seemed to have no stultifying restrictions, and it was just what I needed to keep a glow alive through the long, winter months. I caught myself designing book jackets after every yarn I read—it beat a book report any time. And it was while I was doodling a cover for a book I had just finished that Pete Fox knocked on our cell door, starting a bizarre chain of events that could only happen in a pent-up, frustrated atmosphere such as ours.

He had come to see Margo. When I told him her shift didn't get out for a while, he just said, "May I?" and plopped down on her bed. As he leant back against the wall, the corner of the "SEMPER FI" poster jabbed into his head.

"Shit, it's a conspiracy!" he said, looking over his shoulder at the offending poster.

"What's the matter, still going rounds with 'SEMPER FI?'" I said, laughing.

He straightened the poster and glanced over at what I was doing. Noticing the grotesque design, he asked where it came from.

"It's my interpretation of this book," I said, pointing to a Dennis Wheatley novel on the occult. At his questioning look, I started to recount the strange tale of espionage, conflict, and astral travel.

"Whoa, that's too much!" Peter said.

"Uh-uh! If you can believe Wheatley, when a person sleeps, he dreams, whether he recalls his dreams or not is immaterial, and his soul slips from his body, traveling on an astral plane through space and time. His dreams are usually incoherent and dislocated, because they're an encapsulation of his travels. When his dream ends, his soul is tugged back by a thin filament of silver light to its physical home. He can travel in higher and higher astral planes, depending on the amount of control he has over his sleep patterns and dreams, and he can not only control his own movements, but those of others. For instance, he says, when someone dies in their sleep, we shouldn't always assume it was by natural causes; it could have been brought about by an astral conflict!"

"Hold it, right there! You telling me you can bump someone off in your dreams?" He was so fascinated, he forgot to giggle.

"That's right! If you want to kill someone, all you have to do is to learn how to control your dreams, then venture out when the other party is asleep and dreaming, and sever the cord of silver light, so his soul can't return to his body!"

"Hey, gimme that book when you're through!" Pete said, chuckling.

"Thinking of doing away with someone?"

"Could be!"

"Well, I have to return it first, before I can check out another book; then you can have it. Okay?"

"Are you through with it now?"

"Yeah."

"Okay, let's go. If Margo doesn't get off till three, we've still got plenty of time." With that, we high-tailed over to the library, and Pete checked out the book...and I thought nothing more of it.

That was a mistake, because when Pete was through with the book, it went the rounds of his dorm. There was nothing wrong with that really, except that two of his dorm-mates hated each other's guts—not in the joking way Pete had brought up—and one decided to do something about it.

Starting a regimen of sleeping, dreaming, and waking, he wrote down all his actions till he became confident that he could wipe out his nemesis with no one in camp the wiser. I guess he must've forgotten that his victim-to-be had also read the book, because it didn't take long for the latter to figure out what was going on, and he started working twice as hard, so that he could catch up and not be killed before he had a fighting chance.

According to Pete, the situation went from bad to impossible. Neither party dared fall asleep, as the other might attack him in his dreams. They ended up blabbering idiots, continually at each others' throats and having to be forcibly held apart. Finally, the administration committee found out about it and said, as far as they were concerned, it was a no-win situation. If either man died, the other would be tried and executed for pre-meditated murder, whether they attacked each other asleep or awake. Then they were put in separate dorms and told to get their acts together, or they'd be turned over to the Japs.

*****

Towards the end of November, Margo came off duty with the unbelievable news that crates of desperately needed drugs for the hospital had just materialized out of nowhere. Not even the Japs had a clue—and for once, they didn't even try to play the benevolent benefactor. If *anyone* knew where they came from, they weren't talking.

Needless to say, the hospital staff never questioned the miracle, but went their rounds once more with happy hearts, as surgery could again be performed, and acute pain assuaged.

She also surprised us with the news that she had taken a minor part in *Night Must Fall* and would be wearing two hats, that of prompter and actress. Ursula wasn't in the show for once, having just completed another Noel Coward play, *Tovarich*. But I, of course, was still involved in stage sets and posters.

As busy as we all kept, we still felt Christmas creeping up, and once more, we knew there would be no gifts or goodies to hand out. We tried not to let it get to us, but it was hard. It had always been such a festive season in our family, with grandparents from two continents sending us gifts, not to mention all the lovely ones we exchanged between ourselves.

I was mulling over these glum thoughts while wending my way to K-1 for the usual afternoon stint of cards. When I got there, the others were all in high spirits; even Guy was cutting-up. As we started playing, I realized with smug satisfaction that the boning-up Nico and I had been doing was beginning to pay off. The game was really enjoyable. Hands kept see-sawing back and forth, with lots of kidding but not much concentrated play, and I soon found my grey mood had left me.

Finally, as the afternoon wound down, a hand was dealt Nico that left him with a grin a mile wide that fooled no one. When the bidding started, I knew he was holding a winner, and I played accordingly. With chuckles and smiles, he bid a no-trump grand slam, and the play started.

After all our earlier bantering, the air turned tense, and Guy lost his nonchalance: he was obviously praying René wouldn't goof-up and that he could take a trick and wreck the slam. There was one card unaccounted for, and as dummy, I got up, and walking around the players, spotted it. Not being able to stand the suspense, I went to the kitchen door and looked up Main Street.

The wind, that had been gusting for days, had snapped a tree limb, and it was laying over a heavy electrical line. The civilian camp maintenance crew, with the help of several guards, was trying to trim the branches on the limb back to a workable size so it could be lopped off, and power restored. The equipment they had was limited, and the ladder they were using was far too short for the job. Ed Lewin, who was now our camp interpreter, came over to me and said, "The guards asked for Nico. Do you know where he is?"

"Why?"

"They said he could climb up in the tree and cut off the branches; that ladder's too short."

"How about the power line, isn't that dangerous?"

"Nope, it's turned off."

I debated telling him where Nico was for more reasons than one. I didn't like the man any more: he was involved with the black market and had bartered the respect of his friends for a few goodies the Japs threw his way. He noticed my hesitation and said brusquely, "You know where he is, don't you?"

"In Number One Kitchen," I said reluctantly, "winding up a grand slam, and with any luck, making it."

Ed didn't hesitate, he called to the guards, and two of them followed him to the kitchen. Guy and René looked up as we came in—Nico was lost in concentration.

Lewin ignored the fact that he was interrupting a tense game and came right to the point. "Nico, we've got a problem outside, and the guards insist you're the only one who can help us out."

"Not now! Not now!" Nico said excitedly, ignoring the nods and grins of the young guards.

"Yeah, *now* man! The hand can keep, but the hospital's out of power. It won't take a couple of minutes, and you can come back and wind it up."

I noticed the genuine concern in Ed's tone, and Nico caught it too. Putting his cards face down on the table, he looked at me and said, "Guard them with your life, I'm coming back to take Guy to the cleaners!"

I laughed and slumped over his hand, physically guarding it with my life, as he followed the three men out onto Main Street.

"You're no fun," Guy said after a while, when I wouldn't let them look at Nico's hand. Then turning to René, he said, "Let's go out and watch," and they both pocketed their cards and left the kitchen.

I didn't join them. I just sat there, looking at the rows of white pine tables, long trestle benches, and the walls with their ever-present bulletin boards. The well-worn concrete floors had been swept since the last meal, and except for the table where we sat and had strewn some of our outer garments, the kitchen was neat and clean. *It's much cleaner than Number Two Kitchen*, I thought, *but their cooks aren't as good or imaginative as ours.*

Although the meals at K-2 seldom varied, our menus, written on a blackboard that could be read from the chowline, were good for a chuckle and a reminder that there was another, more civilized world outside. Stew was *never* called stew; it was always Stroganoff, Boeuf Mironton, Hungarian Goulash, Boeuf Bacchanale, or a slew of wilder names printed boldly on the board—even if we couldn't find a piece of "boeuf" in a whole serving! Boiled leeks, a staple for weeks on end, were given every mouth-watering name imaginable; and bread porridge was made to read like some Old World delicacy. And somehow, all the care, and fun, put into the food preparation made it taste much better than it really was. Maybe we couldn't eat imagination, but it sure spiced up our lives.

My reverie ended abruptly as the door opened. I turned to say, *"About time!"*, expecting to see three friendly faces, but there were only two, Guy and René, and they looked ghastly. René's pretty features were blotchy from crying.

"You can forget that hand now," Guy said dully, throwing his cards on the table.

"What do you mean?"

"Nico's dead."

I looked at him in disbelief.

René started to sob uncontrollably as she reached blindly into her pocket and laid her cards down. Then she hugged herself, looking up at the ceiling in a stunned way, rocking back and forth on her heels as though trying to drive some horrible memory away.

"What happened?" I finally managed to ask.

"The branch he climbed out on to reach the broken one had been damaged by the wind, but no one had noticed. It just cracked under his weight, and he fell to the ground. He knew his back was broken, and he asked that no one move him. Ed had left, and the guards didn't understand. Before we could stop them, they lifted him up, and he died in their arms."

"I can't believe it!" I said, looking at his winning hand face-down on the table.

I didn't want to see what tricks he had taken, or if he would have made the slam; I just swept the cards into a stack and put the rubber band back around them.

Guy was speaking again.

"Roger Barton was there. He asked me to tell his old man and his sister." He turned and started to walk out. There were tears in his eyes.

I picked up Nico's coat and handed it to him, then stumbled back to our cell, stunned and still unbelieving.

I didn't want to go in, but I knew I couldn't stay out. The cell light was out, so I knew Margo and Ursula weren't there. Outside, the clouds were low and threatening, and the winds that shoved them around were battering the acacias in the compound and churning up debris and dust as they headed south.

I stepped inside and closed the door. The cell windows rattled even with their paper stripping, and the door pounded as though a body were pushing against it trying to get in. I felt the icy air sneak in through the ill-fitting stoop, whipping around my ankles and mingling with the cold that clung to me.

Everything seemed unreal—especially the thought of Nico. I'd never been that close to death before. The feeling I had at the passing of Elena Maccini and the Japanese general was one of horror more than of hurt. This was different, and I felt a piece of me had been torn away.

"Nico, where *are* you?" It startled me to realize I was speaking out loud.

I thought of his sister and his father: The world must have just stopped turning for them. I knew I'd have to go and see them, but not now, the wound was too raw. Then I thought of Guy, losing his best friend. How would he take it? He had no faith in the hereafter to hold on to. Nothing, but what he could see and feel, and now that was gone. His damn ideology gave no comfort to the bereaved.

The wind struck with such resounding force, I ran to the door to grab it before it flew open; that's when I heard someone call my name. Then I heard more pounding and realized it wasn't the wind. Flustered, I opened the door. Guy was standing there. He didn't speak. It was almost as though he couldn't.

Finally, remembering the errand he'd just been on, I asked, "How'd his dad take it?"

"Well. But I don't think it really hit home."

"And his sister?"

"It *did* hit home with her. She screamed." He winced at the memory. "A neighbor came over and held her. I think they'll be all right."

"And you?" I asked, looking at his drawn face. "How are you taking it?" Then, belatedly, remembering my manners, I asked him to come in.

"No…thank you," he said, looking over my head at the far wall. Then, in a strange, faraway voice, he said, "I have something to tell you. Nico must have known something was going to happen to him. Oh, I don't mean today. But several months ago, he made me promise if it did, I was to tell you that you were the only girl he ever loved." He turned and walked away, grabbing onto his cap so the wind wouldn't whip it off.

I was too numb to speak, his last words seemed to be mocking me. I'd never realized that Nico and I had been cut out of the same cloth, afraid to show our feelings. He had always kidded and joked, and kept everything on an even keel, mostly trying to defuse the arguments Guy and I got into. I felt he was the only person who knew that my fights with Guy covered a much deeper emotion, and

I loved him for not making an issue out of it.
Oh, Lord, how he must have suffered...

I was still numb from the loss when Christmas came around. The frigid weather, almost starvation rations, and the unending monotony took their toll, and the morale of the camp slithered deeper into a bottomless pit. Even those who had planned ahead for little luxuries to be sent in by friends on the outside had exhausted their funds and had to be content with the meager camp fare.

Then, one day in mid-January, when snow and sleet were coming down to add to our misery, the main gates were dragged open, and a line of donkey carts loaded with Red Cross parcels started weaving and side-slipping up the grade!

I stood is total disbelief as load after load came into the camp. In my excitement, I hadn't noticed the crowd that had gathered around me until Pete Fox picked me up and spun me around shouting, "*Now* do you believe in Santa Claus?!"

"They say *American* Red Cross, like those back in July," I said, remembering the handful of parcels that had come in the previous year and been doled out to the Americans.

"Yeah, but I counted a hundred boxes on each cart. And there were fifteen carts; that's more than enough for every one of us in camp!"

Pete had to be right—these parcels were for *all* of us! *So Christmas was late, so what!?!*

I found myself dreaming of their contents, and the anticipation was delicious. I knew what I *needed*: soap. And, luxury of luxuries: *toothpaste*. I knew what I *wanted*: tea, coffee, and maybe some candy; my craving for something sweet was almost unendurable. I would have loved eggs and butter, but knew they were perishable items that could not stand weeks and months in transit. I dreamed on and savored every minute it.

Strangely, the parcels arrived with no instructions, and as there were just over fourteen hundred internees left in the camp now, including two hundred Americans, the Commandant posted a notice stating that the parcels would be given out the following day, one to each internee, and one-and-a-half to each American.

His orders didn't prevail though. He was mobbed by a contingent of angry Americans, who stormed into his office and told him that those parcels were for *them* and no one else, and that he had no right to give away American property; it was not his to give.

I was with Dan when we learned of this turn of events, and he was sick and disgusted with his fellow men. "What the heck would my Mom and I do with fifteen comfort parcels!" he exploded. "How could we possibly enjoy them while all our Allied friends were going without. This is ridiculous! I bet, if they polled the Americans, they'd find most of 'em want everyone to get a parcel."

Dan was wrong though. The *generous* Yanks had made an about-face, and even if the majority didn't like the stand that had been taken, they backed the group that made it, stressing the parcels were American property and reiterating that they were the only ones entitled to receive them.

Afraid of an uprising, the Commandant took immediate control and had all the parcels locked up until he got instructions from Tokyo. While we waited for them, the camp that had once been tolerant of all the different nationals, became bitterly divided.

The ensuing two weeks had to be the slowest I'd ever known, and when the instructions from Tokyo were posted—just in time for my eighteenth birthday—they stated that every American and Allied inmate would get one comfort parcel; anything over would be sent to another camp.

Although this decision was final, the Hattons in our block decided to ignore them, and when the happy block wardens, along with their helpers, starting lining up for the parcels, they were met with a half-ton human blockade.

To our cellblock's embarrassment, the six Hattons were lying on top of the piles of cartons. The parents, over three hundred pounds apiece, were spread-eagled on the larger stacks, and their four pudgy offspring were straddled on top of smaller ones; they were all chanting, "We want our *doo*! We want our *doo*!"

"What the heck's a '*doo*'?" I asked one of the crew, and he explained they meant "due", giving it the English pronunciation. Finally, Roger Barton broke through their silly chant, shouting, *"Shut up!"*

Old man Hatton, purple with rage, and thrashing about like a humongous, bloated fish, screamed, "I *won't* shut up! Those parcels are marked *American* Red Cross, not *International* Red Cross! *Nobody's* getting them except *Americans!*"

I couldn't believe my ears. This man and his family, supposed Christian missionaries, would get seven-and-a-half packages apiece, or a total of forty-five cartons, if he had his way!

I didn't see Rob Connors standing behind me, and was surprised when he said, "Now you know why I can't stand missionaries."

Rob had been transferred from a Shanghai camp with his side-kick, Chad Walker, a year or so after we'd been interned. They both strolled into camp with guitars slung over their shoulders and mischief in their eyes, and from the moment they arrived, they regaled us with bawdy, underground songs that had us in stitches. One still comes to mind...

> *My father was a good missionary,*
> > *He saved little girlies from sin;*
> *He could sell you a blonde for a shillin'*
> > *Lordy, how the money rolled in!*

> *My brother took care of old women;*
> > *My mother made synthetic gin;*
> *My sister made love for a livin'*
> > *Lordy, how the money rolled in!*

There were lots more verses, and I remember being quite shocked when I first heard them.

The only missionaries I'd ever known were really good people, and I couldn't see any of them using the Lord's work to further their own ends. Now, watching the antics of the Hattons, I got to thinking that Rob probably knew a heck of a lot more about the missionary element in China than I did.

Crowds started to converge on the compound when they heard the ruckus, and I saw the anguished faces of the Tucks, Beruldsen's, and Collishaws, and many other upstanding Christians; I felt sorry for them because of what one family was doing to their image in a camp with a pretty low tolerance for their way of life.

Then the Hattons started screaming again, as a group of internees tried to heft their huge bodies off the piles of parcels. Kicking and screaming, Mr. Hatton shouted, "Don't you *dare* touch me!", while Mrs. Hatton, flabby arms waving, started to yell, "Leave our *kids* alone!", as the children, kicking and screaming, were carried out of the compound.

Barton threw up his hands in disgust and charged into the office, coming out with a bullhorn.

"Listen to me, you two idiots!" he bellowed, "You're right, these packages *are* marked *American Red Cross*, but if it wasn't for the *INTERNATIONAL Red Cross* they'd still be sitting on the docks Stateside! There's no way anyone would get them without the help of the Swiss or the Swedes. How the hell do you think they got here!?!"

A rumble of assent ran through the crowd, as he told the Hattons to get down or they would be hosed down. As he spoke, a huge fire hose was hauled out of the building. I didn't see a hydrant anywhere, but the threat worked. The Hattons, flustered and fumbling, tried to get down. As they squirmed and slithered, they dislodged the topmost packages, and they came crashing down on them. Everyone just stood and watched, and not a hand was lifted in help. It was as though the coveted comfort parcels had come alive, playing a role none of us would have dared, flipping and bouncing and clobbering their monstrous human targets till there wasn't an inch of them that wasn't black and blue.

After the Hattons staggered out of the compound and the hubbub died down, the packages were distributed to all the block wardens and their happy band of helpers.

I couldn't believe what they contained!

There was instant coffee, something we'd never seen before. Real tea in tea bags; cans of butter that didn't need refrigeration;

crackers; concentrated chocolate bars; cookies; sugar; scrambled egg mix; Spam; soap; toilet paper...and *toothpaste!* And, now and then, a mash note from some sweet soul who had packed the box. We called it the "fortune cookie touch", comparing handwriting and messages, soon forgetting the Hattons and their rotten behavior. The simple excitement of sharing and trading, knowing that people in the great world beyond the walls remembered us, and *cared,* was an emotion so great, it swept all the previous pettiness before it, and helped make my eighteenth birthday the most memorable one in camp!

We didn't play bridge in Number One Kitchen any more, or anywhere else for that matter, as the memory of Nico was still too raw. Instead, I spent my spare time working on stage sets and costumes, the latter just one more challenge to ingenuity.

I couldn't believe our latest offering, Shaw's *Androcles and the Lion.* I knew we would never have attempted it if it hadn't been for Lena Tavella, but she insisted she could switch the scenes from the forest to the Colosseum with very little effort, and proceeded to show us how it could be done. I was intrigued at her innovative ideas, although it was strange working on the sets during rehearsals and not having either Ursula or Margo involved. They were both taking a well-earned rest.

One would think after all the sets I'd worked on that I'd have learned how to handle paint without getting it all over my one-and-only shirt, but I didn't. Every time I wielded a brush of any size, I ended up having to wash the paint out of my clothes; luckily, it was of the whitewash variety, and pretty easy to rinse out.

One afternoon, while I was doing just that, Mother looked in and asked if I would mind adding one of Dad's shirts to my wash, as she didn't feel up to it. Taking it without comment, I started to dip it into the water—then stopped, feeling in the breast pocket for one of Dad's inevitable hankies. Surprisingly, there wasn't one, but I did find a slip of paper neatly folded up. I put the paper on Margo's bed and got on with the wash. When I was through scrubbing, I humped a fresh bucket of water back to the cell for the rinse, wringing out the clothes and hanging them lengthwise down the middle of the room, so that if they dripped, the water wouldn't land on our beds. I couldn't hang them outside, as they would have frozen into stiff boards.

It wasn't until I was completely through that I remembered the scrap of folded paper on Margo's bed. I was sure it was some of Dad's scribblings, but all that showed was a date, neatly written in his meticulous hand: February 22, 1945—the previous week.

When I opened it up I saw it was a short poem, entitled *Eric Liddell*, and I recalled his recent tragic death.

> *The dreadful reaper came last night*
> *   to levy toll once more—*
> *Eric Liddell, in his prime,*
> *   was borne to the nether shore.*
> *The young will miss the lead he set*
> *   in every branch of sport;*
> *The aged look elsewhere for aid*
> *   that he ever gave, unsought.*
> *And those, left struggling with their doubts*
> *   of that unknown tomorrow,*
> *Might set their creed of life by his,*
> *   and in his footsteps follow.*

I read the lines slowly, and thought of the simple Scottish missionary who loved people, and had done more to unite the diverse elements in camp than anyone else. Dad had told me his missionary parents were in Tientsin in 1902 when he was born, and that he had completed his education at Edinburgh, where he gained renown as an international Rugby player. He insisted though that Eric's greatest claim to fame was the stand he took when he competed as a track star for Britain in the 1924 Olympics. When he found he couldn't enter the hundred-meter dash he had trained for, because it would violate his Sabbath, he switched to the four-hundred meter race and still captured the Gold Medal for his country.

It seemed almost unbelievable that a person could know right from wrong in such strong terms that no person or event could dissuade him. But Eric was such a person. It was that inner strength that had carried him through the Olympics, and through life, that he imparted to others, especially the young, bored, children in the camp. It was not piety or righteousness, but his overwhelming love for humanity that endeared him to everyone, and his sudden death, brought on by a brain tumor, left us all stunned. I was on duty and missed his simple memorial service, but I learned there wasn't a dry eye in the congregation.

As I reread the simple lines, I saw again the light in Nico's eyes when he talked about Eric coaching him in the early morning hours and his dream of one day carrying the Olympic torch, or better yet, being an Olympic athlete. He had loved to talk about the Olympics, and had told me it was his birthright and that he would bring glory to Greece once more.

Eric had given him that pride and drive, and now, somewhere on the other side, they were embracing each other once more...

14

NEARING THE END

Life has a lovely way of evening up the score: for every death in camp, we seemed to have at least one birth. Our cellblock alone had three new arrivals. Emma Allan, who had delivered an adorable little girl named Kay the first year in camp, presented Jock that winter with a second son, Jeremy. And Roy Stone and Deirdre Carver, who were married after a whirlwind courtship, were now residents in our block with a loveable baby boy.

Mrs. Carver had given up her cell to the newlyweds many months back and moved into the women's dorm in the bell-tower building. I had been at loose ends the afternoon of the move so helped her carry a few items, more out of curiosity than anything. At the time, it struck me that I'd been in camp well over a year and had never seen the inside of a women's dorm.

I guess I'd expected it to be neat and orderly like the one at St. Joseph's, and was not ready for the polyglot of beds, suitcases, crates, odd folding-chairs, makeshift shelving, and various decorating themes that seemed to vie with each other in a strange, eclectic way.

Mrs. Carver was given a corner of the dorm, and her closest

neighbor was a Miss Blodgett—I never did learn her given name—
and I found it hard not to smile. Mrs. Carver was the personification
of elegance, her hair neatly coifed, her makeup softly becoming,
and her lovely clothes ironed and immaculate. She always looked
as though she'd stepped out of the proverbial band-box, and I remember Margo saying she must have sat up all night to keep her
hair looking so perfect. Miss Blodgett was her exact opposite. Her
dorm area was neat and Spartan, but it was obvious that she thought
nothing of her personal appearance. She was of medium height,
but she looked tall, because she was so thin and wore long, shape-
less skirts that accentuated her leanness. Her dark hair was caught
back in a loose bun at the nape of her neck and did nothing to help
her rather plain features. Looking at her, I realized she reminded
me of the stern woman in Grant Wood's famous painting, *American Gothic*, only slimmer and younger.

She had just introduced herself to Mrs. Carver when I came up
the stairs with the last suitcase. I noticed her speech was animated
and birdlike; she talked in little bursts, or chirps, as she watched
her new neighbor put her things away.

Seeing there was nothing more I could do, I said my goodbyes
and ran back to our cellblock, where I found Margo hanging up the
few, well-worn clothes she had just washed. I told her what I'd been
doing and said that I thought it was really incongruous to see those
two women together.

"Well, I hear that Miss Blodgett enjoys her solitude, and so does
Mrs. Carver, so they'll probably hit it off beautifully," Margo
remarked.

"Could be. It's funny though—while I was watching Mrs.
Carver put umpteen pairs of little spike-heeled sandals under her
bed, I looked across at Miss Blodgett's feet and noticed she was
wearing tennis shoes with the toes out. I glanced under her bed,
and there was one other pair of sneakers, almost as beat-up as the
ones she had on. Lord, but the war throws the strangest roommates
together!"

*****

There was one blessing that came out of that freezing winter: the Japs decided it would be quicker, and warmer, for all concerned, if we stayed in our compounds and the guards counted us outside our cells. That way they could check on any ill inmates as they took the count, instead of having us stand on the roll-call field till they came back with the tally. The only other people they had to check were the shift workers, like me, and that process was separate from the general roll-call.

It worked out a lot better this way, and went much faster. Jock would stand, looking down Main Street, and as soon as the guards started down Cellblock Twenty, he'd bellow, *"All out Twenty-One!"* and we'd come out of our cells and line up for the count. His little daughter Kay loved to help him at these times and would jump up and down and sing out, "Hello, Mr. Japanese!" as the young guards turned into our compound. They seemed to love little children, and as cold as they were, they'd always smile and pat her on the head...probably thinking of little brothers and sisters back home.

One evening, as our second anniversary in camp was fast approaching, I was engulfed in a feeling of loss and isolation. The only way I could dispel it was by keeping busy or entertained, but neither option was to be found that evening in the aching cold of the camp.

The sets for *Androcles* had been completed, but the play was still in final rehearsal. As neither Ursula nor Margo were involved in it, they were in our cell having a gab-fest with a group of their friends, leaving me with nowhere to go, and nothing to do.

As I trudged through the sloshy snow to Lisa's cellblock, I thought of the dull evening ahead and hoped she could come up with something.

"Hope you're feeling brilliant tonight, 'cos I'm draggin' bottom," I said, as she answered my knock on her door.

"Let me think of something while I put Billie and Jane to bed." After hugging them both, and tucking them in with whispered goodnights, she spun around and said, "I've got it—it's a brainstorm!" Grabbing her coat, and waving to her parents in the adjoining cell to let them know we were going out, she shoved me out the door.

"What's a brainstorm?" I asked excitedly.

"Let's go to the prayer meeting in the assembly hall!"

"You...must...be...kidding?!"

"I'm not!"

"Just the two of us?"

"No, let's round up the gang. It'll be fun, and we can sing our heads off."

"I can't sing," I said dully.

"No one'll know," she said with a smile. And surprisingly, when we rounded up our gang, they all thought it would be a blast.

"Hey, guys, this is a *prayer* meeting," I reminded them.

"So-o-o?" Tom Hazlett responded.

"So no cutting up or fooling around, okay?" I began to feel worried. I enjoyed a good lark as much as the others, but drew a line at offending people, especially in church.

"Yes, mama!" Tom said facetiously.

"We'll behave, Bobby," Dan said, smiling. "Like Lisa says, we gotta do somethin' or we'll go nuts."

When we got to the hall, it was pretty full, and I noticed everyone there, except for us, was from the missionary element in camp. I stood back as the gang slipped into the last pew, then caught myself genuflecting as I stepped in after them. Embarrassed, I looked around to see if anyone had noticed, and saw a sea of faces staring at me in a strange way. I shuddered inwardly, then I heard Lisa whisper to Dan, "Hey, look, they're staring at us!" That made me feel a little better; at least I wasn't the only one getting all the attention.

"Guess we're live meat," Dan said.

I still wasn't comfortable though, and found myself wishing I hadn't come. I'd never been in a Protestant church before. I missed the crucifix, the incense and candles, and the Sisters beautiful singing. People had come from all over North China, and as far south as Shanghai, just to hear them sing. In the evenings, during study hour, I would hear the plaintiff strains of a Gregorian chant and it would act like a gentle hand on my restless brow. How I missed the tranquility of those precious days.

"Oops, look who's going up to the podium," Lisa whispered. Looking up, I followed her gaze. It was none other than the consumptive, young evangelist who had harangued us the day his parents' mission had arrived in camp, and I let out a groan. Now I was positive I shouldn't have come.

He opened the service with the beautiful hymn, *Amazing Grace*, progressing through some Bible readings and a few more hymns. It was rather pleasant, and I found myself relaxing a little. Then, the tone changed, and he called for penitents to come forth. There were stirrings in the congregation, and several members rose and cried out wild, heartfelt confessions that evoked loud "Hallelujahs!" from their fellow Christians.

Somehow, it sounded unreal to me: like a put-on. How could these people stand there and call on the Lord, beating their breasts and making such a show? I was cringing inside. I knew when I called on the Lord, it was in the quiet of my cell, in a moment of deep contemplation, not standing in an assembly hall, packed with Fundamental Protestants and curiosity seekers, and certainly not yelling, at the top of my lungs, that I had seen the Light!

As the meeting wound down, the evangelist called for more penitents to come forward and see the Light and embrace the Lord, and a handful more stepped forward.

Then, to my dismay, as I watched the small procession, I saw one of the "sinners" was Tom Hazlett, who had been at the far end of our line. He had slipped down the side aisle and joined the repentant souls. I was certain he had joined them physically, but not spiritually, as Tom had to be one of the original rough-and-ready boys in camp, who would fight at the drop of a hat, cuss at less, and thoroughly enjoyed being male.

Then, as though I was hearing someone else, I heard him make a genuine plea for forgiveness, and I was so perplexed, I couldn't take it all in.

The consumptive prayer leader's face lit up like a beacon, and joy seemed to radiate from him, as the bare lamp bulb over the lectern spilled a pool of light around him and Tom. I could sense his thoughts: "Lord, I have my one, true, repentant sinner!" And with the thought must've come the belief that his passage to heaven was now assured.

"Brother," he was saying, "Tell me you see the Light!"

"Oh, yeah! Oh, yeah! I see the light!" cried Tom, and pointing to the bare lamp over the head of the young evangelist, he let out a mocking laugh and, waving his arms like a victorious prize fighter, danced up the main aisle and out of the hall.

I could have died!

Oh, Lord, how can we all get out of here without being seen, I thought, as I spun around and silently led the line-up in our pew out through the doors, right on Tom's heels.

"How could you do that to us?" I spat at him, when I caught up with him. He looked at me, unbelieving, as the other boys slapped him on the back and tousled his hair, saying they wished they'd had the guts to do the same thing.

Until that evening, everything to me had been either black or white, right or wrong, mostly judged by what *I* would do in the same circumstance. I didn't realize it fully, but what it boiled down to was, if I wouldn't do it, it had to be wrong. Ah, how smug the righteous are! Now I was left wondering: was what Tom had done blasphemy, or was that what one called the prayer service in the hall?

April, as always, started out as a month full of promise. Dad was writing up a storm in his journal, but he kept pretty quiet about its contents. He was still visiting Guy's mother several evenings a week, and Mother, believing he was in a dorm chewing the fat with the guys, was in blissful ignorance. Mario came over often in the evenings to visit her. When I was in our cell, the bits of conversation that drifted through the thin walls were always nostalgic, sometimes upbeat, as they talked about how life would be after the war. We all now definitely had the feeling that victory for the Allies was just around the corner, but we had no real news to hang our hopes on.

Then, after a total news blackout of more than two years, when the Japs finally posted an official news bulletin on the kitchen boards, we didn't believe the message: it said that Roosevelt had died. We lumped it together with all the other wild rumors and lies we had heard in camp and put it down to wishful thinking on their part. There was one cynic in our crowd who said, "You better believe it, it's Friday the thirteenth." As always, the Orient was a day ahead of the United States.

I'll never forget how crestfallen I was when Peter Fox came over to our cell and told us that the news bulletin had been confirmed. He said he couldn't tell us his source, but that the President was definitely dead. Dan was visiting our cell when Pete made this statement, and in the deadly silence that followed, I watched a stunned expression creep over his face.

"What happens now, Dan?" Pete asked. "Do they have to have an election for a new president?"

"No, the vice-president automatically takes his place."

"Just like that?"

"Yes, that's how it's set up, so that we'll never be without a president over the Union."

"Whose the vice-president?"

"Harry Truman."

"And if anything happens to Truman?"

"Then it's the Speaker of the House."

"You really know your line of succession, don't you?" Pete said admiringly, then added in French, *"Le roi est mort; vivre le roi!"*

"Something like that," Dan said glumly, then added, "I hate to leave, but I better tell Mom. She refused to believe the bulletin. This is really going to hit her."

He unfolded his long length off my cot and went out the door, ducking so he wouldn't hit his head on the lintel. I noticed he was a little wobbly when he stood up, but I put it down to the shattering news, and thought no more of it.

The Japanese magnanimously allowed us to have a memorial

service, and everyone in the camp attended. I can't remember what the day was like, cloudy or clear, I only know my morale was at an all-time low. I was not alone. As I looked at the other faces around me, American, British, Dutch, French, Italian, you name it, I saw tears in their eyes.

Somehow I didn't break down over the touching eulogy, or when the choral group from an American mission sang *The Battle Hymn of the Republic*. But, as the hymn came to an end, I was swept by a deep emotion: I felt I was standing on some remote battlefield, watching my comrades fall all around me. It was horrible, and I couldn't quell the terrible feeling of loss.

As I looked at the faces around me, they appeared to be being sucked down into a bottomless pit, and I thought with dread, *Will we ever get out?*

Then, as we moved sadly away with our heads bowed, a beautiful, clear voice started to sing *God Bless America!*

It was electric!

We stopped to a man, turned around and raised our heads and voices in song, and as the service ended with a feeling of renewal and hope, I looked now at the ever-present guards, and saw the smug looks they had reflected moments earlier turn to ones of disbelief.

After Nico's death, Guy asked for a change in jobs, not being able to face the bakery shift without his buddy. His first short stint was as a stoker in K-1, then he got transferred to the hospital diet kitchen where I worked. His shift followed Dan's, so now I had two stokers I could look forward to working with, and most of all, it gave me a chance to talk with him without feeling shy and awkward. Guy wasn't as helpful as Dan, but he would pitch in and help if I asked him.

One morning, after getting him to help me wrestle with the blending of the soaked millet and boiling water, he stood back and watched while I stirred the mush with the long wooden paddle I used. Feeling his eyes boring into my back, I turned and looked at him, and some of my old animosity started to rear its ugly head, but I stopped when I saw his face. He looked tired, almost ill.

"What's up, you look dreadful," I asked.

"God, I'd love to get some sleep."

"Why can't you?"

"It's your old man. It doesn't seem to matter to him that I have to get up at four in the morning to start stoking; when he comes over, he and my mother have at it till I could scream."

I knew Dad had been coming back to the cell later and later, always well after curfew; many people did, hiding in the shadows while the guards went by, and slipping in unnoticed. Remembering that, and hearing Guy's remarks, I felt my face blazing. I found myself trying to say something, but no words came out.

I must've looked weird, as he gave me a ferocious frown and said, "What the hell do you think goes on in our cell at night?"

I still couldn't find my voice.

"Go on, *say* it!"

I couldn't say it. I was utterly confused, and a dreadful doubt was assailing me. I thought of all the malicious camp gossip I'd heard about his mother, and how it had tainted my thoughts of him. I had never believed the story he told about his father, who was supposedly in the import/export business, and who had been caught away on a business trip when Pearl Harbor was attacked, and was now a prisoner in Singapore, or somewhere. Slowly, I began to realize that everything I'd heard, and had let ruin my life for over two years, was based on rumor, not on fact.

Then, I heard him speaking in a slow, deliberate voice. "I have to admit when he comes over, it's quite an education. You know, your old man is the only capitalist I know who really cares for the peasant, the coolie, the millions of Chinese who never have a say in their lives. He says Pearl Buck is the only foreign writer who really understands the Chinese."

I nodded, remembering Mother and Dad discussing her books.

Then he added, "I think the thing I've found that means the most to me in this camp is a capitalist with a heart. Somehow, all is not lost."

"In other words, all is not black or white? Right or wrong?

There are some grey areas where you and I can meet and even have a civilized discussion...like now?"

"God, someone's going to cut your tongue out one of these days! Your sarcasm is an art!"

I felt I'd been slapped, hard.

"Your old man..." he started.

I interrupted him. "Don't tell me he's a saint. He's *not!*" I'd had enough. I knew Dad. I knew all his little peccadillos. And his cruelty. I knew how he played around...

Then it struck me!

Good God, I thought, *why is it when Mother and Mario get together, all is sweetness and light, but when Dad and Guy's mother get together, it has to be adulterous!*

"I never said he was a saint," Guy was saying, "but, because of his profession, he seems able to cut through all the rot and bally-hoo of war and come down to the bottom line, which is not the acquisition of land and people, but who comes out ahead with the most money in his pocket when it's all over."

"He always was a cynic."

"No, he's honest. That doesn't mean the majority of us don't fight for Empire, or Deutschland, or Mother Russia, or whatever; we do. But the clowns that jerk the strings couldn't give a damn for any of that—it's how *they* come out in the end that counts."

"He must've had a black day," I said.

"No, I don't think so. He said his blackest days were when the Japanese took over Chinwangtao, and he had to work for them. He said his Japanese military counterpart was slippery-fingered and greedy, and that he had a hell of time keeping him in line. The position was twice as hazardous, because if the Jap had been caught juggling the books, or skimming, he would simply have pointed his finger at your dad, and he wouldn't have stood a chance before a Japanese tribunal."

I tried to pretend I knew all about Dad's problems in this respect, but I wasn't being honest. It was the first I had heard about them, and they made his frequent violent outbursts the final months in Chinwangtao much easier to understand.

*****

May arrived with a deep chill still in the evening air, and summer
never seemed to get any closer. Dad didn't notice it though; he was
too busy bubbling over with rumors of all kinds. It was like the last
days in Tientsin before we were interned. As it was impossible to
pick fact from fantasy, I decided to believe nothing till it really
happened, just as we had done then.

One evening, after curfew, I found myself without sleep. I
decided to read, only to realize I had no oil for my wick. I cussed
softly, and my cot squeaked and groaned as I settled down into the
sagging canvas, trying to miss the cross bars of the center support.
Then my mind started to race, and I thought of Lisa: she seemed
to be getting along better with her stepfather now, or was it the other
way around? And Dan flashed in my mind. He wasn't standing
as straight as he always had, there was an arch to his back, and a
strange shuffle to his step. I wondered if I was the only one who
noticed it. Guy loomed up and I saw him with his little shadow,
René. She was always by his side, or two steps behind, like a
dutiful Japanese mama-san. He seemed to be getting over the loss
of Nico slowly, and had moved into our little circle of friends. I
also got a feeling that he wasn't quite as sure of his political beliefs
as he had been. Either that, or he decided discretion the better part
of valor; better to have friends and keep your beliefs under wraps,
than the other way around. I stretched, and my cot creaked loudly.

"Lord, you're restless tonight," Margo said.

"Sorry, I thought you were asleep."

"Who can sleep?" Ursula mumbled.

We started to talk desultorily after that, about nothing in particular. Suddenly, during one of our long pauses, the silence was
shattered by the clanging of a loud bell. It rang, and rang, and rang,
and our whole cellblock seemed to rock with the vibration of its
clangor.

"My God! What's *that!?!*"

"The bell in the bell tower!"

And just as suddenly as it started, it stopped, and the silence was ominous. I found myself holding my breath, unable to say a word, just listening. Then, Margo started to say something, but Ursula stopped her with a soft, "Hey, sssh...*l-i-s-t-e-n!*" I found myself straining to hear once more.

"Footsteps. Someone's running," Ursula whispered.

Then I heard them; they were coming closer. We heard Japanese being shouted back and forth between guards who were double-timing up and down the roads and through the compounds.

Margo peered out of the window and whispered, "The guards are up and at it."

"Think someone's escaped again?" I asked.

"Well, ringing the bell won't bring 'em back," Ursula said, drily.

About half an hour later, after lots of weird, undefinable noises, Jock banged on our cell door and shouted, "All out for roll-call on the roll-call field!"

"What the heck...?" Margo started, as we clambered out of our beds, threw on some warm clothes, and trotted over to the ball field, with Mother and Dad making up the rear.

The internees closest to the field were already in line. Babies were bawling, kids were whimpering because they'd been dragged out of their warm beds, and everyone was in a foul mood. The air was biting cold. Half the internees turned up in inadequate clothing and were chilled to the bone. The only thing keeping them from getting hypothermia was their overheated tempers.

Everyone looked accusingly at the other, assuming he was the only one left in the dark about what was going on. And Jock didn't help matters when he whispered to each of us that we were not to talk to each other or make a sound. He carried little Kay on his shoulders and tried to keep her quiet as he delivered the individual warnings, but every time he bent over to whisper in someone's ear, she would yell like a banshee. The situation would've been really comical if it hadn't been bristling with would-be incidents.

Although I noticed only a few guards, their tempers were more frazzled than ours. The night was extremely dark, and the few internees near the perimeter of the field were the only ones who could be seen under the dimly lit lamp standards. I wouldn't have liked to have been a guard under such circumstances, and I wondered if they were fearful like we were.

We waited what seemed like hours. When finally the main contingent of guards came out of the guard shack, we saw to our horror that they weren't carrying clipboards, but machine guns. They placed themselves strategically around us, and I felt a sudden wave of real fear sweep through the crowd as the guards stared at us with cold, blank eyes, as though they'd never seen us before.

There were no instructions or demands. Just silence. Deadly silence, broken here and there by the whimpering of a child and the shushing of a parent.

The Commandant was nowhere to be seen.

Then, Ed Lewin came quietly down the lines and whispered to each of the block wardens, who in turn whispered to each of us. The message was simple. We would stand there all night, and all day if necessary, until someone confessed to ringing the bell.

Well, at least *that* was cleared up; we now knew one of us had rung the bell. But why? For God's sake…*why?*"

Another hour passed, and the older internees tried to sit down on the ground, but the guards shouted at them and they were held up between their more robust neighbors.

I looked at my family. Ursula and Margo were expressionless. Dad resigned. Mother defiant. I shrugged and looked up the line. The Collishaws were standing quietly holding hands. Towering Jim Tuck had a faraway look on his face as he stared over the heads of the rows of people, but his equally tall wife was beginning to crack. The Beruldsen's were standing like Stoics, while the obnoxious Hatton clan was quiet for once, quiet and scared. Emma Allan had little Jeremy in her arms, while Douglas and Kay clutched at her skirt as they watched Jock silently walk up and down the line trying to look calm and unperturbed, smiling at those who needed encouragement.

Gladys Tabor, irrepressible as ever, gave him an outrageous wink, and nodding toward the guard at the end of our line, made an obscene gesture with her hand that I couldn't help catching and smiling at. The Stones were silent; Deirdre holding her precious new baby, a look of terror in her eyes.

One of the guards had trouble with his automatic and let out a burst over our heads. That was all Mrs. Tuck needed. She snapped and started screaming, "We're all going to be killed! We're going to die! We're going to die!"

Mother brushed my sleeve as she stepped out of line, marched up to her, and reaching up, slapped her hard on both cheeks. Her face crumpled like tissue paper, as Mother quietly hissed, *"Shut up! We are not going to die!* They haven't kept us alive for almost three years to kill us now. They could have done it ages ago, if that's what they'd wanted to do. *Shut up! Stand straight…*and don't let them get to you!"

Jock quietly led Mother back to her place in line, and the silence was complete.

A long while later, King Kong marched onto the field, flanked by Gold Tooth, who handed him a bullhorn, which he used to yell at us in Japanese. Ed Lewin quickly rushed up beside him and tried to translate, tossing the bullhorn back and forth between commands. "You are to return to your cells…there will be *no rations…*until the perpetrator of this monstrous act…turns himself in for punishment."

There was a rustle in the lines, and everyone looked at his neighbor, trying to figure out who had rung the bell. The wardens rushed up and down the rows whispering, "No confessions, absolutely *no* confessions!" We nodded in agreement, and after another interminable wait, we were finally dismissed and sent back to our cells.

Dawn was breaking when we got back to our compound, and not knowing whether the restricted rations applied to the hospital, I went to work. That turned out to be the last meal I fixed for a while. As the grain had been soaking all night, the guards let me prepare it so that it wouldn't be wasted, then the rest of the supplies were hauled away.

Rumor went rampant in camp, the most persistent of which was that the war was over in Europe! We figured we would happily starve if that was the case, and to the Japanese's surprise, our spirits went up instead of down. People with remains of comfort parcels and hoarded food meted it out to the children, so they wouldn't go without, and we just cinched our belts tighter. After almost a week of no food, we were walking zombies, but we never missed a roll-call, or let the Japanese know how badly off we were. On the sixth morning, we were told that breakfast would be served as usual.

I hoped we had won without a confession, but found that was not the case.

Peter Fox had turned himself in during the night while everyone was asleep, because he couldn't stand seeing the people suffer for what, it turned out, he had done. He hadn't been very smart though. When he confessed to ringing the bell, he couldn't help telling the Japanese why he had done it...*the war was over in Europe!*

Whether they had known it or not was moot; the fact that Pete knew meant there had to be a shortwave set in the camp, and they tried to find out from him where it was.

Realizing his big mouth had put him, and everyone else, in jeopardy, Pete clammed up, forcing an absolutely livid King Kong to put him in solitary without rations. The little jail was at the farthest end of the tree-studded Jap compound, and next to impossible for us to reach. It was then that a twelve-year-old human fly named Dennis Carter stepped forward and offered to get food to him. It was a calculated risk, but we were banking on the Japanese not hurting a child if he got caught, so we let him do his stuff. It was amazing. He could cling and climb on anything that rose above the ground, and swing himself across unbelievable expanses with the ease of a trapeze artist. The trees, with their dense foliage, gave him great cover, and he was able to "Tarzan" it through their upper limbs, and lower food and messages to Pete without the guards being any the wiser.

This went on at least once a day, week in and week out, and the Japanese couldn't understand how Pete could hold out without food. He'd hide the food container between drops, then, when Dennis lowered a meal, he would attach the earlier container and return it, so there was never more than one in the cell at any time, and that one well hidden.

Needless to say, we didn't send Pete just any food—it was always something special. We pooled stashed goodies to make desserts, and sent little thinking-of-you notes that he chuckled over and carefully returned. His morale was great, his weight remained the same, and his captors were completely baffled!

And for us the days slipped slowly by. There seemed to be an unreal feeling about that summer. We needed to hear how the war in the Pacific was progressing, but once again we couldn't tell fact from fiction. Dad said the *"Axis Rag"*, as he called the *Peking Chronicle* that always arrived in camp three weeks late, admitted to heavy bombing of the Japanese homeland. From that, we deduced we must have retaken many of the islands. It was quite a change from their usual drivel about sinking the United States Navy. Dad said, through the years, according to the *Chronicle*, the total U.S. fleet had been sunk at least three times!

I don't know if the guards knew any more than we did, but some of them appeared to be coming apart and were getting drunk at night, roaming through the camp singing bawdy Japanese songs, and making a pathetic spectacle of themselves. It was usually after curfew though, so we heard them more than saw them.

Camp life continued to go on its muddled way, and Saturday night dances moved outdoors as the weather got warmer. Our favorite dance floor was a concrete circle in front of the bell-tower dorm, with a bank and benches around it, like a little amphitheater. Some nights, when the music wafted on the air, and the moon sailed through a starless sky touched now and then by wisps of clouds, it reminded me of summers in Chinwangtao and Mother's Harvest Moon parties. Then my mind would play tricks, and I'd see the dancers—not in their bedraggled clothes, most of them barefoot—but beautifully dressed in crepes, voiles, and satins, the men in dress whites, and I'd keep up this charade till the last note drifted away on the evening air.

It was at one of these dances in early June that Dan, all lean six-foot-something of him, started to collapse in my arms. I looked at him, and my panic was reflected in his eyes.

"Get me to a bench, quick!" he pleaded.

I half-danced half-dragged him to the sidelines, then eased him down onto the bank, as the benches were all taken.

"What happened?" I asked, scared.

"Oh, nothing," he said, trying to make light of it. "My legs seemed to give out on me. I'm all right now."

"Level with me, Dan!"

"I'm fine, let's go dance," he said, and started to get up again.

His legs buckled once more, and he dropped back down and looked at me, his face ashen with mingled horror and fear.

"Don't say anything to Ian and Lisa, please."

"I won't. They're still dancing. No one saw what happened." I put my hand over his and tried to smile—"Want to talk about it?"

"It's been going on for quite a while. I don't want Mom to know about it. There's nothing anyone can do. I feel fine. Only every once in a while, I seem to lose control, and my legs give out." Then lightly, "I guess I'm growing too fast!"

I gave his hand a squeeze, as Lisa and Ian came over. For once they were relaxed and enjoying each other's company. "We're going for a walk," Ian said, and they sauntered off.

Dan and I sat and talked till the dance broke up, then he got up carefully, and I walked slowly back with him to his cell. I watched him closely after that, but he seemed to be doing all right. His shuffle was a little more pronounced, and his back slightly more arched, but he was still fun and easy-going, and if he hurt, no one knew about it.

Several weeks after the episode on the dance floor, he was the stoker on my shift, and while I was cleaning up the kitchen and putting out the rations for the lunch crew, I heard a frightening groan and thud.

I rushed out into the hall and down to the boiler room. Dan's legs had given out, and he had fallen against the blistering boiler. I screamed and screamed, and tried to pull him away, but he was a dead weight, and I couldn't move him.

Guy came rushing in just then—for some miraculous reason he was early—and we dragged Dan away from the heat and laid him down. He was badly burned. While Guy rushed upstairs for an orderly, I knelt and cradled his head in my lap and prayed he would be okay.

There was no keeping his condition from his mother now. He was all she had left, and she watched him like a hawk. To pacify her, when he got out of the hospital, he walked with a cane. At first, he would tuck it under his arm when he was out of her sight, but after a while, I noticed he didn't do that any more. He didn't have to say anything; I could see he was getting worse, and I felt so helpless.

As July rolled around, the mood in the camp became erratic. It swung from light-hearted highs to panicky lows, and for me, sleep was almost impossible. I found the only way to beat the pendulum effect was to work and play as hard as I could, so that I'd drop into bed at night exhausted, and force sleep to come.

The evening ball games became hectic, with the onlookers getting as worked up as the players. The dances got more boisterous, and the music wilder, as if sheer noise would keep our spirits up. But as the month ground on and our rations got lower and lower, we started to succumb to depression no matter how hard we tried not to. Once again, bread was all that saved us: we had it morning and night, with either water or weak tea. Our midday meal was usually a ladle of leek soup. Through it all, I knew I was running on utter willpower, and wondered how long I would be able to keep it up.

Pete was still in solitary, and his smuggled meals were getting harder and harder to come by. One thing helped us a great deal: the guards were getting very lax, and sometimes he wouldn't be guarded for hours on end. It was as though they didn't give a damn what happened to him, or us.

Finally, muggy August arrived, still rampant with rumors, but with no news we could verify or sink our teeth into. Dad's journal of August seventh was a tale of hunger and little hope. His usual up-beat scribblings were few and far between.

On the fifteenth, the camp was swamped with the rumor that the war was over, but the Japanese would neither "confirm nor deny". It was not surprising, as we knew all along that they had been fed the same propaganda we had.

We could only hope...

Little did Dad know that his lifeless journal entry of the sixteenth, "Nothing of any interest marked life in camp today," would presage an overwhelming day of joy and chaos.

15

LIBERATION!

I was standing in the breakfast line at K-2 when I first heard the gentle purr. I wasn't the only one. There was a hush in the chow-line as the hum of the plane got louder. It struck me that the sound was different; not the funny, tinny drone of the Japanese Zeros and Judys, or the rattling-roar of their bombers, but a strong, steady, comforting sound that seemed to push up against the heavens and reverberate back down to earth. I knew instinctively *this was one of ours!*

The foliage over the camp was dense and we couldn't see the plane's approach, but the drone got louder...and louder...and then there it was! Directly overhead—its wings painted with a huge POW and a Red Cross on the fuselage!

A cry went up, "Oh, God, it's over! It's *over! They've FOUND US!*"

I lost it completely! I started jumping up and down and shouting deliriously. The yells, screams, and pandemonium that broke out all around me drowned out the roar of the plane's engines as it skimmed over the camp. We were hugging each other, laughing and crying at the same time.

The plane made another pass, and I rushed out of the kitchen compound and started down Main Street to the prison gates, forgetting my soggy breakfast in the excitement of the moment.

Suddenly, the joyous shouting turned into a long moan. The plane had left and was roaring off to the west, towards China's mountainous heartland...

The crew hadn't seen us after all!

The guards were coming out of their quarters, heavily armed, jogging down to the main gates and the guard shack, their faces grim. Gold Tooth looked sallow and sick.

I stood still for a moment, looking up and down the street trying to decide where I could find some high ground to watch the plane's flight. Then, remembering the forbidden bell-tower, I raced towards the women's dorm. Not surprisingly, everyone else had the same thought, and scores of us pounded up the stairs looking for a vantage spot.

I could see the plane again in the far distance, like a little fly speck against billowing thunderheads. I watched till it looked as though it would disappear into white nothingness, then it turned south and flew along the face of the clouds.

"It's heading home—maybe to Kunming."

I couldn't believe the voice I was hearing. It was Pete Fox! But before I could say anything, he let out an, "Oh, *hell...*" and started back down the stairs on the heels of a disappointed, disbelieving crowd.

"Hey, wait a minute, how did you get out?" I yelled, running after him.

"When the guards left, I wriggled out through the vent," he said over his shoulder.

"Great!" I sang out, clumping down the stairs.

As I passed the second floor dorm, I saw Miss Blodgett standing by her bed, mumbling to herself and throwing things out of an old suitcase like a demented customs official. Suddenly, she gave a little cry of triumph, grabbed a piece of rolled up cloth, kissed it, and tucking it under her arm, raced down the stairs behind the motley mob.

I followed her, churning with excitement.

"Whatchagot?" I asked, coming up behind her.

"Old Glory. I've hidden it all these years. It used to fly over our mission compound, and I just couldn't leave it for the Japs to get." Her eyes began to water, and she brushed away a tear, as she stopped and cocked her head to one side, birdlike, listening.

"They'll come back," she said, confidently, "I know it...and this time we'll be ready for them!"

The few times I'd seen her, I had thought she was quiet and rather meek, but when she started to sprint after the crowd again, her long, black skirt flapping against her thin legs, I realized I had never really known her. She was dynamite!

When she got in front of the crowd, she stopped and waved her arms till she had everyone's attention, then she started unfurling Old Glory. We all just stared. As I finally grabbed one side of the flag and helped her hold it aloft, I felt goose-bumps crawling all over me again...

"Those planes flew over us, because they didn't know we were here," she shouted. "If they saw us at all, we were just a bunch of running people...*any* people. If we go out the gates and lay Old Glory in a wide, open field, they'll *know* we're here!"

"What makes you think they'll come back?" someone yelled.

"They're looking for us!" Pete said. "Miss Blodgett's right, they'll be back. Let's help them find us!"

From somewhere in the milling crowd, there was a bellow of, "Let's *G-O-O-O!*", and like lemmings streaming off a cliff, we started running toward the main gates.

We saw Gold Tooth, standing with his binoculars looking up into the sky, cussing a blue streak, and stopped dead. It was obvious he had spotted the plane returning. With that realization, we started yelling all over again. My throat was raw, and as I ran with the crowd, I tripped over a slab of granite that had broken loose from the wall around the assembly hall compound. I picked myself up and kept on going. Then I saw King Kong. He was yelling at his men, as they formed a solid line across the heavy wooden gates, their machine guns aimed at us, point blank.

I looked at the guards, especially the young ones who were the same age as us, wondering if they would fire. We had known them for almost three years; we had seen them become forgotten by their country, suffering from homesickness, their uniforms in tatters, their teeth chattering in the cold, their bodies sweating in the heat—but they'd always been good soldiers, following commands without flinching...

God, help us! I prayed silently.

Just then, someone yelled, *"Buggayara!"*, and as if on cue, we all let out a roaring, *"B-A-N-Z-A-I!"*, and charged the gates.

The yell caught the men off-guard, and they lowered their guns, as Pete shot the gate-bolt and Miss Blodgett rushed through, Old Glory streaming out behind her, followed by the most ragtag bunch of scarecrows I'd ever seen.

The feeling of freedom was intoxicating. I'd almost forgotten how beautiful the Chinese countryside could be. Wind-scarred willows clung to the banks of a running stream, and little bare-bodied children ran splashing through the water, waving bamboo sticks with bright paper windmills pinned to them. They were giggling and shouting, *"Mei kuo jen! Mei kuo jen!"* (Americans! Americans!), pointing to the skies.

I looked up too and saw the plane circling. There was a lump in my throat as I kept up with the crowd racing out to the *kaoliang* fields. The plants, like corn, were tall and ready for harvest. I knew that throwing Old Glory over the tassels and pulling her out straight and square would be tricky to do, but there was nowhere else to lay her down, as the fields were planted to *kaoliang* as far as the eye could see.

While we wrestled with the flag, the plane dropped lower and lower, and then, as I looked up, it made a roaring pass, the cargo doors opened, and seven paratroopers rolled out like marbles from a bag, followed a few moments later by huge metal drums of supplies.

Hysteria swept over us once again as we raced out to where they were landing, fighting our way down the long rows of *kaoliang* and jumping up to spot their location. Some of the brightly colored supply parachutes didn't open, and we could hear their cargo landing with a ominous thud.

When we finally came upon the men releasing their 'chutes, we were surprised to see them in full combat gear, and laughed when they told us to stay back, as they might have to fight their way into the camp. We also found one tragic victim: a little Chinese boy, who had sustained a glancing blow from a drum that had landed with an unopened parachute. Pete gently lifted the little fellow in his arms, and then, before the paratroopers knew what had happened, the stronger of our men had raised them shoulder-high, and we swarmed back down the road and through the prison gates.

The older people and young children were standing in a semicircle just inside, their faces flushed with excitement, while the jubilant Salvation Army band was playing *God Bless America!*

There weren't any Japanese to be seen.

I turned and looked at the guardhouse to the left of the entrance; a white flag was flying from a hastily erected pole.

I smiled at Miss Blodgett, who was happily draped in Old Glory. Her neat bun had broken loose, and her dark hair cascaded down her back. Her face was flushed with joy and excitement, and she looked like a young girl. Pete, who had handed the injured boy over to a hospital orderly, gave her a big hug, and spinning her off her feet, shouted, "You're one helluva lady!"

That day, August seventeenth, 1945, that had started with a gentle drone, and then a happy roar, kept building to an unending crescendo. We learned from the OSS paratroopers that the war had been officially over since the fifteenth, and that Emperor Hirohito's decision to surrender had been hastened by the detonation of an atomic bomb over Hiroshima that obliterated the city—decimating bodies and buildings with equal impartiality as it rose into the sky like a huge, defiant mushroom. There was a second one dropped over Nagasaki, but that was tragically anticlimactic.

To our added surprise, it appeared that the paratroopers, who were from Kunming, had been searching for our camp for almost

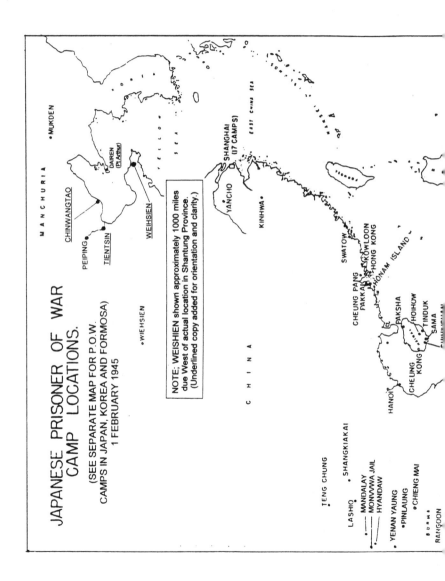

JAPANESE PRISONER OF WAR CAMP LOCATIONS.

(SEE SEPARATE MAP FOR P.O.W. CAMPS IN JAPAN, KOREA AND FORMOSA) 1 FEBRUARY 1945

NOTE; WEISHIEN shown approximately 1000 miles due West of actual location in Shantung Province. (Underlined copy added for orientation and clarity.)

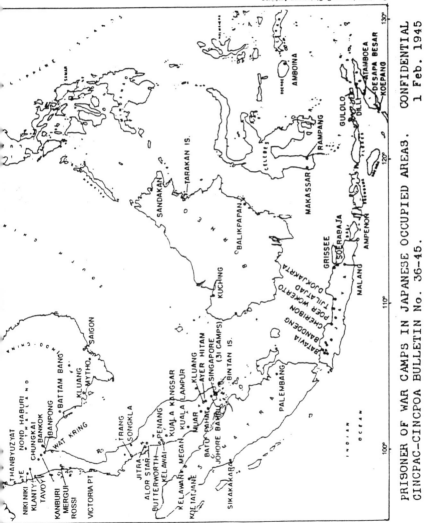

Courtesy Jerome P. Steigmann Archives

PRISONER OF WAR CAMPS IN JAPANESE OCCUPIED AREAS. CONFIDENTIAL
CINCPAC-CINCPOA BULLETIN No. 36-45. 1 Feb. 1945.

a week. When they couldn't find us, the horror of other camps they had liberated made them fear the worst. They had been on the verge of desperation when they finally spotted the flag in the *kaoliang* field. All they kept saying was, "Thank God for Old Glory!" I wasn't to learn till much later, when the war crimes trials were held, that the treatment accorded us by the Commandant and the consular guards was infinitely more humane than that of the Japanese army in the field. To this day I can't understand why we were spared. Could it be, as Mother Superior said, that one act of kindness, thousands of miles away, started a ripple that couldn't be quelled?

While Major Staiger and his men were accepting the surrender of the Japanese, a camp work crew went out to the fields to bring in the supplies, and Lisa and I, too excited to stand still, ran out of the gates again and splashed through the stream running by the camp. Chinese children ran after us and impishly splashed our legs by smacking the flowing water. We laughed and splashed them back. After a lot of giggling and bantering back and forth, the game ended, and we slipped out of the stream and stood on the far bank eyeing the grey walls of the camp with their terrifying wire and ugly guard towers.

"It doesn't look so bad from the outside, does it?" Lisa mused.

"No, and the walls don't look half as high; but look at all those trenches and barbed-wire entanglements. They were really afraid we'd try to escape. How the heck did Tip and Arthur make it?"

"Maybe the Japs installed all that mess *after* their escape."

"Could be..."

As we talked, I heard the drone of planes again, and felt blood rushing to my head, my scalp tingling.

This time they weren't troop transports, but bombers—B-29s from Okinawa, we learned later—and as they approached, their bomb-bays opened, and the sky was filled with brightly colored supply parachutes, dropping like manna from heaven.

As I watched, two drums with unopened parachutes came down, collided in mid-air, and burst, raining peaches and cream over the Chinese countryside!

"Hey, let's have breakfast!" I yelled, as we rushed over to the spill and plonked down in the field, dipping the sliced peaches into condensed milk and gorging ourselves. A group of Chinese children joined us, giggling and slurping the goodies along with us. Finally, sated and sticky, we headed back to the camp. On the way, we found a quiet little Chinese boy, sitting by a burst carton, happily squirting toothpaste down his throat.

"Pu ch'ih la! Pu hao!" I cried, rubbing my tummy and pretending to up-chuck.

He looked startled, got up, and ran away crying.

"Poor little bugger," I said, "I hated to tell him not to eat it, he was obviously enjoying the minty flavor."

"Bet he has the cleanest innards in China tomorrow," Lisa said, laughing. Then she looked at me and really cracked up.

"What's so funny?"

"You!"

"What do you mean?"

"God, if you could see yourself! Your hair's full of peaches and condensed milk!"

"Oh, n-o-o-o!"

"Oh, yeah!"

"Well, here goes!" I shouted, and running back to the stream, I plopped down and rinsed my hair with the sparkling, cold water. Then I lay full length in it and let it flow over me. Laughing, Lisa joined me.

After we cooled off, we got up, and straightening our soggy clothes and smoothing our wet hair, we sauntered back to the camp. As I got to the huge main gates, I stopped and looked at them, and the forbidding grey walls, and vowed silently I would never allow anyone to imprison me again.

Everyone was laughing and cracking jokes in our cellblock when I got back. Gladys was being a complete cut-up, and the dear little lady she had been caring for was sitting with tears of happiness running down her thin old wrinkled cheeks.

Jock came up smiling about then, and asked, "Want to hear the latest poop? Those OSS boys escorted King Kong and his men back to their quarters, but Gold Tooth refused to go with them. He said he wouldn't leave the guard shack till the OSS gave him safe-conduct out of the camp—he's afraid we're going to lynch him!"

"Hey, that might be fun!" Gladys said.

"No…it's over," Dad said quietly, "he doesn't need our help to go to hell."

Then, I looked around for Mother, but I didn't see her in the group. I peeped in her cell and found her sitting on the bed, a suitcase open at her feet, and in her hands she was lovingly holding Kuan-yin, running her fingers over the beautiful white porcelain figure. She looked up and smiled as I came in and said simply, "My beautiful Goddess of Mercy has looked after us again."

Two more planes came in that afternoon from Kunming and made a bumpy landing in a field a few miles from the camp. The men aboard commandeered a Chinese truck and drove into camp with more supplies, mostly medical, and crates of assorted equipment. I also saw my first cases of C and K Rations. When I finally got back to our compound, it was well past our evening chow time.

"I wonder if we're going to have dinner tonight," Margo said, as I joined her outside our cell. "I've got a feeling no one took their jobs seriously today."

"Oh, you had the duty, didn't you?"

"Yep. I was there when they brought the Chinese kid in. He was pretty badly hurt, but he took it like a trooper, and I'm sure he'll be fine before long. One of the men, Lieutenant Jim Hannon, hurt his shoulder when he landed. Seems he tensed up a bit when he realized they were landing in *kaoliang* and not some low ground crop. Don't know much about it, but I guess you have to be totally relaxed as you land so you won't jar any bones."

The talk about bumps and busted bones made be realize my left foot hurt terribly. I looked at my canvas sneaker and saw a horrid purple ankle protruding out of the shredded shoe. Carefully untying the laces, I slipped my foot out and stared at it. My middle toe was a huge black sausage, and the rest of my foot was discolored by a ghastly bruise.

I looked at Margo and back at my foot, and all of a sudden, the pain hit me, and I thought I was going to scream.

"When did that happen?" she asked, concerned.

"I don't know. But it hurts like *aitch!*"

"I'll bet it does. I'm going to get you some cold water to soak it in. Looks like you've broken a toe. There's not much anyone can do about it, except tape it to the next toe. Try and keep your weight off it."

As I sat soaking my foot in icy water, it all came back to me. "My God, I've been going on it all day!" I said. "I remember when it happened! Early this morning, I tripped over a slab of granite by the assembly hall when we made our *banzai* charge!"

"And you didn't feel the pain till now?!"

"I can't believe it! I guess hysteria kills pain."

Until now I'd always thought war stories about soldiers fighting on with limbs blown off, and bodies clobbered by shrapnel, rather far-fetched.

16

LEARNING TO LIVE AGAIN

Raindrops woke me around four-thirty the following morning, hitting the makeshift tin cookstove outside Mother and Dad's cell door. They landed like bursting water balloons, first with a thud, followed by a splash; then they came faster and louder till they sounded like a roar, and I knew the monsoons had arrived once more.

I got up as quietly as I could, trying not to yelp as I put my foot down for the first time, then scrambled into my threadbare clothes and groped for the comb to run through my hair. As I tucked my ragged shirt into my crumpled khaki shorts, a fabulous idea hit me: when I got off at noon, I was going to find one of those gorgeous, bright colored supply parachutes and make myself some new clothes.

A *dress!* Lord, I hadn't had a dress on in ages! The few I'd brought to the camp I had grown out of the first year, and had given away. I chuckled, thinking about camp life—it was like a huge hand-me-down family, with the littlest getting the "mostest".

I crept past sleeping Ursula, and then Margo. The light at the corner of the compound shone dimly through the window and lit up the "SEMPER FI" poster. *It won't be long now, Margo*, I thought, as I looked at her sleeping figure.

Stepping out into the warm, soggy morning, I made an awkward, hobbling dash to work—out of our compound, through Number Two Kitchen, where a stoker was already working on the fires, through the mens' dorm area that seemed to go on forever (only at this hour there were no catcalls), and across the ball court to the hospital. I started to slow down as I approached the building. What was the use of hurrying? My foot hurt like the devil, and I was already drenched to the skin. I could feel my hair hanging down my shoulders like a heavy, black cloth; my patchwork shirt was sticking to me and threatening to rip with every move; and the cuffs of my old shorts were like rain gutters, filling up with the run-off from my shirt. Soft mud squelched through my torn canvas shoes giving gentle relief to my throbbing toe. I clumsily stepped down the couple of steps to the kitchen and pushed the door open. The one bare lamp bulb in the hall cast a moving shadow as the wet air rushed in with me. I saw a glow coming out of the boiler room, and then the stoker stepped backwards out of the door and looked over his shoulder: it was Guy, and he looked strange.

"What's up?" I asked, seeing his clouded blue eyes.

"He's gone!"

I stopped and looked at him, wondering who he was talking about.

"Dan," he added.

"Oh, God, he died?" My voice broke, and in a moment of panic I thought, *Not Nico* and *Dan!*

"No, he's not dead. They flew him out yesterday evening—Stateside. The doctor from Kunming said he had spinal meningitis, and if they didn't airlift him right away, he wouldn't make it."

"Will he now?"

"Maybe."

Guy turned back to the boiler and kicked the iron door shut with such force it echoed all through the halls. When the din died down, I said quietly, "That's not fair, I didn't even get to say goodbye. The States are so big, I'll never see him again." Tears joined the rain on my face, mingling with the puddle I was making on the hall floor.

"You better go into the kitchen and dry out," Guy said gruffly, "I got your fire going first, as nothing is drawing right today."

I obeyed numbly.

I did everything by rote after that, and somehow got through the breakfast. I didn't have to ask Guy for help; it was as though he didn't want to be alone with his thoughts, so he pitched right in. For once, the mush had a minimum of lumps in it; the toast, prepared last over the smoldering coals, turned out crisp and golden; and when the orderlies came down for the food, my mood began to lift. I helped them load the pans and platters onto the cart, and ran after them down the hall with the usual forgotten serving pieces, then turned back to the kitchen.

The room was hot and stifling from the steam of the cooking. I went over to the high windows that had sills at ground level on the outside, and pushed one open. There was a rush of moist air, and the pounding rain sounded like horses hoofs as it hit the concrete apron around the building. I stepped back as the water bounced into the kitchen and splashed onto me.

Suddenly a loudspeaker blasted in my ear—it must've been rigged to the electric pole just outside the window—and a voice sang out, "*Good* morning! This is Captain Casey. Hope you have a great day!"

I shook my head in disbelief, and looking at Guy slouching in the doorway, I asked, "Who the heck's Casey? He must be totally demented!"

"He came in yesterday with the medical group from Kunming. He's here to orientate us and get us ready to face the real world."

"Maybe we should tell *him* about the real world!" I said.

Before I could comment further, there was another crackle on the PA system, and a strong, male voice belted out a song I'd never heard before, the notes bouncing off the kitchen walls.

"Oh, what a beautiful mornin'!
Oh, what a beautiful day!
I've got a beautiful feelin'
Ev'rythin's goin' my way."

"Shit!" Guy bellowed, as he rushed to the open window, sliding as he hit the rain slick floor. Slamming the window shut, he turned to me and started to laugh. The darn song and the damn weather tickled his perverse humor. He laughed so hard and so long, he got me started, and we stood like a couple of mindless hyenas, laughing till we ached.

When we finally stopped, I felt the tragic spell of the morning had lifted, and later, when I went off duty, my thoughts of Dan were happy ones. Maybe, with his speedy release, he would be cured. "Please, God..." I whispered.

The rain had stopped when I went back to the cell, but the heavens were still low, as the Chinese say, and I knew it was only a break in the deluge. Ursula wasn't there, and Margo's shift at the hospital still had three hours to go.

I scraped the mud off my shoes on the cement stoop, and went in. There was a copy of *LIFE* magazine lying on Margo's bed. I looked at the date; it was a couple of months old. *Only* a couple of months old! I grabbed it with a sense of excitement.

Hey, there is *a whole new world out there,* I thought, as I flipped over the pages and drank in the news. It was all so fabulous. Maybe that nut, Captain Casey, was right after all—what was a little rain when there was a beautiful world waiting for us outside. There was a whole crew of new movie stars I'd never heard of, and a guy called Frank Sinatra who had bobby-soxers swooning and screaming; he didn't look like much to me, but then, I hadn't heard him sing. There was also a new peace group called the United Nations meeting in San Francisco. I gathered they were something like the old League of Nations that had fallen flat on it's kazoo back in the late thirties. I wished them luck, and turned the page.

I gave a gasp. Looked harder. Then grabbed the chipped washbowl by my bed and brought up my breakfast.

I shut my eyes, as I had done ever since my childhood, and tried to will the horrifying sight away, and as always, it didn't work. I slowly opened the magazine again, and stared in disbelief at the pictures: they were of a German concentration camp, where emaciated bodies were stacked like so much cordwood, and the living dead, too weak to stand or cheer their liberators, stared at me from the pages like hollow-eyed cadavers.

Oh, God, this can't be real! No man could do this to his fellow men. Please, God, don't let this be true! My heart started to thump like mad, and I felt a wave of nausea sweep over me again. I put down the book and stood up and went outside.

Dad was sitting in front of his cell. He looked across at me and said, "What's the matter? You look awful."

"Did you see that *LIFE* magazine?"

"Yes."

He looked away and got a tattered handkerchief out of his pocket, then, taking off his glasses, he breathed on them, wiped them with the handkerchief, and put them back on. I knew he was playing for time and that he felt as sick as I did.

I thought of his old World War One sketchbook entitled *Man's Inhumanity to Man* with its beautifully rendered pen-and-ink drawings of French villages lying in rubble; a gutted cathedral standing like an eternal promise over a city that had nothing left to live for; the broken body of a dead horse, half-decayed, lying by the side of the road with a couple of shovels of earth scattered over it, and a sign scribbled by some Tommy, "Horse Buried Here".

Dad had been a captain with the British Expeditionary Forces in that "war to end all wars", and because he spoke Chinese fluently, he was put in charge of transporting a contingent of coolies to the Western Front. That trip triggered his sketches, his drawings reflecting the anguish of the seasick Chinese as they pitched about in the hold of the old *SS Kaiping* wallowing across the Pacific. He told me when they arrived in Vancouver, British Columbia, he had no trouble getting the men off the old collier-cum-troopship, but it was a different story when he had to herd them onto the Canadian Pacific to cross Canada. Every time the train stopped for water or fuel, the men would jump off and run like hell. Some they would catch, but most got away. Realizing he would arrive in France without any men if he didn't do something drastic, he reluctantly had them locked into the cars, where they lived like cattle till they reached the east coast. Then, when they saw the ocean again, they went berserk. Trying to get them onto another ship, while the memory of the pitching Pacific was still vivid in their minds, was a nightmare beyond belief. He said, somehow, they finally got to the Front where they had the back-breaking job of digging Allied trenches and graves.

When I looked at him again, he was staring at me, or rather through me, and he said in a sad, tired voice, "I thought I had seen all that man could do to man…how wrong I was!"

He stood up, his back bowed, his shoulders drooping, and I hesitantly went over and gave him a hug.

"Daddy, it's all over. We'll never let it happen again, *EVER!*" I was so young and so sure, and he looked so old, and so sad.

In a world gone completely mad, it didn't seem incongruous that our enemies had now became our allies!

The seven paratroopers, realizing they were outnumbered, but, surprisingly, in control of the camp, had enlisted the help of the Japanese guards to protect us from possible attack from the Chinese Communists who surrounded us. Needless to say, Gold Tooth was not one of their number.

It must have been two days after "liberation", when I was down at the main gates inhaling the intoxication of freedom, that four Chinese horsemen came riding slowly up to the camp. As they alit, Rob Connors, a very recently appointed member of our new Camp Police Force, and a Jap guard challenged them. The challenge abruptly turned into a cheer when two of the Chinese turned into Laurie Tipton and Arthur Hummel, the escapees of the previous year! With recognition came an ear-splitting war-whoop that rang all through the camp, and before you could spit, noisy crowds of well wishers gathered from all over. It was an unforgettable re-union, and as the day progressed, the plotting and planning of the breakout, and the miraculous appearance of the medication and drugs, all came to light.

It turned out that the escape in June of '44 hadn't been an impromptu affair, but very well orchestrated, and a necessity in more ways than one.

Surprisingly, the first order of business after Arthur and Tip got over the wall was to convince the Nationalist guerrillas on the outside *not* to try and rescue us and have us all air-lifted to Kunming! The select few who were in secret contact with the Chinese had tried to convince them that an airlift would be disastrous, as there were too many elderly and ill people, pregnant women, and tiny children, who could not face the hardships of trekking out to an airfield even if the guerrillas could secure the area. The second order of business was to contact Kunming and request a medical supply drop.

I guess that was the beginning of Arthur Hummel's diplomatic career, as they were successful on both counts. They didn't have time to celebrate though, as they soon learned they were in a very unenviable position: the Nationalist guerilla army they had linked up with, under General Wang Yu-min, was completely surrounded by Japanese forces, Chinese puppet forces under Japanese control, and Chinese Communists. For the medical supply drop to be successful, it was going to have to be made with almost pinpoint precision, and after the drop, the crates would have to be retrieved without alerting any of the opposing forces.

Somehow, the sortie was carried out without any casualties, but the drama had just begun. Now came the challenge of getting Allied medical supplies into a Jap prison camp without incurring the suspicion of King Kong and Gold Tooth! The problem appeared insurmountable, and in desperation, Tip and Art sent a note by Chinese courier to Mr. Egger, the Swiss consul and International Red Cross representative in Tsingtao. The note said that four unmarked crates of medical supplies would be left with Egger in the early dawn hours of the following day, and that it was left to him to find a way to get them into the camp.

Egger was a timid little businessman who had been pressed into consular service by an act of war. Although he had made many visits to Weihsien to check on our welfare, the Japanese treated him with distrust, and we were unable to give him any messages that weren't first approved by our captors. It soon became evident that, even if he had found anything amiss, he had little or no authority to change our circumstances. His was a token position, and as such, he never thought he would ever be called upon to show extreme cunning and courage under enemy fire. But that was just what Hummel and Tipton were expecting of him.

If anyone knew how badly we needed medical supplies, Egger did. He also knew that the only way he could get them into the camp was through the main gates with a signed manifest from the Japanese authorities in Tsingtao. After mulling over the situation for while, inspiration hit him, and he had his Swiss secretary go into the city and purchase all the antacid, aspirin, cough syrup and bandages she could round up. Taking them, item by item, he had her type up a manifest, leaving many lines between each entry, then, armed with this document, he went to the Japanese consulate requesting their approval. After an interminable wait outside the consul's office, where his mind conjured up all sorts of harrowing situations, the paperwork was finally returned to him with the coveted "chop" on it.

Racing back to his office, he had his still bewildered secretary fill in all the blank lines with the names of the supplies in the unmarked crates. It was a stroke of genius!

The following day, when he arrived in Weihsien with his precious cargo, he had to face King Kong and Gold Tooth. His queasy stomach tied in knots once more as they went meticulously through the entire contents of the crates. Although he couldn't understand their comments, it was obvious they were completely baffled how Allied medical supplies could be sanctioned by Japanese consular authorities, and the tone of their remarks made his skin creep. He kept waiting for someone to pick up the phone and call Tsingtao, but it never happened, and finally, cussing under his breath, King Kong pounded his "chop" on the paperwork and allowed the crates to be taken to the hospital.

I'll never forget Margo's surprise when I repeated the story to her.

The next day, she was the one who dropped the bomb on me. I was sleeping in that morning; we didn't have roll-call any more, and

I felt positively wicked as I snuggled back under the covers and watched her leave for her early shift. I'd barely fallen back to sleep, when she came rushing into the cell. Both Ursula and I sat up with a start.

"What's up?" we said in unison.

"I'm leaving tomorrow!"

"What?!"

"That's right. Tomorrow. Captain Casey says all war-brides must be ready to leave tomorrow morning. There's a troopship leaving Shanghai for the States before the week's up and we have to be on it.

Part of me was happy for her, and part of me was dying inside. It was 1941 all over again, and the thought of losing her was more than I could bear. I knew she had mixed emotions too, but it wasn't until late in the evening, after we'd helped her pack her few precious mementos, and the three of us were talking together for possibly the last time in years, that she bared her soul.

"I don't know if Jack's alive or dead. I haven't got a buck to my name. I'm going to a strange country where I don't know a soul. And I'm scared to death!"

It wasn't hard to put myself in her shoes. Supposing Jack wasn't at San Francisco to meet her? I didn't want to think of that one…I heard her tossing and turning all night long, and the next morning when she got up, I could see she was running on raw nerve alone.

To add to the gloom of the day, it was raining. The Chinese say it's nature's way of sympathizing with man and call rain "the tears of heaven".

We'd just grabbed a hurried breakfast and were entering our compound, when we were almost knocked over by an OSS officer. "Ah, there you are Mrs. Bishop," he said, relief in his voice, "the truck taking all war-brides to Weihsien station is leaving in thirty minutes—hope you're ready!"

"Ready as I'll ever be," she said, managing a wan smile.

Twenty minutes later, following her out of the cell for the last time, I noticed she had left the "SEMPER FI" poster on the wall; it had been half-devoured by creepy-crawlies that had roamed through the flaking plaster. She left her cot, of course; the canvas had broken on it long ago, and like Ursula's and mine, it barely held her weight when she lay on it. But most of all, she was leaving *us* behind.

When we got to the main gate, things started to move very fast; one moment we were helping Margo up onto the back of the big troop truck with its flapping canvas cover, and the next moment she was gone. The wheels spun for a minute in the slimy mud on Main Street, then they got traction, and the old vehicle waddled out of the gates.

I ran behind it waving for a minute or two, but the sheets of rain were merciless, and I turned back and followed the others, bereft as I, into the gloomy camp.

Mother was standing outside her cell, where she had clung to Margo minutes earlier. She didn't seem to know it was raining. She was oblivious to everything, and I was loath to go up and break the spell. Finally, when I saw her getting drenched to the skin, I said, "Mother, you'll catch your death," and led her gently indoors. I didn't see Dad. He might have been there in the shadows, but I didn't see him. All I saw was the look on Mother's face, and I knew her heart must be breaking like mine.

When I eventually went into our cell, Ursula was standing looking at Margo's bed with a numb expression on her lovely face. She turned to me, and I put my arms around her, and we just stood there in a soggy hug, too full of emotion to speak.

When the rain cleared up, I went for a walk. I had to get out of the cell, as everywhere I looked I could see Margo, and as lonely as I felt, I knew it couldn't touch on what she must be going through. I started to walk fast; I guess I was just about running, as Lisa called after me, when I turned down Rocky Road, "Hey Bobby, what's your hurry?!"

I spun around at the sound of my name.

"I'll join you," she said, catching up with me, then, noticing my tear-streaked face, added, "What's up?"

"Margo just left...and I feel there's a hole inside that nothing can fill."

She frowned for a moment, then her eyes twinkled, and she said slowly, "Yeah, I seem to remember—'You don't stop loving other people just because you've lost someone'."

I had to smile; she was dishing it back to me, and I loved her for it. "Thanks," I said simply, and after a while, we slipped into lighter subjects, and I found myself telling her about my plan to make clothes out of parachutes.

"You're too late, at least today. They've been taken out to the roll-call field and draped over the walls and benches to make it festive for the Victory Dance tomorrow."

"Who says?"

"Captain Casey. Have you met him?"

"No, but I sure have *heard* him!"

"Yes, he does like that loudspeaker of his, doesn't he?"

Just then Pete Fox came up with a face as long as a foot.

"What's eating you?" Lisa asked.

"The same thing that's eating me, I expect," I said smiling. "You miss her, Pete, don't you?"

"Sure do! Hope everything goes right for her for a change. She deserves it."

"She'll be okay, Peter—I know it," I said, trying to keep the doubt out of my voice.

Changing the subject abruptly, he asked, "Are you going to be off tomorrow?"

"Yes, they're rescheduling our shifts."

"How about Urs?"

"I don't know. Why?"

"They need a whole crew to bake a batch of chocolate cake for the Victory Dance tomorrow night."

"Chocolate! Where the blazes did they get chocolate for cakes?"

"There was cocoa in one of those supply drums."

"How about eggs...and sugar?"

"We've got hundreds of eggs, and gobs of sugar. Believe me, we've got *everything* to make chocolate cake, except a crew!"

"I'll be your first volunteer!" Lisa said.

"Thanks," then turning to me, he added, "think you can round up Ursula, Bea, and Lettie, and maybe Claire and Tess...?"

"How many do you really need?" I asked.

"At least eight—ten would be better."

"We'll get 'em! What time and where?"

"Sun-up at Number Two Kitchen. The bakers want the cakes baked before they put the bread in the ovens."

"That might be a little tough, but I think chocolate cake's enough of a incentive to get most of them up at that hour."

Then the logistics hit me, and I asked, "What the heck are we going to mix them in? Do you realize how much cake we'll have to make for fourteen hundred people?!"

"Oh, they're bringing over an old clawfoot bathtub from the Commandant's quarters. You're to mix the batter in that."

"Sure we are!" I said with a grin.

We had a lot of fun rounding up the crew. Not a girl turned the assignment down. Bea's comment, when we asked her, was, "Sure, I'll do it if they'll let me lick the spoon."

"What spoon? We're going to use paddles!"

The next morning, while the rest of the camp was still asleep, our cake-baking crew assembled in Number Two Kitchen. The first thing we were handed was forty-dozen eggs to beat—without a single egg-beater between us. To the ten-girl crew, that came out to over forty eggs a piece, to be beaten with a fork in a long loaf pan! Although we didn't attempt to beat all forty at once, the job was still arm-aching beyond belief.

While we were beating our hearts out, Pete and his team of men were measuring and dumping flour, sugar, cocoa, and baking powder into the ancient bathtub. The monstrous old clawfoot had been raised up on blocks, so that the work would be less backbreaking, but it was still as awkward as the devil.

After the dry ingredients had been dumped and thoroughly paddle-mixed, we made wells in the mixture and dropped the beaten eggs into them, then added powdered milk liquids, and peanut oil, and stirred like crazy.

We tried everything, from ten girls running around the tub with paddles swishing to standing still and just stirring in one place. Whatever we did, we must have done it right, because the batter turned out beautifully smooth, and we were soon filling the loaf pans.

"Hey, hurry it up! The ovens are ready, and we have to bake those dumb cakes before we can put the bread in!" shouted one of the bakery crew coming into the compound.

"We're going as fast as we can," Pete yelled back, as we went on dipping and filling pans, cake batter splattering up to our elbows.

I looked at the tub, and a thought struck me. "I know we haven't had a bath in ages, but when we do, how do we empty the tub?"

"We pull the plug!" someone said.

"*S-o-o-o-o?*"

Chalk one more up to inspiration. We laid an old one-by-eight piece of shelving we found in the kitchen under the bath, loaded it with pans, end to end, pulled the plug, and slowly pushed the "conveyor belt" along. It took about ten seconds to fill a pan, and as the first plank went through, we found a second and followed with it, while we loaded the first one back up with empty pans. The job was done in minutes, and we all stood back and had a good laugh, as the last pan was filled.

"Say *cheese!*" someone said over my shoulder, and turning, I saw a movie camera grinding away.

"How long have you been filming this operation?" I asked with a giggle.

"O-o-o-oh, from when you broads started chasing each other around the tub," the cameraman drawled.

While the cakes were baking in the big brick ovens, five B-29s flew over from Saipan, and figuring the beautifully draped roll-call field was intended for a drop zone, they obliged us by unloading their cargo right over the field!

It was Day One all over again, but this time we had nowhere to run!

The pinpoint drop was very accurate, with only a few missing the roll-call field, but the ones that did, dropped through cell roofs and into compounds, crushing everything they hit.

Pandemonium reigned. Mothers screamed for their children. Children wailed for their mothers. And the men swore in frustration.

"I can't believe I've survived four years of war, only to be killed by kindness," someone said in exasperation.

After the panic had subsided, we found that no one had been hurt, and the three drums that had crashed through cell roofs had done surprisingly little damage. The only really peeved people were the members of the Victory Dance Committee: they had to call in an extra work detail to clean up the mess and help them roll the drums away to a distribution area.

Nothing spoiled the Victory Dinner-Dance though. Major Staiger and his paratroopers, along with Captain Casey and his men, traded their C and K Rations for our stew and fresh bread, insisting it tasted "just like home cookin'", and the meal was topped off with fruit and chocolate cake, two treats we hadn't had in over three years.

After the meal, what was left of our fabulous dance band played up a storm for us. Roy, Deirdre, and their little son had left with Margo and the war-brides. The rest of the band was leaving for the States the next day; this was their last night in camp, and they were *celebrating!* Late in the evening, Captain Georgia, one of the new men replacing the OSS, took over Smitty's bass and introduced us to the boogie beat. We'd heard a little of it over the PA system, but nothing like this! It was contagious, and before we knew it, the whole camp was jiving!

17

PAWNS OF WAR

After the Victory Dance, the camp started to empty fast. Most of the American missionaries and business people had left for the States along with the remainder of the band; their British counterparts had also shipped out, and within a week, all the Italians had gone back to their homes in Shanghai. I wept no tears when Claire left for New Zealand, although I had to admit everyone needs a Claire in their lives just to keep them on their toes. It was different with Lisa though: when she left for England, I felt she'd taken a piece of me with her, and I wandered around lost for days with no one to turn to.

Then, it was Gladys's turn to put her feeble little friend onto a bus to the train station, on the first leg of a long trip to Australia, and hopefully, a reunion with her family down-under.

Gladys had smiled all the while, checking to see her little friend had her passport and her few precious belongings, then she'd handed her over, with a big hug and kiss, to a man in the truck who promised to see she got safely on the train. She laughed and smiled to keep her friend's spirits up, but when the truck rolled out of the camp, she let out a filthy stream of cuss words. Remembering the last time I'd heard her swear, I knew she was darn close to tears.

I couldn't think of anything to say as we walked slowly back to the cellblock, but by the time we got there, she was her old self again. She had spoken several times in the past of a kid brother in India whom she loved dearly. She hadn't seen or heard from him in years though, and didn't know if he was alive or dead. All I could think of was, *There must be someone in the world for Gladys to care for. Right now she has no man, no home, and no job waiting for her. She has nothing!* Then I looked at her, and she was cutting up once more, and I thought, *So what, she'll never let it get her down!*

I was right. After that, she slipped into the hole Lisa had left, and as each one of my friends took off for parts unknown and I felt the chasm getting wider and wider, she'd say, "Don't worry, honey, it'll be your turn next. You'll see, it'll be your turn next!"

I wanted to believe her, but the days dragged on till finally the only members left of our old gang were Guy and myself; even René had left, sobbing, for French Equatorial Africa.

Chad and Rob, the troubadours from Shanghai, Pete and Mike, Bea and Lettie, and a handful of Tientsin-ites were still around. They had been part of Ursula's group of friends, and now Guy and I gravitated over to them. Some were quite a bit older than we were, but somehow in the last few weeks, we'd grown up fast, and now there didn't seem to be any age difference to speak of.

I remember one evening all of us sitting around discussing what we would do with our futures. The guys made me envious; most of them were planning to travel, hoping to sign on with any tub that plied the seven seas. Girls couldn't do that. Pete was going to offer his services to UNRRA as an interpreter; I found myself kicking my butt around the block for not learning how to read and write Chinese; I could speak it pretty well, but without being able to read or write, I knew I could never get a job as an interpreter. Oh, well, there was always shorthand and typing and a secretary's job in the wings…

It was after one such interesting evening, following a couple of shots of good American whiskey, that I had a weird dream. It was the first time I recalled dreaming in color—something someone had once told me was impossible. I was on the roll-call field, only it was huge and looked strangely like the playing field at North Hollywood Junior High. There were rows and rows of seats and benches and a podium. The Commandant was there with a group of dignitaries, and in the distance, I could see grey walls, electrified wire, and forbidding guard towers.

I was in line, in cap and gown, and suddenly, I heard Elgar's *Pomp and Circumstance*, and I started to tingle. I looked down at my legs. My darn robe had shrunk up over my knees, and I tried desperately to yank it down, the goose-bumps on my legs making me look like a dumb plucked chicken.

I don't remember getting a diploma. I do remember hearing the Commandant saying, in his precise English, with a slight American twang, "Goodbye, my friends, it wasn't a bowl of cherries, but at least we survived." And strangely, in my dream I realized, it had been a matter of survival for him too. Then, the world got horribly dark, and Guy was there saying, "It's over. It's *all* over! Goodbye…I *will* forget you. I *must!*" And I was looking into his pale blue eyes, feeling the strength of his taut, hard body, like the first day we had met. I shuddered as an icy wind hit us, and looking up, I saw a colossal, black mushroom with a seething red stem, rising higher and higher into the sky, blotting out the sun. Then someone yelled, *"The Japs have the atomic bomb!"* and I woke up screaming…with a cold wind rushing in through the open cell door.

"What's up?" Ursula shouted.

"Nothing," I said, still shaking, "Just a nightmare." And I got up, closed the door, and stumbled back to bed.

Another week passed, and the day was dry for a change. Hot air swirled around the camp. I knew there were things I had to do: mending, cleaning, and umpteen menial little chores, but I couldn't work up the energy; I was still brooding over an incident that happened the previous night; in fact, it was hounding me.

I looked at the wall calendar I had started to keep on "Liberation Day" and realized it had been a full month since the Americans had taken over the running of the camp, the U.S. Army having taken over after the OSS left. Living conditions hadn't changed much in that time, but the food was a lot better, and we never went hungry any more. Clothing was still in short supply, unless one opted for GI fatigues, which were better than the clothes we already had, but about as sexy as hopsacks. I had been able to make a full-skirted dress out of a red parachute, but the job had turned out to be very time-consuming, as the fabric frayed faster than I could work it. There was more room in the cell now that Margo wasn't there, but I would rather have been cramped and had her company. Ursula was okay, but she was totally surrounded by admiring Yanks, much to faithful Alex's disgust, and I didn't get to have two words with her on any given day. And Dad and Mother were busy making plans for the future, now that there was one.

Then, my mind flashed back to the incident of the previous evening, and I thought, *Damn Lieutenant Newman!* He was one of the new army contingent. I really enjoyed his company and had spent several delightful evenings with him, kidding and joking and catching up on news from all over the world. It was as though I could never hear enough, and I hungered for every scrap he could remember. But suddenly, the evening before, our relationship did a complete flip, and I found myself having to fight off a physical attack that left me hurt and stunned.

"You little bitch!" he shouted at me, "You lead a guy on, tease and flirt, then act shocked when he gets ideas. Damn you!" He slid off the low compound wall we'd been sitting on, and stormed off without looking back. I was crushed. I wasn't prepared for anything so crude, and I felt my face turn scarlet with embarrassment.

"Your convent upbringing has made you a prisoner more than these grey walls ever could," a voice said from the shadows, and I recognized it was Mike, Pete's cynical brother and ex-leader of the now-defunct "Suicide Squad". And he wasn't the least bit embarrassed that he had been eavesdropping on a very personal situation.

"*Shut up,* you clod!" I shouted, and dashed off to the privacy of our cell and one of the longest, most tortuous nights of my life. It didn't help matters much the following morning when a girl ahead of me in the chowline said she had taken a tumble with Newman the previous night in a pile of supply parachutes on the ballfield.

"Okay," I said to myself, "so much for knights in shining armor..."

I was still smarting from the hurtful memory when Pete came up with a great big grin, and said, "There's an empty supply truck returning to Weihsien in about twenty minutes, and a group of us are going to town...want to come?"

I knew a trip to the city would do me good, and said, "Be ready in a jiffy!"

As I touched up my makeup and combed my hair, I watched Pete through the cell window. He was standing in fatigues, smoking an American cigarette, looking the epitome of a regular GI; the only things missing were a patch and rating on his sleeve. A few minutes later, I slipped out of the cell, and the two of us moseyed up Main Street to the small group that had already gathered at the assembly hall compound: Rob, Chad, Norm, and a vivacious Lettie.

The truck turned out to be a jolting monster with slatted side panels for hauling produce. It smelled as if it had hauled more than vegetables in its time, and I unwisely commented on the fact.

"Think you're right," Rob said. "Isn't this the one they hauled that old camel in a year or so ago?" he asked Pete.

"You mean that green job that was so rotten it bubbled and heaved and came back to life?" Chad said, joining in, watching Lettie and me wince.

I couldn't help remembering that slimy carcass; its fly-covered flesh had rumbled by me one hot summer afternoon and I tried not to think what K-2 would do to disguise the meat. I recall we ate it though, and none of us got ill.

"That's the one," Rob was saying. "Remember, we ground it all up into hamburger, even the eyeballs, and everyone *loved* it!"

"Stuff it!" Norm said, with disgust. He enjoyed eating, and I knew his stomach was churning like mine.

The rest of the guys laughed, joking and swapping tall tales about

Gold Tooth and the perennial hassle for supplies. I half-listened, but my eyes were taking in the colorful scenery. The children playing in the dirt by the roadside, their little split-ass pants exposing cute little round bottoms, while milling peasants hauled their wares on their shoulders, or in two-wheeled carts.

As we approached the old walled city, the crowds got thicker and tighter, and the mood of the people started to change. The truck rattled on, barely doing five miles an hour, and I stood up to look over the top of its antique cab.

"Hey, we've just about stopped! What's happening?"

"See those three people in the middle of the crowd with their hands tied behind their backs?" Pete said, joining me.

"Where?" I said.

"There!" Pete replied, pointing them out. "See, someone just threw a rock at one of them!"

"Oh, yeah! One's a girl with long braids. I wonder what they've done."

"Probably nothing. They're Communists and they're being taken to be executed."

"Oh, n-o-o-o..."

I didn't get to say any more, as the crowd started to press in closer and yell and hurl more rocks at them. I felt my stomach give a lurch, and simultaneously, there were three bursts of gunfire, and the figures crumpled and fell, their heads demolished by dum-dum bullets, their brains splattering the violent crowd.

I rushed to the side of the truck and wretched into the street. The others, who had been laughing loudly and missed the short bursts of fire, looked at me, and then Pete, and asked what had happened.

"Nothing. The jolting got to her," he said, as the truck driver wisely turned, and we rolled through a wide gate in the city wall and continued on into town.

When I stopped heaving, Pete came and sat beside me and said softly, "It was much more merciful that way. If the soldiers hadn't done it, they would've been torn to bits by the mob." I knew he was right, but nothing could erase the horror from my mind.

The jarring ride took us deeper into the city, and before long, the cobbled road got narrower, and the air became filled with the smell of pungent cooking. Finally, we stopped in front of an old Chinese restaurant.

"We're here!" Rob shouted, jumping off. The rest of the men followed, turning to help Lettie and me down.

Pete went up and paid the driver, who, seeming more than happy with the fare, asked if he could take us back after the meal; it was just as well he did, as no one had thought about our three mile return trip to camp. After some friendly haggling, arrangements were made, and we all went inside.

The interior was dark and steamy. Chinese men were tipping rice bowls to their lips and shoveling food in with bamboo chopsticks. As we watched them and savored the luscious smells from the kitchen, a beaming, rotund little man came up and led us to a round table with a slightly soiled white tablecloth. He helped us pull up a couple of additional chairs, then asked if we would like a menu. There was a chorus of, "No, just bring on the *chiao tzes!*" and they ordered a couple of dozen apiece. Twelve would have been a meal at any other time, but everyone except me was ravenous, the aroma of the food at the other tables whetting appetites even more.

It took quite a while to steam the huge order, so we passed the time sipping hot tea and cold beer, and discussing the rotten luck that kept us in the camp. As I couldn't get the picture of the bloody execution out of my mind, I sat quietly listening in a half-hearted way while the conversation rambled on. It seemed to me that Pete was the only one who had a handle on the situation, and I heard him saying, "I know this is hard to believe, but the Japanese in Tientsin haven't surrendered yet. On top of that, the Communists are in control of Shantung Province, with only Tsingtao and Weihsien in Nationalist hands."

I leapt into the conversation at the mention of Tientsin, "What do you mean, the Japs *haven't surrendered in Tientsin?"*

"That's right. They're still living in our homes. Why do you think we haven't been shipped out before now?"

"I thought it was because the Commies kept blowing up the airstrip," I said lamely.

"Well, that's one of the reasons. But the real one is that there is nowhere to send us, even if they could fly us out."

"Well, I hear fifty-thousand marines are landing in North China," Rob said with a grin, "and if that doesn't put an end to all this mess, nothing will."

I caught myself smiling in spite of myself. "Natch! Whenever something has to be done...*bring on the MARINES!*"

"Oh, Lord, Margo really got to you, didn't she?" Pete said with his crazy little giggle. Everyone was still laughing when the platters of pork-filled dumplings were placed on the table.

There were calls for more beer, tea, and *bai gar*, and as dishes and chopsticks were passed around and food mercilessly scooped off the huge platters, I found my appetite leaving me completely, and in its place the ugly mob scene replaying itself, over and over again.

God, why couldn't I get it out of my mind?

As I watched Norm pop a whole *chiao-tze* in his mouth, I saw his head explode, and I started to jump up and run out of the room. Pete gently took my arm and sat me back down. "Come on, I ordered some for you; try and eat, you'll feel better."

I smiled wanly, but it was no good.

Lettie got stuck after eating seven of her *chiao-tzes,* and Norm asked if he could finish them for her. After he ate hers, he looked at my untouched plate with melting eyes, and I shoved it over to him, saying, "Go for it!"

"I've been counting," Rob said, "and you've had close to forty of those darn things. If you finish Bobby's, that'll make it sixty! Where the hell are you putting them?"

"I'm still hungry," Norm said, grabbing the soy sauce, "And I'm making up for almost three years of being hungry. So, keep counting, I don't give a damn!"

It was a numb, drowsy crew that scrambled up into the old truck for the ride back to camp. I kept my eyes shut as we jolted along, hoping to miss seeing where the execution had taken place.

*****

A week later, the last internees leaving for points all over—except for those returning to Tientsin—pulled out of Weihsien station, and to be sure no one else would follow them, the railroad tracks were blown up between Weihsien and Tsingtao! Both sides claimed responsibility for the act, as though it were some clever achievement.

I couldn't see any reasoning behind it, until I tried to think like a Chinese. Then it dawned on me: if the rest of us internees couldn't leave, we would have to be protected by the Americans, and the fallout would be that the Nationalists would also be being protected by the Americans. Pretty smart!

I realized that scenario didn't apply to the Communists. They would want us to leave, so they could pick off the Nationalists at will; why the heck were they doing anything to stop us making it out of the camp? Finding I was back to square one, I turned to Dad.

"The Communists are trying to show they're in control and are fighting for a seat at the peace parleys," he explained. "They insist on being included in any surrender deals."

"And how do the Americans feel about it?"

"How do any of us feel about Communism?"

He saw I didn't like his response, so he smiled and said, "All is not as dark as it seems."

"Meaning…?"

"Well, if one can believe the latest rumor, the rail lines have just been re-opened to Tientsin, and we should be out of here in a day or two."

"I don't believe it! What about the Japs in Tientsin?" Then I asked, "Will we get our old home back? Or will they send us to Chinwangtao?" I couldn't contain my excitement.

"Hold it! You can forget Chinwangtao. A British colonel briefed us yesterday: there are no more Treaty Ports. The Kailan is still operating, and we're definitely going back to the house on Edinburgh Road. As for the Nips, I don't know what their status is; but, damn it all, we should put *them* all into prison camps like *they* did us!"

I found myself nodding in agreement. "I wonder what the house is going to be like, and if the Japs took care of it. Margo said Mr. Araki and his family took over our old place in Chinwangtao. Bet they kept it immaculate."

"Wonder what's going to happen to that poor bugger and his family now," Dad said, with a faraway look, "...or all the decent Japanese civilians. God, war has a way of making our enemies friends, and our friends enemies!"

Two days later, we were still in camp. The rails to the north had been blown up again in several places, and as September came to a close, it was obvious that the only way we were going to get out was by plane, between running attacks on the local airfield. On the morning of October the sixth, we learned that the Japanese forces in the Tientsin area had surrendered to the United States Marines and we could finally go home. After what the Japs had done to the Fourth Marines in China in '41, it was poetic justice.

I was still musing over this happy news item, when I turned into our cellblock and saw unsinkable Gladys awash in tears.

That can't be Gladys! I thought. But it was.

A young officer was standing in front of her, his back to me, and he was moving uncomfortably from foot to foot and trying to speak, but she wouldn't stop bawling. She looked so pathetic I wanted to hug her, but I knew that would only make matters worse, so I tried to sound casual, and asked what had happened—dreading to hear her response.

The officer, obviously British by his khaki shorts and knee socks, said in a halting voice, "I don't know why she's crying. I'm her brother, and I've come to take her home." The voice was strangely familiar, and as he turned, I let out a shriek. It was Cosmo, the piss-pouring bachelor who'd slipped out of Chinwangtao without a trace!

I shouted, *"Daddy! Mummy! COSMO'S here!"*

Gladys looked at me as though I were nuts. "Why do you call him Cosmo? He's my brother, Alge—" She never got the name out as Cosmo slapped his hand over her mouth and said, *"C-o-s-*

m-o", very softly, slowly, and deliberately.

She looked from him to me, and then to approaching Dad, and said, demurely, "Yes, Cosmo."

"Where the hell have you been, and what the hell are you doing here?" Dad asked, clapping him on the back.

"I've come for my sister, Gladys, you old reprobate, you. And if I'd known she was in the same camp as you, I'd have gotten here sooner!"

"Gladys, you never told me your brother's name was Cosmo," Dad said, perplexed.

She started to say something, then looked at Cosmo's frown, and said, "Didn't I? I thought I did."

"You got out of Chinwangtao just in time," Dad said, "the fireworks really started after you left."

"Really?" I saw his eyebrow arch, moustache twitch, and monocle flash—it was the old Cosmo all over again. "Yes," Dad was saying, "we kept losing tonnage, and the Nips climbed all over me thinking I was privy to the show. I was sure glad when the girls spotted a sub out in the bay. Guess the Yanks or someone were up there canceling out our collaboration. God, those months were a nightmare!"

"So you thought the Yanks were sinking the colliers?" Cosmo said, "You know I *can* do more than piss into champagne."

I looked at him, stunned, and then at Dad whose face was a study. "Come again," he said quietly.

"I didn't leave Chinwangtao. I slipped into the native city and lined up a few coal coolies, and we scrounged up some dynamite from the old granite quarry. I showed them how to place the charges in the holds while they were coaling the ships. It was tricky, especially getting them to set the timing devices, but they caught on real fast."

"But what about the sub we saw?" I asked.

"That was Japanese. I heard about it from the coolies. I guess the Japs figured the only way the ships could've been sunk was by a sub—one of ours—and they were on the prowl. If they'd thought about it, they would have realized that the bay was far too shallow for effective submarine warfare."

"I'll be damned!" Dad said slowly, putting his arm around Cosmo's shoulder. "Cosmo, you old son-of-a-bitch, we all owe you a debt of gratitude. All I can say is, thank you!"

Cosmo started to look uncomfortable, and cleared his throat noisily several times, then he said gruffly, "Come on Gladys, grab your things if you're coming with me, we have to leave *now!* The guys won't wait. They allowed me to sneak aboard when I told them my mission. We're due back in Kunming before nightfall."

"Grab *what* things? I don't have anything here I want, except my passport." And she ran into the cell, coming out with a couple of items she stuffed in a pocket, then she grabbed Cosmo's arm and started to say, "Hey, Alge—!" She corrected herself. "Hey, *Cosmo, let's g-o-o-o!*" And she flounced out of the compound, giving us one of her wicked winks and shouting over her shoulder, "Tell all my friends my *baby brother* came to take me home!" Then she slapped Cosmo across the butt and sashayed down Main Street to the waiting military truck.

"I'll miss Glad-Eyes," Dad said softly, "she was one hell of a lady."

After that, the days seemed to dragged interminably. Even with movies almost nightly in the assembly hall, and lots of late magazines to read, I couldn't get my mind off returning to the world outside and becoming a part of it again. As there were only a handful of us left, all the kitchens had been shut down except for Number Two. Even the hospital kitchen, where I had worked, was no longer in operation. There was no need for it: all the ill, infirm, and little children that it had fed were gone.

We were the only ones left in our cellblock except for the Hattons. Jock and Emma and their three bubbling offspring had said goodbye many weeks ago. And the Tucks, Collishaws, and Beruldsens had hugged us and wished us well as they left the camp behind. Now I found myself trying to spend as little time as possible in the compound, as the Hattons never stopped complaining about everyone and everything at the top of their very loud voices.

I couldn't help wondering why they hadn't gone home to the

States, or back to their mission, like all the others. It was strange, and I said so one evening to Guy and Rob as we waited in the assembly hall for a movie to start.

"What's strange about it?" Rob asked. "I bet they never did belong to any *bona fide* mission." And he started to sing out with a wicked grin—

> *"My father was a good missionary,*
> *He saved little girlies from sin.*
> *He could sell you a blonde for a shillin',*
> *Lordy, how the money rolled in!"*

"You'll never change, will you?" I said, laughing.

"Why should he?" Guy said. "He knows more about this crazy country than you ever will."

"What brought that on?" Rob asked, sensing an undercurrent to Guy's words.

"Oh, some unfinished business. Bobby knows what I'm talking about."

"I do?"

"The bet," Guy replied, "remember the bet, about the rich getting richer and the poor getting poorer?"

Rob, in a playful mood, couldn't help himself, and sang out, *"In the mean time, in between time, don't we have fun!"*

"Hey, Rob, this is serious," Guy said.

"It doesn't sound like it."

"Well, you've never locked horns with Bobby then. On our way to camp she made a bet with me. She called it the 'Grand Experiment'. She contended that, although we were all coming here with what we could carry in one suitcase and a few bucks in our pocket, when it was all over the rich..."

"...would be richer and the poor would be poorer," Rob interrupted soberly, adding, "I think she's right!"

"I don't see it. I might be dense, but I don't see it!" It was also easy to see Guy was wishing he hadn't brought the bet up, at least not in front of Rob.

"Hey, come to think of it, you're a Commie, aren't you?" Rob said without guile.

"More like *was*, I think," I said slowly, looking into Guy's troubled face.

"What makes you think I've changed my thinking?"

"Oh, something you said about my Dad being a capitalist you could like," I said, smiling.

"That doesn't change a thing."

"Really?"

I thought of the fight that Chilton, Dad, and the port engineer had put up to save the jobs of thousands of coal coolies when the head office wanted to install mechanical handling. And how those same coolies had taken their lives in their hands, not to mention jeopardizing their precious jobs, by placing dynamite in the holds of the colliers to frustrate the Japanese war effort. They were simple souls, and that was their way of repaying us for going to battle for them and their families.

I told Guy Cosmo's story, keeping my voice calm and level. I ended with, "The coolies knew we couldn't do anything to stop the Japs, so they did it for us. Does that sound like exploited people who despise us?"

"Maybe they hated the Japs more."

That's when I lost it.

"Okay, have it your way!" I exploded.

"What's that got to do with the rich getting richer?" Rob asked, perplexed.

"Everything...and nothing. Wealth isn't just measured in currency. It comes with respect...and friendship, especially from the Chinese people. You can call us imperialists, or capitalists, or whatever you like..." I could hear my voice rising, but I couldn't stop, "I'm fed up being accused of exploiting the Chinese. I don't excuse some of the early things we did, especially the Opium Wars, but my grandfather helped start the railroads in China against overwhelming court intrigue and opposition, and look at the millions of Chinese today who travel everywhere by train. My Dad worked for the Peking Syndicate Mines, and after I was born, the Kailan, and the Chinese fought to get jobs with both companies, as they took care of their workers and paid better than anything that China had to offer. *Dammit*, I refuse to apologize for our role in the Orient!" I knew I was shouting.

"Okay, okay! My family goes back as far as yours," Rob said with a smile, "and," he added thoughtfully, "I *do* see what you're driving at. And, if you think about it, our life in camp was something like the everyday life of the Chinese masses. We were starved, subjugated, and fed propaganda, but like them, we've survived. I can't believe I'm saying this, but I think I do feel richer for what I've been through."

"*That* makes you richer?" Guy's tone was incredulous. "I think you're just trying to help Bobby weasel out of her bet!"

"I'm *not* weaseling out of a bet. I'm not like you. I don't put a price tag on everything. To you wealth is spelt with a dollar sign, I equate it with gaining knowledge and understanding, along with bucks. And if we got nothing more out of our stay here, we have to admit we learned a hell of a lot, even if it was only how to get along together."

"Speak for yourself!" Guy sneered.

"There you go!" I said smugly, "You're just bearing out my hypothesis. You're class conscious. You've always thought yourself poor—ergo, *you're poor!*"

Rob grinned. "What did I hear about learning how to get along together?"

I gave him a friendly shove as the projector started to whirr and someone killed the lights.

While I was stewing over the interminable delay in leaving, Dad was trying to get news of Granny and the rest of his large family in London. When he finally heard, he was desolate. Everyone had been wiped out at a reunion just before VE Day, when the solid old house in Mill Hill had sustained a direct hit by a buzz bomb. He was inconsolable and kept mumbling, "There's nothing left... *nothing left!*"

Finally, Mother was able to reach him and remind him there was still one side of the family alive and well in the States.

"Guess I'm going to have to be a Yank whether I want to or not," he said sadly.

After that tragic incident, time crept by on a shaky treadmill going nowhere. I was ready to scream at the inactivity. Just when everyone's nerves were frayed to the limit and about to snap, we heard the outside world had been at the negotiating table, and we were finally given a hard-and-fast date for our departure: October 13th, 1945.

The night before we were to leave, we held one last dance in Number Two Kitchen.

I'd packed my few meager belongings that afternoon—laying out the GI gear I'd been issued to wear on the flight home the next day. I'd even been given socks and sneakers. I wondered how my feet would feel with decent shoes on.

That evening, I got into the red parachute dress and splashed my lips with a vibrant new lipstick one of the GI's had given me earlier in the week. I felt almost beautiful for the first time in ages, as I twirled around in the full skirt just to see it swish. "Goodbye Weihsien! Hello world!" I sang out, as I slammed the cell door behind me.

There seemed to be a smile on old K-2 when I waltzed in the door. The steamy windows, the banged up tables, the bow-legged trestles all added to the ambience, holding everyone in a gentle spell of friendship. A few army men were there, but I sensed they also felt that special mood, understanding what this last evening meant to us civilians. I'd hoped Guy would be there. We hadn't spoken since the night of the movie; he'd maintained an icy silence all through the evening and had let Rob walk me home afterwards.

We didn't have our wonderful dance band any more, so the music was canned. It was good, but it seemed to lack something I couldn't put my finger on.

When Norm came over and asked me for a dance, I realized sadly this would be the last evening we would dance together, and as the piece ended he said, "That music is okay, but it isn't *us!*"

"Your right! It *isn't*, is it?"

"Nope. We don't need it tonight. We need Rob and Chad and a bunch of our zany old pieces. Maybe the army will laugh at our taste in music, but I don't think there's a soul here who gives a damn."

As if on cue, Chad and Rob came in with their guitars, and after a hurried tune-up, broke into our old favorite rendition of *My Blue Heaven*. I still remember most of the numbers they played that night: *Cocktails for Two, Harbor Lights, Deep Purple*, and my favorite of all time, *Blue Moon*.

That was the dance Guy asked me for, and as we stepped out onto the floor, he put his arm around me and kissed my hair. It was so unlike him, I looked up in astonishment.

"I will get over you, you know," he said softly. "This isn't love. It hasn't ever been. It's infatuation. You never get over your first love, but you do recover from infatuation." He gave me a hard hug, and looking over my head, said, "You're the only person in the world who can turn my legs into putty, and make me want to hide when I see you come into a room. I'm crazy about you, and I loath you, all at the same time...but I *will* get over you. I *must!*"

The words were eerie. My nightmare was coming alive! I found myself willing the dream to stop. There mustn't be an atomic bomb. No red-stemmed mushroom...no terror.

The moment passed, and all I could think of was the three wasted years. How could we have been so dumb. We were so busy circling each other and fighting, we hadn't sorted out our true feelings. It would be different from now on.

I don't remember the rest of the evening, except that we danced every number in a happy whirl. At midnight, when Rob and Chad rang out the old life with *Auld Lang Syne*, everyone sang...and hugged...and cried, then sang some more, seemingly loath to start back to their cells and dorms for the last time.

Alex was kissing Ursula goodnight when Guy and I stepped into our compound. He held me close and kissed me. "One day I will see you, and my legs won't buckle, and I'll know it's over. And I'll tell you...and it won't hurt any more. Good night."

*****

The next morning, we climbed aboard an old C-47 that must've logged many more hours than it was ever intended to fly. I'd never been on a plane before, and I wasn't sure this was the one I wanted to be in on my maiden flight.

As always, I found myself focused on where I was going, not where I'd been, and I hardly noticed the people around me in the building excitement of the trip ahead.

Mother and Dad had been one of the first couples to board, and when Ursula and I finally clambered in, we saw them sitting on one of the few webbed sling seats, holding hands dreamily, lost in contemplation of yet another joyous homecoming.

How many times had they lost everything and had to start all over again? It had been quite a while since the last time. That had been the year I was born, eighteen years earlier. They survived that, and so did I. China had a unique way of taking everything, then giving it all back, full measure and brimming over. Was this to be one of the times?

I thought of Guy again, and the promise that lay ahead. He stirred feelings in me that I never knew existed. I had hoped he'd be on the plane with us going home, as he had been on that fateful train ride years earlier, but I hadn't even seen him in camp before we boarded the old bus that jolted us out to the airstrip.

Well, Tientsin was not the States; I wouldn't lose touch with Guy as I was sure I had with Dan.

Oh, God, I wanted to get home! The yen for all that was dear and familiar was almost more than I could bear. I couldn't help feeling that the war had changed more than just me.

Oh, Guy, where are you when I need you so?

I looked around at the tight, little clump of people, all talking excitedly, and wondered in horror if I'd spoken out loud!

"Come on girls, come up front with us," one of the crew said, showing Ursula and me into the cockpit, where the pilot was checking out the controls. He turned and gave us a smile and a thumbs up, then the plane coughed a few times and the props started to turn.

As I looked out the window at the handful of people on the ground moving back as the plane readied for take off, I repeated my happy challenge, "Goodbye Weihsien! Hello world!"

"Amen!" Ursula said.

"You gals been in camp with your folks?" the pilot asked.

"Yep, Mother and Dad are on the plane with us."

"You're lucky. The guy that left ahead of you for Kunming just learned his father's in Burma; he hasn't seen him in over four years. Sure hope he finds his old man."

My stomach gave a lurch.

"His name?" I asked abruptly.

"Guy Woodruff. Know him?"

EPILOGUE

I don't remember my "maiden flight". I could have been blindfolded for all I saw. Where excitement and anticipation had crowded my thoughts, there was now nothing but a bottomless well of self pity. Oh, sure, I should've been happy for Guy, but I was too busy wallowing in my own misery. I lost all sense of time, and the light background chatter of Ursula and the crew did nothing to ease my pain. Finally a voice broke into my self-imposed silence—"If Tientsin's your hometown, we've arrived."

It was the co-pilot speaking, and as I looked down on Tientsin I was amazed by its misty, sprawling size. Dropping down over the airport, details became sharper: I saw none of the ornate buildings, native carts, and jostling crowds I had expected, but instead, seas of endless macadam, stacks of supplies and fuel drums, and racing Jeeps scuttling around like mice in a maze.

This can't be Tientsin, I thought, bewildered.

The jolt of the plane as we touched down jarred me into the present, and when the doors were opened, the stink of black-top and high-octane fuel awakened me further. *"It doesn't even SMELL like Tientsin!"*

As trucks rolled up to the plane and the ex-internees were assisted aboard, Urs and I stood back and eyed the hundreds of marines, in khaki fatigues like us, scooting around in seemingly happy "make-work".

"Okay gals, it's your turn," the debarkation officer said with a grin as Ursula got off the plane and started to climb into the last truck. Suddenly a yell broke out over the airfield. *"DAMES!"* And as hundreds of pairs of eyes shot in our direction, the Jeeps wheeled around to a man and sped towards us. The officer, panicking, gave my butt an unceremonious boost up into the truck and shouted to the driver, "Go like hell! Get outta here, *now!*"

The truck was no match for the bouncing Jeeps that careened alongside, the marines hanging out whistling and shouting, *"Hub-ba! Hubba!"* Their exuberance was contagious and I laughed outright, all thought of my broken heart lost in the fun of the moment. Mother and Dad, sitting up next to the cab, were smiling broadly, and I heard Dad say, wistfully, "Oh, to be young again!"

The days that followed held nothing but surprises. The first happy one was a letter waiting from Margo, c/o the Kailan. In it she told of the hectic trip to the States on a troop carrier loaded with homeward bound marines. She tried to catch their festive mood, but, every time she thought of arriving in San Francisco, panic would set in. When the ship finally docked all the family members waiting on the pier for their loved ones were pushed back from the railings as a resplendent band marched up blaring *The Marine Hymn.*

While the ship was being secured the crew wished the war-brides good luck in their new homeland. Margo thanked them and nervously looked at the pier. The band was jubilant, playing and marking time in perfect formation.

She frowned. Even though she was distraught and apprehensive, she could see something was wrong with the front line. There was an odd-man-out at the end playing an invisible instrument. As she stared at him he broke into a wide grin and started to wave frantically.

It was Jack!

He'd been waiting in full uniform since sun-up for the ship's arrival, and when everyone was pushed back into the shadow of the warehouse, he ran around the end of the band and slipped into the front line making believe he was a piccolo player!

*****

A not so happy surprise came when we moved back into the house on Edinburgh Road and Mother and Dad went to the Swiss compound to redeem their precious belongings.

There were none.

The day after we were shipped to the prison camp the Japanese military raided the godowns and took every single Allied crate—some holding irreplaceable mementos of our lives in China. Apart from all of Mother's priceless ivory, jade, porcelain, and cloisonné pieces, they took all our family memorabilia; our photo albums; Dad's marksman and racing trophies; portraits, paintings, and a priceless library. I looked in shock at Mother and Dad when they walked into the house, their faces a picture of stoic resignation.

"What's the matter?" I asked, scared.

Dad was the first to find his voice. "The filthy little bastards took *everything!* The Swiss didn't lift a hand to stop them. So much for bloody neutrality!"

Without a word, Mother slipped out of the room and a few minutes later came in and put Kuan-yin on the mantelpiece. Then she looked around the living room, through the massive curtained archway to the dining room, and said quietly, "The place is clean and liveable. After all we've been through, what more can we ask."

Just after we settled in we had a visit from the Red Cross and Ursula and I were asked if we would become hostesses at the Liberty Lounge and Amerine Club—the new names given the old French Club and Tientsin Men's Club. A few evenings later, with barely time to get new dresses made, we were whisked away in a plywood canopied Jeep to the Liberty Lounge. It was snowing, and a huge Sikh policeman, with frost on his formidable whiskers, gave us a rare, welcoming smile as he opened the club's massive glass doors. Gingerly stepping up the stairs to the vestibule, my feet still not used to heels, I saw Monique greeting servicemen with a Red Cross girl by her side. When she saw us she waved wildly and rushed over.

An angry old memory coiled itself around me, and staring at her rudely I said, "Hello, Monique, it's been a long time. Is that your hair or a wig?" She knew I was referring to what loyal Frenchmen had done to collaborators after the German retreat, and grabbing me aside she said with tears in her eyes, "Please, Bobby, *please...*"

I shook my head in disgust, and as I moved away I said, "Please don't call me Bobby. I'm not a tom-boy any more—in fact, I never was. My name is Pamela."

A week later, while I was at the convent brushing up on my typing and shorthand, a bird colonel came in looking for Chefoo lace from a blind orphanage the Sisters ran in that city. It was unbelievably delicate, and much sought after by those in the know. Seeing me pounding away on an old Royal, he asked if I could start work in the legal office of the First Marine Division the following Monday. I was on cloud nine. I figured I'd be doing clerical work and filing and making enough money to put a new wardrobe together, the last the only thing on my mind.

To my dismay, when I reported for work, I found my first assignment was to go out to the Tank Battalion at the old French Arsenal to record a Court of Enquiry into the death of a marine. From there I went on to general courts-martial and cases of manslaughter, rape, and armed robbery. For a girl who raised in a convent, I certainly grew up in a hurry!

At the end of each case, when the young defendants stood for their sentencing—only one got off—I thought of the life that spread out before me and what *they* could look forward to, and my shorthand notes would blur, and I'd search feverishly for a handkerchief. Time and again I'd slam back into the legal office to type up my notes, fuming at the injustice of the sentence some kid, younger than I, received. "That damn 'boot-lieut' was more interested in plotting football plays than following the case," I'd storm. "I kept trying to give him questions to shoot but he ignored them. Even the judge advocate got mad at him. It was no good. He couldn't've cared less what happened to that kid. Now he's got twenty years!"

"It's okay, Pam," Major Brooks would say, "Everything's reviewed in Washington."

"How can you review evidence that wasn't taken!"

"They compare cases," he'd say, trying to calm me.

"Compare them to *what?!*"

Ursula, who got the job I wanted, would come up then and tell me "to let it go".

But I couldn't. Injustice was not part of the plan I had for my brave new world.

Dad was happy once more, working proudly for the Kailan, one of the few British enterprises still operating in mainland China. And Mother was busy too. She was getting necessary permits and visas so that she, Ursula, and I could go to the States—the only home we had left to us.

Everything was going swimmingly until the actual date of departure was finalized: September 6, 1946. Ursula's twenty-first birthday was on August 4, and according to American immigration law, anyone who lived twenty-one years in one country automatically became a citizen of that country! It didn't matter to the United States that British subjects could *never* lose their citizenship. Nothing counted but the letter of the law, unreasonable as it was.

Strangely it was that same "unreasonable" law that had turned Mother's father into an American citizen without her or Grandma knowing it.

Her dad, William Lawson Henderson, was a reporter for the *Manchester Guardian*. At the turn of the century, when Mother was seven, the Spanish-American War broke out, and Grandpa was assigned as a war correspondent to the *New York Herald-Tribune*. He died at Manila Bay while covering the Philippines operation, and later was buried as a war hero in the Presidio at San Francisco.

When we visited Grandma in California in '39, she'd just learned she was considered an American war widow. She told how a social worker had come up to her little home in North Hollywood and said, "Mrs. Henderson, why have you never claimed your pension as an American war widow? The government always considered you a person of means, but I don't see you in that light."

"What do you mean, an American war widow? I'm a British subject. My husband was a British subject."

"No, not actually. When he died under the American colors, he automatically became a citizen of this country, and you, as his widow, have been entitled to an allotment since 1901."

Mother thought of all that the pension would've meant to Grandma, the headmistress of a girl's school in London, and how hard she'd had to work to raise two sons and a daughter. She remembered how when Grandma retired in 1927, she had cashed her meager savings and come to the States to visit Grandpa's grave, and how the big, sprawling country had stolen her heart and she'd decided to stay.

Mother told Grandpa's story to the American authorities; they listened politely, then said, "Sorry, that doesn't alter a thing. By September your daughter will have been in China over twenty-one years; she'll have to enter the States under the Chinese quota, and there are over fifty-thousand people already on it."

"How long will it take for her name to come up?" Mother asked.

"Five to ten years," was the unconcerned reply.

The dumb law that "automatically" made Grandpa an American, "automatically" made Ursula Chinese.

"We'll see about *that!*" Mother said, and stormed out clutching the still unsigned papers.

A week or so later she threw one of her famous parties. The house was bristling with brass and dignitaries, and when everyone was well sloshed, Mother got the necessary signatures on Ursula's exit papers.

Time flew after that.

It seemed we'd no sooner celebrated Ursula's twenty-first birthday than we were boarding a train for Chinwangtao to catch a freighter on the first leg of our journey to the States.

Passing through Kaiping, I thought of Jung-ya. We hadn't been able to find him when we got back from the prison camp. We hoped against hope that he was doing so well on his farm that he didn't need to work for us, but deep down inside we knew Kaiping was the Communist headquarters for Hopei Province and that they didn't look kindly on landed gentry, especially if they had once worked for foreigners. All I could offer up was a silent prayer.

When we got to Chinwangtao, we were whisked out to the pier in a charcoal-burning taxi. The fumes were nauseating and we tumbled out of the car in relief when it came to a jolting stop in front of Dad's old office. As our luggage was being unloaded we looked around for the freighter, and noticed one out to sea.

"That must be it," Mother said. "Guess we're going to have to take the old *Fuping* out to it."

A very precise voice cut in, "You're right. The bay has been terribly neglected and needs dredging badly. We're going to have to sit out to sea and wait for the evening tide." It was the skipper, and he had come ashore to escort us out to his ship.

"If we're not leaving till this evening, can't we go and see our old home one last time?" Ursula asked.

"No, the area isn't secure; Communists are everywhere." It was obvious all the captain wanted was to get us out of port safely.

As we boarded the tugboat and headed out to sea, I scanned the shore, the bobbing boats, the purple hills—everything looked the same, yet it didn't feel the same. After our bags were stowed in the tiny stateroom, Ursula and I got into our swimsuits and went on deck. There was no breeze, and the air was still and hot. We asked the captain if we could go swimming, and he kindly had a ladder lowered for us. The cool waters of the bay felt wonderful, and we swam and floated, enjoying every minute. Suddenly, looking up at the looming side of the ship, I noticed the crew lined up. I looked at Ursula, and she was smiling and waving at them gaily. They weren't smiling back: they were yelling and beckoning for us to come in.

We both shook our heads and struck out further.

The captain came out with a bullhorn and shouted, "Get back

aboard! We're sailing!"

I noticed the sun was still high in the sky, and as I swam back, I wondered what on earth was going on. Ursula was ahead of me on the ladder, and it was swinging precariously as I tried to get a foothold. The ascent was a lot harder than the climb down had been, and I was having a terrible time getting up. It seemed ages before the deck loomed into view and burly arms pulled me on board.

As I thanked the men and stood up, I saw they were armed, and looking back down the ladder into the lovely cool, blue bay, I saw sharks circling.

"That was *close!* Why didn't you tell us there were sharks?"

"You might've panicked!" was all the captain said.

We spent the rest of the day up on deck, and from our vantage point, we noticed an ugly lighthouse out on the promontory between our old cove and that of the commissioner of customs. Later in the day, when the sun set behind the western hills and we finally weighed anchor, we saw barbed wire entanglements etched along the waving green bluff line. I couldn't help thinking—*the Japs who had scaled those cliffs so many years before must have been waiting for an invasion that never came!*

As I enjoyed the cool sea breeze that swept over the deck, I remembered the courage of the coal coolies who had blown up the colliers; no poems would be written to their glory. I thought of the Chinese people: Dad's business associates, my school friends, and our servants who had shown us that service can be an honorable profession, and I wondered if I would ever feel at home in another country.

The trip to Shanghai was full of mixed emotions. Of despondent feelings of loss, and excited dreams of the future. I'd never thought my life in China would end like this. I'd always thought it would go on and on. Sadly I realized that although the Japanese were vanquished and the war was over, the Chinese would still keep on fighting...only now with each other. Then a niggling thought started to surface: could it be that the sharks in the bay circling the freighter were really *déjà vu*—a vision of Communists waiting to take over China after we left?

I found their numbers much greater in Shanghai, and their contempt for foreigners permeated the waves of humanity overflowing the streets and the cluttered chaos of the waterfront.

I felt strangely dispossessed.

When we finally boarded the *USS General Meiggs* for San Francisco, I realized I was genuinely looking forward to my new home in the United States.

AFTER WORDS

Now, fifty years later, as I mull over memories of China and what followed, I recall moments of humor…and sadness, that, like the prison camp years, wove themselves into the quilt of my life.

The first was just months after our arrival in the States, when we received an invitation to Chinese chow and movies at the California home of Phil Malmstead, the military photographer who had recorded our last days in camp. The food was superlative, but the *pièce de resistance* of the evening was the showing of camp movies. As he was setting up for the screening he told us of the unending runaround he'd had in Washington to get the material de-classified because of its serious nature. There was a twinkle in his eye as he completed his remarks and asked for the lights to be dimmed. The first few minutes were of camp conditions when they found us. To anyone who hadn't gotten accustomed to them, as we had, they must have seemed pretty grim. I could visualize the Pentagon brass viewing them with concern, mingled with smug satisfaction at the part the military had played in our liberation. But then the mood changed. After a few happy shots of cart-wheeling kids and internees gushing over their liberators, the camera cut to a closeup of a girl's cute behind, then panned upwards to chocolate spattered arms; backing off, it got a lens-full of flashing legs and swishing paddles, and the Chocolate Cake Caper came alive in all its slapstick humor.

*****

Well over two decades were to pass before I was to be touched again by a spectre from my China years. I'd had a hectic but interesting career, all in different fields of art and design, and was now an art director in the private sector of the space program. There was something special in contemplating that, minute as my efforts might have been, I helped put a man on the moon! I found I was glued to the news channels on television through all those exciting days.

Strangely, it wasn't outer space that caught my eye one Saturday morning, but rather an on-the-spot interview from Kowloon, across from Hongkong.

The hot sun was not kind to the freckled face that glowered out from under a rumpled coif. Mother Thomas à Becket's lips were cracked as she tried to speak, hatred and anguish fighting in her eyes. "They are pigs! Soul-less pigs!" she exploded.

The interviewer, audibly taken aback at the un-Christian remarks of this hot, sweaty nun, said softly, "You are speaking of the Chinese people?"

"I am speaking of the Chinese *Communists*. The animals that took over that land. We've been their prisoners for twenty years, allowed to live in Peking to teach the children of the foreign embassies. When Mother Superior became ill, we begged our captors to let us leave. But they wouldn't. Finally, when she was so ill that they realized her care would become a burden on the State, they told us we could go."

"How did you get from Peking to Kowloon?" I could sense the interviewer was finally warming up to her feisty little subject.

"On foot."

"On foot?!" There was an distinct pause that the cameraman grabbed to pan the diminutive Sister in her tattered habit and shredded shoes.

"And Mother Superior?" the interviewer persisted.

"In a wheelbarrow!"

Mother Thomas did nothing to hide her disgust and loathing. "Those pigs spat on us, hurled stones, and insulted us all the way. A few Christians tried to feed us, but they were afraid for their families and their lives."

"How did Mother Superior take the trip?" The questions now showed genuine concern.

"She died as we entered Kowloon."

There was no hatred left in Mother Thomas's eyes. Her tears flowed unashamedly, and as she reached into her habit for a grimy handkerchief and loudly blew her nose, my eyes brimmed too, and I thought of the love, sacrifice, and loss of those gallant Christ-like women. And with the thought came the memory of the last time I'd seen Mother Superior in the prison camp, and I wondered if she died still believing in the ultimate humanity of man.

BIBLIOGRAPHY

P. H. Kent   "Railway Enterprise in China"
Arnold Publishers, London, 1907

Carroll Alcott   "My War with Japan"
Henry Holt & Co., New York, NY, 1943

Chang Kia-Ngau   "China's Struggle for Railroad Development"
The John Day Company, New York, NY, 1943

George Simmons   Prison Camp Journal (unpublished)
1943 - 1945

Laurance Tipton   "Chinese Escapade"
MacMillan, London, 1949

Langdon Gilkey   "Shantung Compound"
Harper & Row, New York, NY, 1966

Henry I. Shaw Jr   "The United States Marines in North China,
1945-1949" Historical Branch, G-3 Div. HQ
USMC, Washington, DC, 1968

John A. White   "The United States Marines in North China"
Col., USMC Ret.   Self-published, 1974

W. G. Winslow   "The Fleet the Gods Forgot"
Naval Institute Press, Annapolis, MD, 1982

George H. Nash   "The Life of Herbert Hoover—The Engineer"
W. W. Norton & Co. Inc., New York, NY,
1983

ORDER FORM

Fax: (530) 622-0851

Phone: (530) 647-2000

E-Mail: pamela@hendersonhouse.com

Mail: Henderson House Publishing
            1390 Broadway, Suite B-295
            Placerville, CA 95667

_____ books @ $19.95 each $ _____

Shipping (first book $4, each additional copy $2) $ _____

Sales Tax (California residents only, $1.45/book) $ _____

                                              TOTAL $ _____

Name _____

Address _____

City _____

State _____   Zip _____

Country _____   Phone (____) _____

Payment: ❏ Check   ❏ Credit Card
              ❏ Visa   ❏ MasterCard   ❏ American Express

Card Number _____

Name on Card _____   Exp. Date __ / __

THANK YOU FOR YOUR ORDER!

ORDER FORM

Fax: (530) 622-0851

Phone: (530) 647-2000

E-Mail: pamela@hendersonhouse.com

Mail: Henderson House Publishing
          1390 Broadway, Suite B-295
          Placerville, CA 95667

_____ books @ $19.95 each $ _____

Shipping (first book $4, each additional copy $2) $ _____

Sales Tax (California residents only, $1.45/book) $ _____

                                        TOTAL $ _____

Name _____

Address _____

City _____

State _____ Zip _____

Country _____ Phone (____) _____

Payment: ❑ Check   ❑ Credit Card
          ❑ Visa   ❑ MasterCard   ❑ American Express

Card Number _____

Name on Card _____ Exp. Date __ / __

THANK YOU FOR YOUR ORDER!

ORDER FORM

Fax: (530) 622-0851

Phone: (530) 647-2000

E-Mail: pamela@hendersonhouse.com

Mail: Henderson House Publishing
            1390 Broadway, Suite B-295
            Placerville, CA 95667

_____ books @ $19.95 each $ _____

Shipping (first book $4, each additional copy $2) $ _____

Sales Tax (California residents only, $1.45/book) $ _____

                                    TOTAL $ _____

Name _____

Address _____

City _____

State _____ Zip _____

Country _____ Phone (____) _____

Payment: ❏ Check   ❏ Credit Card
            ❏ Visa   ❏ MasterCard   ❏ American Express

Card Number _____

Name on Card _____ Exp. Date ___ / ___

THANK YOU FOR YOUR ORDER!

ORDER FORM

Fax: (530) 622-0851

Phone: (530) 647-2000

E-Mail: pamela@hendersonhouse.com

Mail: Henderson House Publishing
            1390 Broadway, Suite B-295
            Placerville, CA 95667

_____ books @ $19.95 each $ _____

Shipping (first book $4, each additional copy $2) $ _____

Sales Tax (California residents only, $1.45/book) $ _____

                                        TOTAL $ _____

Name _____

Address _____

City _____

State _____ Zip _____

Country _____ Phone (___) _____

Payment: ❑ Check   ❑ Credit Card
            ❑ Visa ❑ MasterCard ❑ American Express

Card Number _____

Name on Card _____ Exp. Date __ / __

THANK YOU FOR YOUR ORDER!